WORLDING AMERICA

WORLDING AMERICA

A Transnational Anthology of Short Narratives before 1800

EDITED AND WITH AN INTRODUCTION
AND CRITICAL NOTES BY
OLIVER SCHEIDING AND MARTIN SEIDL

STANFORD UNIVERSITY PRESS
STANFORD, CALIFORNIA

Stanford University Press
Stanford, California

Printed in the United States of America on acid-free, archival-quality paper

Library of Congress Cataloging-in-Publication Data

Worlding America : a transnational anthology of short narratives before 1800 / edited and with an introduction and critical notes by Oliver Scheiding and Martin Seidl.
pages cm
Includes bibliographical references and index.
ISBN 978-0-8047-9080-2 (cloth : alk. paper)
1. America--Literatures--17th century. 2. America--Literatures--18th century.
I. Scheiding, Oliver, editor, writer of introduction. II. Seidl, Martin (Martin Johannes), editor, writer of introduction.
PN845.W67 2015
808.8'03587003--dc23
2014017369

ISBN 978-0-8047-9259-2 (electronic)

Typeset by Bruce Lundquist in 10/15 Minion Pro

For Alfred Weber
(1925–2006)

CONTENTS

ILLUSTRATIONS

ACKNOWLEDGMENTS

As it is with other books, this one results from a personal history and involves numerous people who were decisive in making this project come through. It has its beginnings in the mid-1990s when I was sharing an office with Alfred Weber at the Universität Tübingen. Through our many conversations I discovered a new world of early American narratives that were, to a large extent, unknown or excluded from existing anthologies, but were texts that enriched my own teaching and scholarship for years to come. Looking back to those moments of collegiality, it is a pleasure to thank Alfred Weber for his advice, encouragement, and support, since this book evolves in one way or another from our inspirational "lucubrations."

With all the hum and buzz of academic life, particularly during my years as a young scholar with its numerous posts, unexpected opportunities, and the requisite completion of other projects, I lost sight of an earlier plan to publish a volume on early short narratives until financial support from the University of Mainz and the German Research Foundation made it possible to resume this work. In doing so, I count it as my good fortune to have worked alongside so many stimulating colleagues, friends, and students both in Mainz and abroad. Among them, I must first thank my co-editor, who accompanied this project in all things intellectual and practical with great enthusiasm and scholarly productivity. I would also like to acknowledge the warm encouragement and sound advice of James Nagel and his inspiring commitment to study the history of the short story. Conversations that emerged from our annual meetings of the American Literature Association were immensely beneficial, and I owe a special debt of gratitude to his generosity and friendship. I am particularly grateful to Alfred Bendixen for his personal counsel and to Werner Sollors for his many suggestions that reinvigorated this book immensely.

This book also owes a particular thanks to Patricia Godsave, who gave up her time to read the entire manuscript; her revisions and succinct comments improved the book immeasurably. The editors would also like to thank a number of our student assistants for investing their time and energy into typing up the original documents and preparing the manuscript. We are grateful to Laura Audrit, Lukas Dausend, Sabrina Herzig, Ann-Kathrin Michaelis, and Frank Newton. We especially thank Anette Vollrath for her infinite patience and administrative expertise.

We would also like to thank Emily-Jane Cohen of Stanford University Press for her unflagging support of this project.

Last, but not least, we would like to thank our families for their patience and support.

Mainz, September 2013

A NOTE ON THE TEXT

The narratives in this anthology have been transcribed from original seventeenth- and eighteenth-century sources (when available). All texts have been preserved in their original spelling and punctuation according to the source quoted for each text, except for the modernization of idiosyncrasies and special letters of seventeenth- and eighteenth-century print or where the absence of punctuation renders specific passages of a text unreadable. Emphases in quotations and extracts are in all cases as they appear in the original. In terms of em dashes and other paratextual events, the texts of each section retain the typographical conventions of seventeenth- and eighteenth-century print culture.

WORLDING AMERICA

INTRODUCTION
The Worlds of Short Narratives

THIS BOOK TAKES A NEW APPROACH to the history and circulation of short narratives in a global context by exploring the diverse textual economies in the Americas before 1800. Until recently these early short narratives remained largely obscure and marginalized, and their neglect in critical discussion has been mirrored by their absence from curricula and anthologies.[1] Given this legacy, *Worlding America* seeks not to trace the origin of the American short story, but instead aims to respond to the reevaluation of American literature as a network of transnational literary exchanges. Rather than focusing on the birthplace of the short story and the emergence of an exceptional national print culture, this volume unearths the circulation of prose compositions and textual networks written in various Native and European languages. *Worlding America* provides a basis for studying the constant movements of stories, writers, and themes from the seventeenth into the nineteenth centuries. It thus exceeds notions of origination and sheds new light on the formative period of American literature.

The texts assembled in *Worlding America* reveal a literary market and culture of reprinting that existed side by side and independent of the novel, while providing a new context to existing theories of the later short story.[2] Most scholars agree that the short story evolved out of the Romantic interest in oral storytelling. Critics trace the origin of the short story back to folklore and regard the history of the genre as a development of psychological and descriptive realism that replaces older models of storytelling. Accordingly, Washington

Irving's *The Sketch Book of Geoffrey Crayon, Gent.* (1819–20) marks the starting point of the short story as it combines written and oral discourse with a vivid and realistic portrayal of life, rendered through the perspective of the teller.[3] While the nineteenth-century short story has played a prominent role in American literary history, the tendency to reduce earlier short narratives to forerunners of a nineteenth-century form not only levels the variety of oral and written narratives that existed before this date, but also leads to their dismissal because of a lack of moral and artistic complexity.[4]

Such an assessment overlooks how those works that are now called short stories have been influenced by and existed side by side with narrative traditions that reach back to the Middle Ages. They are products not of a Romantic imagination but of a vibrant print market that valued storytelling as it was revealed in integral pieces of letters, histories, collections, and—later—newspapers and magazines. Irving's experience as a writer depended much on his earlier work in periodicals. Before the American version of *The Sketch Book* was published in seven installments and became a best seller in England and later in North America, Irving edited the *Analectic Magazine* (1813–14) and coauthored essays and tales in *Salmagundi* (1807–9). Though Irving was commonly labeled as a "chronicler of American life," his tales are actually inspired by a variety of European myths, and his later works are set in medieval England and southern Spain. While the term "short story" was first used in America by William Gilmore Simms in 1866, and gained widespread recognition with Brander Matthews's 1885 essay "The Philosophy of the Short Story," it developed from Edgar Allan Poe's 1846 description of the prose tale as a tightly plotted text that evokes a unified effect and can be read in one sitting.[5] However, Poe's definition was only retrospectively adopted as the first and still influential theory of short prose compositions and proclaimed as a typical American genre, invalidating the transatlantic literary influences and exchanges of material that have characterized earlier short forms (cf. Levy 1993, 1–9; Curnutt 1997).

In the seventeenth century, the terms "story" and "tale" existed side by side, and they were used interchangeably in eighteenth-century magazine publications, which also applied a range of other labels, like "novel," "tale," "sketch," and "essay," to all forms of short narrative. Although the label "short narrative" was current neither in magazines nor in colonial writing, it serves as an umbrella term for the texts assembled in this volume. Rather than using periodicals to demonstrate the development of short narration before the advent of the short story, *Worlding America* aims to show the continuous participation of short narrative prose in networks of storytelling that reach across time to link, for example, Protestant wonder tales with eighteenth-century magazines (see Parts IV and V). Traditional concepts of literary history, such as genre and period, have combined with the retrospective application of aesthetic and critical standards to exclude these mobile and highly popular narratives from the agenda of American literary history and short story theory.[6]

Transatlantic religious, print, and communication networks have become a standard frame of reference to reassess the literary worlds of the early Americas and the postrevolutionary era (Amory and Hall 2007; Gross and Kelley 2010). In the seventeenth century, one encounters "worlds of wonder" (Hall 1990) that reach from Elizabethan England to early eighteenth-century North America, and in which folklore, commercial texts, and Protestant writings mingled on both sides of the Atlantic. The growth of reading publics and their interest in entertaining and edifying literature between 1560 and 1640 contributed to the popularity of "strange newes," under which printers comprised all kinds of disasters, accidents, and bizarre prodigies. Public demand was answered by sermons and collections of wonder tales like those of Increase and Cotton Mather, but also by cheap prints of ballads, pamphlets, and eventually newspapers. Similar to medieval exempla and legends, such publications gave sensational accounts of contemporary events, and drew on classical sources, such as Pliny's *Natural History* (AD 77–79), that had become available during the Renaissance. In England as well as in the Americas, the seventeenth century witnessed the parallel use of sources from radically different times and places, mixing Christian and pagan accounts of supernatural and wonder. Colonial providence tales—which have been associated with the birth of American literature—simply adapt formal conventions and subjects that recur across cultural and temporal boundaries.[7]

Early modern Protestantism derives many of its narrative practices from medieval Catholicism, as their literary interactions in the Atlantic world demonstrate. Apart from having spiritual centers in England and on the Continent, religion is considered "an expanding cultural field" (Round 1999, 6) involved in communication networks that were both transatlantic and colonial. While colonial politics played as large a role in this cultural field as religion did, scholars maintain that the rise of reform movements—quietism, pietism, and evangelicalism—created a religious vernacular in the Atlantic world that actively encouraged people to write and participate in the literary market. These global religious movements resulted in both a manuscript and a print culture that "displaced most of the traditional hierarchies that writing involved, substituting a geography of dispersed production and distribution for a geography of a cosmopolitan center, and . . . the sociability of like-minded Protestants for the coteries that practiced literary connoisseurship" (Hall 2008, 12). Written to teach religion in a language that was easy to understand, and largely based on personal experience, narratives in collections, sermons, and cheap prints were steady sellers and created an expanding market demand for short tales, such as exemplary life writing (Brown 2006; Imbarrato 2012).

At the same time, diaries, letters, and other handwritten manuscripts circulated, were copied, and again influenced other printed texts to constitute "scribal publication" (Love 1993), a practice used not only by colonial authorities such as John Winthrop and William Bradford, but also by many anonymous commentators who satirized social and political events. Ministers like Cotton Mather engaged in an extensive correspondence with many of the foremost theologians and politicians on both sides of the Atlantic. These textual networks become particularly obvious in collections of providence tales, where Continental and colonial examples are placed side by side. For instance, Increase Mather's *Essay for the Recording of Illustrious Providences* (1684) was based on a manuscript by English minister Matthew Poole and also on James Janeway's *Legacy to His Friends* (1674). Cotton Mather's account of Joseph Beacon's encounter with the ghost of his brother (see Part V) was in turn quoted by William Turner's *Compleat History of the Most Remarkable Providences* (1697), and then crudely investigated by Daniel Defoe (Baine 1962). Moreover, the conventions of Protestant writing were quickly adopted by commercial producers as well. Thus, over time it became impossible to distinguish between the wonder tales produced by religious writers and those written by commercial authors who used similar narrative conventions to instruct and entertain their readerships (Hunter 1990).

The above examples show the ways in which texts traveled and were published, through scribal publication, reprint, or editing in Europe or the Americas, and established a larger circum-Atlantic literary network. All published texts from that period have been subject to a "network of intentions" (Hall 2008, 3) involving intermediaries and cultural brokers like the printers and booksellers who took license to adapt or edit and reprint texts as they saw fit. Next to practical matters such as access to a printer and capital, political constellations and controversies determined which texts were printed or how they were altered—perhaps, for example, by a printer editing out controversial passages (Bryant 2002). Taken all together, these influences and the fluidity of texts make it impossible to analyze the texts collected in this volume according to categories such as authorship, genre, and period. Instead of reconstructing original texts and their intentions, historians of print culture propose a decentralized concept of authorship, with editors, writers, collectors, readers, and correspondents interacting as nodes of textual transmission. In moving from the work itself to the network in which public and private realms overlap, any attempt to use literary artifacts as building blocks for identity formations becomes obsolete.[8]

Decentralized concepts of authorship also apply to the records of Native American storytelling that have been preserved in the documents of the colonizers and literate Natives through a process of transliteration (see the Penobscot story of "Corn Mother" in Part V). Throughout the Americas, Native peoples developed elaborate traditions of both oral storytelling and writing systems, or what Friedrich Kittler (1990) calls "notation systems." Supporting the notion that narrative is a human universal, practiced in all cultures and times, Roberto Echevarría (1997, 5) states that like the Old Testament and Greek mythology in the Western tradition, Native short narratives revolved around the origins of the world with the intention to perceive and understand their present situation (Brander Rasmussen 2012). While many of these narratives belong to the oral tradition—stories passed from generation to generation—some cultures developed systems for recording information, such as the quipu (see illustration in Part V).[9] The *Popol Vuh*—a mid-sixteenth-century record of Guatemalan K'iche' Maya oral traditions—originated in the efforts of literate Mayas to preserve their culture. In addition, many Native narratives that circulated in the mid-Atlantic colonies and Canada were recorded by missionaries such as the Jesuits and Moravians (Engel 2008). Yet these colonial intermediaries often lacked the language and cultural knowledge to adequately translate Native myths or texts, and their perspective, prejudices, and technical limitations inevitably distorted the outcome as well. The sources in which these native stories could be found differ according to the changing intentions pursued by their publication, ranging from informing a European audience (such as missionary reports and travel accounts) to laying the foundation for a national literature in nineteenth-century Latin America.[10]

In contrast to the network of Protestants on both sides of the Atlantic, the French and Spanish colonies produced different types of texts but used similar strategies of narration. The French possessions in North America were military, missionary, and trading outposts from which Jesuit priests sent frequent reports—compiled in *The Jesuit Relations*—to the church leaders in Paris. After their conquest, the Spanish erected a number of viceroyalties in their South and Central American colonies in response to the expansive Aztec, Inca, and Maya empires that they encountered. Similar to the French, the Spanish explorers, military commanders, and administrators wrote letters, records, and annual reports to their superiors in which they dramatized their role in the conquest, but they also included a number of narrative episodes (see Part I). Their perspectives were countered, however, by racially mixed historians and writers such as Garcilaso de la Vega, el Inca (1539–1616), who used the conquerors' hegemonic practices of religion and historiography to reassess the Spanish claim of superiority (Bauer and Mazzotti 2009).

In North America, Native tribes were less of a threat to the settlers' expansion as they joined shifting political and trade alliances during the frequent border conflicts between the French and British empires. During the Enlightenment, Native Americans came to represent the perfect harmony between humankind and nature, resulting in an increasing popularity of Native American representations throughout Europe and North America. Stories such as "Azakia: A Canadian Story" (1783; see Part IV) portray wise and deeply moral Native characters, and were translated from French into German and then into English. At the same time, they hint at the plurality of migrant stories that circulated in magazines and whose subtitles indicate the different readerly appropriations of Native Americans. Narratives of bizarre frontier killings and the violent interaction of Natives with white women can equally be found, as exemplified by the story of Hannah Duston, whose legacy was both fortified by local historians, newspapers, poems, and periodicals, and subverted by Nathaniel Hawthorne's scathing revision of Cotton Mather's original text (see Part II). The unabated interest in graphic violence, and sensational descriptions of death, rape, and deformity, are thus also visible in the treatment of the otherwise sentimentalized Native Americans (see Parts I and IV).

In addition to depicting sensationalist themes, early short narratives also engaged with the multiple forms of servitude and the African slave trade practiced in the eighteenth-century Atlantic world. Since the earliest colonial times, millions of Africans were enslaved and brought to the Americas to work on plantations and in households or as indentured servants (see Part III headnote). The atrocities of the Middle Passage as well as the exploitation and cruel treatment by slave owners and traders can be found in narratives such as "Zimeo: A Tale" (1798; see Part III) and many other slave narratives of that time (Carretta 1996; for the topic of white slaves, see Baepler 1999). The Caribbean became a setting for many of these narratives dealing with themes of exploitation, slave rebellion, and the Maroon communities of fugitive slaves on Jamaica and Haiti (see Part III; Goudie 2006). Simultaneously, the global movement of abolitionism shows how narratives can be used to a political end, as, for example, in Benjamin Rush's pro-Anthony Benezet story, "The Paradise of Negro Slaves," which appeared in his *Essays, Literary, Moral, Philosophical* (1798; see Jackson 2009). As these narratives are accessible via a number of anthologies (Carretta 1996; Krise 1999), *Worlding America* focuses on a few examples from a transatlantic culture of reprint revolving around global ideas of abolitionism and emancipation.

Worlding America seeks to do justice to the multilingual dimension of colonial short narration by highlighting marginalized groups such as the Scotch-Irish and German-speaking immigrants. Unlike the host of French, Spanish, English, and German sources, there is little evidence of narratives written or published during the short-lived Dutch and Swedish colonial undertakings (Schmidt 2001). Yet radical Protestants from those countries immigrated to the mid-Atlantic colonies where German-speaking immigrants founded towns like Germantown or Lancaster that to this day are reminiscent of their influence. Christopher Sauer, a German immigrant whose career as a successful printer and influential public figure has been compared to that of Benjamin Franklin, set up one of the largest printshops in prerevolutionary America. Established in 1738 in Germantown, Pennsylvania, this first German press published almanacs and various papers that focused on local life. Records of this press show how the Pennsylvania Germans, contrary to their image as low farmers and dumb pioneers, were interested in religious and educational matters and produced their own Bible translation, as well as many other types of publications (Wilsdorf 1999; Erben 2012).

As diverse as its readerships were, the eighteenth century also witnessed a rise in public participation in the print market, especially through religious pamphlets and the spread of magazines and newspapers. Beginning with Samuel Keimer's *Pennsylvania Gazette* (1728), which was later published by Benjamin Franklin, newspapers and magazines relied on a network of correspondents for local stories, opinion pieces, letters, poetry, and tales. Many seasoned writers and editors, but also first-time authors, both female and male, filled the pages of the magazines with their own stories or the translations of popular foreign pieces, mostly published anonymously. Similar to the decentralized authorship of seventeenth-century narratives, the exchange, adaptation, and circulation of short prose in the periodicals of the eighteenth and early nineteenth centuries resemble the fluid and participatory culture of the Internet age.[11] A survey of reprints and adaptations of Defoe's *Robinson Crusoe* (1719), for example, shows that many reprints had either condensed or elaborated the plot, and indicates the currency of subjects such as the international trade, slavery, and piracy (Bannet 2011). The lack of copyright protection also facilitated the colonial reprint of any successful British or European publication. Reprints often appeared in a slightly adapted version, or even as a continuation of the original story (see Part IV). The diverse literary production of the early Atlantic world is therefore best described as a literary commons, a term leaning on the "textual commons" established by David Brewer (2005, 12–14) for the habit of imaginative appropriation and the formation of virtual communities of readers in the Atlantic world.

Another so-far-neglected aspect of eighteenth-century literary production in the Americas is the emergence of a periodical culture and the role of the editor. Current studies shift critical attention to the specific conditions of editing, writing for, and reading periodicals (Lanzendörfer 2013). With their wide circulation, short narratives in magazines and newspapers reached a broad and diverse audience (see Part IV). From the Caribbean *Antigua Gazette* (1755–1815) to the *Quebec Gazette* (1764–98), periodical publications enabled swift reactions to political events. Their circulation was also much wider than the number of subscribers suggests, as many periodicals were shared among friends and neighbors or hung up in public places. While single-essay periodicals like the *Tatler* (1709–11) and *The Spectator* (1711–12) were highly successful in England, the leading periodical format in North America was the miscellany—a magazine characterized by the diversity and brevity of its contents. Contrary to expectations of literary merit and "art for art's sake," periodicals and their short textual commodities became objects of daily use and were highly popular among all classes and readerships.[12]

A Worlding Approach to Literature

As a dialogue between scholarship and the rich archive of storytelling in the Americas before 1800, *Worlding America* combines recent critical trends that reassess American literature in a global context with a new approach that focuses on textual circulation rather than on the emergence of the American short story. Americanists have, in recent years, moved away from the traditional categorization of genre, period, and author; this, in turn, has led to a shift in the object and method of their inquiry (Rhodes 2012). Current literary histories no longer seek to preserve a canon of texts and authors. Instead of maintaining a U.S.-centric bias, they reconstruct a mixed body of texts and offer diverse interpretive strategies that take "the reader through the matrix of American culture" (Marcus and Sollors 2009, xxv) and raise questions about what constitutes American literature. Critics frequently summarize this shift as a move from a national to a global frame for analysis that corresponds to the present relationship of the United States to the world. While Americanists have traditionally worked with a "limited number of objects that were produced at the intersection of periodization and generic concepts" (Pease 2007, 9), they must now account for the various influences connected with the global movements of capital, people, and culture. To avoid endorsing a national fallacy, critics reconceptualize America from both a transnational and a localized perspective to make visible the global conditions of literary production.

But if we want to study literature in light of a globalized world order, what categories—besides the larger analytic frameworks launched by the transnational turn in current literary and cultural studies—could replace genre, period, and author, all allegedly predicated by the nation? Critics have recently made numerous propositions. Some suggest forms, spaces, and practices (Levander and Levine 2011, 1) as key terms for analysis, whereas others seek to combine space and time to form a geography of American literature. Spatial paradigms claim a specific locality in which global flows and imperial influences become visible. From a comparative point of view, critics set out to link South America with the southern United States, or show the global dimension in the literature of the Pacific Northwest, spanning the United States and Canada (Giles 2011). Frequently, such reterritorializations of American literature complement, and are partially based upon, the notion of "deep time" (Dimock 2001), connecting literary texts from different periods and backgrounds, making them a subset of larger literary arrangements. Others disagree with such a classification of literature's worldedness by pointing out that the global logics of capital and territory shape literary production at the structural level of literature itself, and are used to reorganize the new spatial arrangements in forms of allegorical local and world histories.[13] In one way or another, all of these approaches seek to emphasize the similarities and cultural connecting points in literature that transcend historical periods and national borders and claim that both have outlived their usefulness as critical terms.[14] In their variety, post-national and transnational methodologies have often been associated with comparative literature. As such, however, they frequently result in two-way comparisons that continue to center in the United States. Other critics, in contrast, rather than regarding comparative literature as an approach of its own, consider it only one among many methods of practicing transnational American studies.

In addition to transnational reassessments of the literary history, the concept of worlding has been recently introduced by a number of scholars. The term "worlding," coined in 1927 by the German philosopher Martin Heidegger (2010), has been expanded into a critical paradigm for studying American literature in relation to a larger horizon of cultural influences and networks of publication. Engaging with ontology—the branch of philosophy that considers the nature of being and what makes human existence and reality—Heidegger states that worlding is a basic process that allows humans to make meaning of their surroundings. Instead of pure sense impressions, human beings receive meaning by engaging with the objects surrounding them in an ongoing process. This processual quality also distinguishes worlding from the static construct of world literature that frequently insulates its object of study from the world.[15] In American literary studies, the notion of world*ing* has been recently introduced as a multilayered and dynamic process of analysis for a "text-network model" (Gillman and Gruesz 2011, 232). This model is based on iteration rather than origination and examines the pluridirectional flow of texts across different languages, cultures, and nations.[16] At the same time, in regard to its critical practice, worlding remains an open activity of constant reinterpretation whenever different texts are examined together. As such, any study or collection of texts can only highlight a finite number of the networks that are potentially even more complex and layered in each cultural and historical situation (Levander 2013, 7).

Worlding America argues that "American" literature is not only a product of the global flow of literary objects, but also a local node from which connections and transformations can be reconstructed. By using a worlding approach, this volume aims to reconstruct literary histories of transmission and circulation in the Americas that have so far received little critical attention and have been disregarded as not fitting modern criteria of aesthetic value or the concept of originality. Two types of text are constituent for *Worlding America*: short narratives that deal with the exchange of ideas, people, and goods across temporal and spatial boundaries, and those that are subject to constant movements and shifting meanings. Early America's manuscript and print cultures provide material contexts in which texts are not fixed but are being freely translated, copied, and adapted. These "worlding" processes result in a new understanding of the literary text not so much as a work that can be ascribed to a particular author, place, and time of publication, but rather as a network of multiple intentions, writing practices, and print traditions that stretch across time and space.

To put theory into practice, *Worlding America* reconsiders the short narrative as a vehicle for expanding literary history with its focus on the predominance of specific genres (frequently the novel), national origins, and periods. By avoiding critical notions of generic development that trace the origin of the short story to the Romantic period or to a specific national history, *Worlding America* seeks to reassess early short narrations within the framework of the early modern literary production and reception. Instead of concentrating, as many anthologies still do, on the New England heritage or the cultural hegemony of British America, *Worlding America* builds on recent anthologies that extend their collections to Native, French, English, German, and Spanish sources that illustrate how the Americas were perceived and reflected upon in diverse forms of short narratives.[17] Without reflecting present-day aesthetic notions or a teleological trajectory of genre history that assumes all earlier narratives are precursors of the "American" short story, *Worlding America* presents short narratives embedded within a wider network of reprints, multiple authorships, and changing literary productions. By applying thematic clustering rather than chronological order, this volume reflects recent findings on how American literature evolves in the context of circum-Atlantic cultural relations and influences that can, in turn, be studied in the form and content of the volume's selected narratives.

Subjects and Forms in Worlding America

The five parts of this volume identify key themes and agents in the literary networks of the early modern Atlantic world. Yet the selected texts can only exemplify the transnational scope of this network through their subjects, publication history, and the figures involved in their production and dissemination, as it is impossible to do justice to the variety of short narration throughout the geographical and temporal expanse tackled in this volume. *Worlding America* defines a short narrative as a brief, self-contained series of events that can be published individually or within a larger text or collection. As is the case with existing short story definitions, brevity remains relative rather than absolute, and the above criteria have been adapted to cover the different types of embedded short narration—in diaries and letters, for example—to demonstrate its various forms and purposes rather than a stringent generic development. The volume's arrangement of short narratives and their publication histories also reveal various connecting points between American and European narratives and between different moments of time that would have otherwise remained invisible—pairing narratives that demonstrate the scope of specific issues or themes. By including regions outside of the national trajectories of American literary history, *Worlding America* provides an opportunity for readers to explore larger publics by highlighting the overlapping literary productions in the pre- and postrevolutionary Americas.

Part I, "Life Writing," assembles personal records of those who have traveled to and lived in the Americas. These documents illustrate the experience of various groups of travelers: French missionaries, English- and German-speaking settlers, Spanish adventurers, and two convicts—one Irish and one African American. This section also contains three narratives from private correspondence that participate to various degrees in the process of scribal publication and deal with experiences of transatlantic or American sea travel. While Edward Taylor's and Christopher Sauer's accounts deal with the difficulties and pleasures of sea travel, the story of Anthony Thacher's shipwreck was transformed into a harrowing account in the collection titled *An Essay for the Recording of Illustrious Providences* (1684), and was edited by Increase Mather in the tradition of the "books of Wonder" he encountered in the England of the 1680s during the "height of the Wonders craze" (Hunter 1990, 215).

In the transatlantic exchange of cultures, storytelling becomes a means of expression for previously marginalized groups as they supersede local distinctions of gender and class. Accordingly, *Worlding America* highlights female authors, African American narratives, stories by Irish and German immigrants, and the oral tales of Native Americans that are taken up by American writers as indictments of their own colonial practices. Part II, "Female Agency," shows how women negotiate and assert their position, both as writers and as protagonists of the narratives themselves. Ann Eliza Bleecker and her daughter Margaretta, as well as the unknown author using the female pseudonym "Sabina" in the *Massachusetts Magazine* (Part IV), were important and respected contributors to a variety of periodicals. Active and assertive female figures were already included in many seventeenth-century captivity narratives, and Cotton Mather's 1697 version of Hannah Duston's violent escape has since inspired many literary treatments, such as "The Duston Family" (1836), which is attributed to Hawthorne.

Part III, "The Circum-Atlantic World," contributes to the expansion of "worldedness" in the Americas with narratives such as "Zimeo: A Tale" (1789) and Freneau's "Inexorable Captain" (1788). Both stories are set in the West Indies and explore the hardships and moral questions surrounding the Atlantic economy and the slave trade. Freneau's short narrative is probably one of the first to address the relationship between profit and social agency in a capitalist trade system. Slaves enter this economic system through the Middle Passage, and "Zimeo" presents two alternatives to exploitation embodied by a benevolent plantation owner, or a slave rebellion and the subsequent erection of a Maroon community of escaped slaves. "Zimeo" also exemplifies the use of translation in a creation of a transnational abolitionist public as eighteenth-century magazines took over and then recirculated the story from the French Marquis de Saint-Lambert's *Les Saisons* (1769). Both stories exemplify how narratives were augmented by sensational, political, and historical elements, and how the worldliness of the periodical evolves from re-editing, translating, and copying texts from different linguistic, cultural, and geographical backgrounds.

Similarly, migrant fictions such as "Azakia: A Canadian Story" (1783) and "The Child of Snow" (1792), which are included in Part IV, "Cultures of Print," can either depict the cultural encounter between French settlers and Native American tribes in Canada or be read as timeless stories of unfaithfulness and revenge. "The Child of Snow," a German fairy tale, and "Azakia," an eighteenth-century French story, passed through various stages of translation and adaptation before being printed in North American magazines. Other stories have been originally published in German: "The Ghost of Falkner Swamp," which first appeared in a German pietist magazine and as part of Sauer's 1744 collection *Of Sundry Old and New Tales of Appearances of Ghosts and Glimpses of the Souls' Condition after Death as it Happened in Oly*, and Marie Le Roy and Barbara Leininger's captivity narrative (1759). Together with the English narratives of Part V, "Ghost Stories," such as Cotton Mather's "A Narrative of an Apparition" (1692) and "A Notable Deliverance from Captivity" (1697), they offer different perspectives on themes like captivity, ghosts and apparitions, and Orientalism. In the multilingual context of the Americas, any retrospective categorization or generic systematization disregards the semantic variety and playfulness as well as the geographical and temporal boundlessness of short narratives; for instance, stories of ghosts and apparitions have proven one of the most diverse and vibrant genres in world literature.

Each part of *Worlding America* is divided into units of interrelated narratives of different times and backgrounds. With their introduction to the themes and backgrounds of the narratives, headnotes serve as a reference guide for a close reading of each story in the context of its publication history, modes of production and consumption, and relevant cultural backgrounds. To demonstrate participation in a literary network and a culture of reprinting, the headnotes also establish cross-references to other parts of this volume. As the selections can act only as a starting point to study individual themes, types of narratives, and publications, the further reading suggestions provide additional narratives that can be read in combination with those published in the volume. A detailed publication history contains all available versions of a narrative, as well as possible foreign language sources, to demonstrate their transmission across countries and over time. This anthology invites readers to explore a story alongside other stories found via the bibliography at the end of each headnote, or by following, for example, the development of Native American or African American storytelling across the various parts and time periods covered in this volume. *Worlding America* ultimately encourages readers to explore stories in ways that re-create modes of world-making grounded in cross-cultural and cross-temporal texts in motion.

Notes

1. Some scholars (see Voss 1973) acknowledge the variety of literary production in the seventeenth and eighteenth centuries. Yet the assumed lack of literary merit, or what O'Brien ([1931] 1969, 20) disparagingly calls the "primitive formlessness" of early short narratives, has prevented any attempt to examine more seriously the widespread use of short narratives in the context of America's colonial literature (cf. Current-García 1985, 14). Weber (1987, ix) sums up the underlying assumptions of normative and retrospective short story definitions and their effects: "Their [Matthew's and Pattee's] thesis that the short story constitutes a particular genre with its own specific qualities, essentially different from the novel, and that it is a peculiarly American accomplishment, became a critical norm for them. It may have been valid for their own period, but they also projected it back onto earlier times. The result was that many forms of short story writing that had emerged during the 18th and early 19th centuries did not fulfill their criteria and were ignored" (cf. Matthews [1885] 1994; Pattee [1924] 1966). For a first comprehensive overview and categorization of early short narratives, see Pitcher (2000, 1); for reevaluations of early forms of storytelling, see Nagel (2008, 11–19); Hochbruck, Erdogan, and Fidler (2008); and Scheiding and Seidl (2011).

2. See, for example, Gardner (2012), who qualifies the rise of the novel by looking at magazine literature, and McGill (2003, 5), who regards the use of reprints as vital for the

reconstruction of a historical "culture and its audiences." For the transmission of short narratives in early American magazines, see Scheiding (2012).

3. See the surveys by Werlock (2000), May (2002), Scofield (2006), March-Russell (2009), and Bendixen and Nagel (2010). According to Pitcher (2000, 1:1), short magazine fiction saw the "gradual coming together" of elements from different oral genres that form the modern short story.

4. Many of the currently available anthologies evaluate eighteenth- and nineteenth-century short narratives from an essentialist point of view that relates the later short story to notions of origin, fictionality, and literary quality. Literary histories and anthologies frequently begin their chronology with one of Irving's tales as the first short story; see Boddy (2011).

5. Poe's (1846) definition of the short "prose composition" (164) as a text that can be perused "in one sitting" (163) and uses a tight structure, multiple levels of meanings, and effective language to achieve a "unity of impression" (163) upon the reader has become a critical commonplace and can be found even in the most recent surveys of the genre (cf. Basseler 2011, 44). Its usefulness for defining the short story has nevertheless been questioned, as its criteria are difficult to quantify, such as brevity or the unity of effect, and generally distinguish short stories from longer prose forms like the novel (Bonheim 1982; Lohafer and Clarey 1989).

6. Among those tales that fail to conform to modern aesthetic standards are popular tales of the supernatural, graphic violence, sexual deviancy, and moral depravity that can be found in narratives in eighteenth- and nineteenth-century magazines and newspapers (Scheiding, forthcoming). For a survey of sensationalist literature in early American magazines, see Pitcher and Hartigan (2000).

7. James Hartman (1999) develops a history of American literature out of wonder and providential tales, under which he also subsumes captivity and apparition tales, based on the importance of religious literature for the origins of the English novel (see McKeon 1987). Dorothy Baker (2007, 8–9, 38–39) establishes a continuation of supernatural themes and forms from the providence tale of Cotton Mather's works to the fiction of Melville, Hawthorne, and Poe.

8. The vibrant scholarly field of eighteenth- and nineteenth-century print culture and the reassessment of literary production, genres of print, and reading audiences have exchanged notions of author and origination for circulatory patterns of textual commodities and the denaturalization of authorship over the emergence of a specific genre (frequently the novel) or a literary movement. For theoretical implications of "cultures of circulation," see Lee and LiPuma (2002) and Edwards (2011). For changing attitudes toward early American literary history in terms of what Bourdieu (1993) calls the "field of cultural production," see Loughran (2007), Jackson (2008), Dowling (2011), and Weyler (2013).

9. The quipu consists of a system of strings and knots used by the Incas to record and communicate data; it contains both numerical and other information in a writing system that has not yet been fully decoded. As Lindstrom (2004) presumes, the quipu could potentially also entail "folktales and poetry" as a cultural memory in narrative form. For the shift from oral traditions to Native literacies, see Bross and Wyss (2008).

10. Following independence, Latin American nations aimed at forging a literary tradition of their own, leading to an adaptation of the *costumbrista* movement, which rediscovers folk and indigenous ways of life and evokes a "usable" and mythic past in collections of short narratives and magazines, such as Ricardo Palma's *Peruvian Traditions* (1872–1910; see Echevarría 1997, 11–15).

11. For current reevaluations of American and British magazine culture, see Kamrath and Harris (2005, 221–364) and Powell (2011, 241).

12. Recent studies (see Fergus 2006) on readership in eighteenth-century England reveal that readers were more interested in short tales, fragments, and essays than in the novels that define the period from a modern critical perspective. This distortion is partly the result of the ephemeral nature and lower cost of pamphlets, periodicals, and chapbooks, only a fraction of which have survived. The predominance of the novel has far-reaching implications for the study of narrative in its variety and productivity. Altman (2008, 4) concludes that "romance, epic, pastoral, sacred history, the *fabliau* and other comic tales—all of these were effectively written out of the definition of narrative by developments associated with the rise of novel." For a recent attempt to reconstruct the "rise of the American novel," see Gura (2013).

13. Rather than part of a world system or a global comparative approach, Hayot (2012, 49) regards worldedness as an "aesthetic effect," namely the "world-oriented force of any given work of art." Approaching narratives as literary objects shaped by multiple intentions and mediators, *Worlding America* uses worldedness to describe their reference to the actual world of the Americas. The sections in this volume consider how the various functions of narrative relate to it, as ways to explore localities, meet popular demand for information and entertainment, or defy marginalization and participate in the discussion of social and political questions. The concept of worlding captures the processes of cultural exchange, whereas worldedness refers to the relationship between the texts and the actual world of the Americas and the ways in which the social finds symbolic expression within formal and aesthetic patterns of short narrations; for recent hemispheric, transnational, and global theories and methodologies in early American literature, see the special section "Theories and Methodologies" in *PMLA* (2013).

14. Giles (2011) links the uncertainty of geographical boundaries and the mingling of ethnicities in seventeenth- through early nineteenth-century America to the ongoing cultural, economic, and political globalization starting late in the twentieth century. For a critical evaluation of the concept of global literature, see Prendergast (2001) and White (2008).

15. Gillman and Gruesz (2011, 230) go beyond the transnational turn and argue for a "worlded analysis" that implies three scales: time, space, and language. In practice, many of the approaches to world literature studies have focused on a specific genre, primarily the novel, and tried to demonstrate its development empirically (see Moretti 2005). With its focus on genre and binary comparisons, comparative literature, however, does not account for literary networks of production and consumption (see Flint 2011); for authorial economies, see Jackson (2008), and for "literary capitalism," see Cohen (2012).

16. As a critical concept, worlding implies the world as the horizon for analyzing literary production and circulation, foregrounding the material conditions and the cultures of circulation in which constant movements of textual commodities take place, making the nation only "one point on the spatial scale . . . along with region, hemisphere, climactic zone, trade zone, and so on" (Gillman and Gruesz 2011, 229; Lee and LiPuma 2002). A worlding approach draws upon multiple circles—geographical, temporal, and linguistic—while constantly shifting its centers. As a result, the United States would lose the "conceptual power that comes with being the center from which a comparison is made" (Gillman and Gruesz 2011, 230). Medovoi (2011, 657) investigates literature that is "*about* US power" and reads it as "politico-libidinal forms of allegory" that represent "unequal exchanges around the globe." For Medovoi, "worlding" is not a mapping device or concord fiction—i.e., ordinary views—of global developments, but literature itself is a "textually complex symptom of a world-system in transition" (657).

17. In the field of early American literature, recent anthologies go beyond an Anglocentric collection of texts by stressing the multilingual dimension of literary production in the colonial Americas, assigning only a minor role to the transatlantic workings of reprint and storytelling; see especially Mulford (2002), Bauer (2009), and Moore, Brooks, and Wigginton (2012).

PART I

LIFE WRITING

LIFE WRITING IS A BURGEONING FIELD—especially in combination with a transnational perspective—not only as a subject for literary scholarship, but also with the diversification of its practices in the Internet age. Across cultures and ages, the various practices of biographical and personal writings have provided important ways of constructing one's identity in relation to the surrounding culture and society. "Life writing" generally refers to the various types of writing that take a life as the subject, including both self-referential and biographical texts.[1] It raises awareness and yields power that can challenge mainstream and hegemonic discourses, such as in the life narratives of women, indigenous groups, ethnic minorities, and migrants. In British North America, for example, the biographies of the New England governors, military officials, and church leaders featured in Cotton Mather's *Magnalia Christi Americana* (1702) contrast with the lives of servants, slaves, and minorities who emerge from the selection of late eighteenth-century confession narratives. Similarly, the oral records of Native American lives found their way into the writings of colonial officials, ministers, and missionaries, leading to the combination of authoritative texts and marginalized voices that are included, for example, in both the *Jesuit Relations* and Christopher Sauer's "Description of Pennsylvania."

Exploring, conquering, and traveling the new continent are mirrored in a host of autographed and printed documents ranging from informal diaries to the highly stylized journals of Columbus. Rather than full-fledged autobiographies, the documents selected for this chapter represent only episodes or turning points in the lives of the writers. However, the construction of a subject position has to balance individual experience with the influence of conventions as well as the intentions of the writers, printers, editors, and other intermediaries involved in publishing life writings of the seventeenth and eighteenth centuries. The most prevalent autobiographical form of the seventeenth century—the spiritual autobiography—is a retrospective account that divides a life into three stages that sometimes repeat themselves. The subject first revels in worldly behavior, is then awakened through a religious experience, and subsequently decides to lead a holy life. Going back to Augustine's *Confessions* (c. 398) and flourishing in the seventeenth and eighteenth centuries among Protestants on both sides of the Atlantic, the spiritual autobiography fashions its subject's life according to biblical patterns to legitimate the writing and its writer, much like the lives of saints related in Catholic hagiography (Bertsch 2004, 4). For their authors to be considered exemplary Christians and their writings truthful and instructive, these writings had to conform to biblical models and norms, as many of them were addressed to the members of the author's family. Consequently, elements of the spiritual autobiography—such as a conventionalized plot and biblical formulations—have influenced Protestant narratives of all kinds; this can be seen in Mary Rowlandson's *Souvereignty of God* (1682), in "The Narrative of Marie le Roy and Barbara Leininger" (1759; see Part II) where the experience of captivity is compared to a spiritual journey, and also in many of Daniel Defoe's novels. At the same time, personal writings—from letters to diaries and reports—were a primary source for information about the New World that both captivated the European readership and "kept communities connected and informed" (Imbarrato 2012, 65). The *Jesuit Relations*, for example, comprise a number of letters, journals, and formal communications that were sent by Jesuit missionaries in modern-day Canada to their superiors in France. These reports not only document the progress of the missionary activities, but also describe Native life, folklore, language, and religion, and trace the health and personal thoughts of each writer. Between 1632 and 1673 the *Relations* were collected and published annually in Paris, but then forgotten about until the Canadian government reissued them in 1894 along with other archival material. The excerpt printed in this volume illustrates the tensions between French colonial rule, the Jesuits' willingness to accommodate and live among the Natives, and the complex relationships among the various Native tribes both with the French and among themselves. When the French commander Samuel de Champlain refuses to liberate a Huron murderer, his explanation of French law is at first accepted but then challenged by the family of the accused, and the Jesuits act as mediators even though they are unable to pacify all the Natives. Colonial law emerges as a "master discourse that delimits subjects, geographies, and knowledge" (Boyer 2010, 26), as illustrated by the negotiations between missionaries Paul Le Jeune and Jean de Brébeuf with the Wyandot people ("Hurons" in French) in a report that is similar to that of Carlos de Sigüenza y Góngora's historical account of the *Misfortunes of Alonso Ramírez* (1690). The *Jesuit Relations* thus register the complicated and dangerous position of the missionaries who found themselves caught between the intentions of French colonization and the policies of the different Native tribes. The Jesuits' interest in understanding the Hurons' customs and principles is obvious; as they record the Hurons' argumentation, they endow the indigenous peoples with a distinct voice and offer multiple perspectives on the issues.

For Puritans like Edward Taylor, diaries relate individual experience to patterns of religious history as they search for divine communications in daily events. Confronted with the question of whether their souls were elected for eternal communion with God or doomed to damnation, Puritans carefully noted what happened to them and to their surroundings, searching for signs of God's approval or discipline as demonstrated by the journals of John Winthrop, William Bradford, and John Hull. In contrast, the diaries of Samuel Sewall and of John Pike, a minister in Dover, New Hampshire, present events in an objective and succinct style, using a chronological sequence for short remarks on the weather and activities of each day with few theological references. Still, they are all involved in the Puritan practice of self-examination in which the status of the soul is assessed and its progress made visible. As the personal records in Part I deal with transatlantic travel and life on the new continent, they also participate in the network of texts and intentions surrounding the voyage to and exploration of America.

Edward Taylor was an English minister who immigrated to Massachusetts in 1668, where he studied at Harvard and worked as a pastor and physician in Westfield. Considered one of the most eminent colonial poets, he continued the tradition of the metaphysical poets in England of a generation earlier, most notably John Donne and George Herbert, whom Taylor greatly admired. Poetry, like diary-keeping, was regarded as a tool for private meditation and reflection; it was not considered an artistic activity deserving publication (Mather 1726, 42). Taylor's diary is preserved in manuscript form, and its material condition becomes visible when individual words are missing or unclear due to a torn page or to Taylor's use of shorthand (also a typical element of Puritan diaries), all of which are indicated in the text by the original editor.

While Taylor exemplified the Puritan production of devotional texts and scribal publication, Christopher Sauer was one of the most active publishers and printers in eighteenth-century Pennsylvania. At his press in Germantown, he published almanacs, pamphlets, primers, and books (such as a German Bible translation), along with newspapers and periodicals. Born in 1693, he immigrated to Pennsylvania by way of Rotterdam in 1724, and worked as a pharmacist, a clockmaker, and a farmer before acquiring a printing press from German pietists in 1738. His German Bible was the first Bible printed in America, and his almanac, *Der Hoch-deutsch americanische Calender* (1739–77), and newspaper, *Der Hoch-Deutsch Pennsylvanische Geschicht-Schreiber* (1739–77), were widely read among Germans in Pennsylvania and Maryland. Both Taylor's and Sauer's reports of their journeys to and arrivals in America can be related to a number of similar texts and forms of travel writing, which were not only promotional tracts but also shipwreck and providence tales.

The arduous and dangerous sea journey becomes a defining experience for colonial settlers, explorers, and missionaries alike. With its exceptional length of at least six weeks, and dangers that ranged from unpredictable weather conditions to starvation, political conflicts, and pirates, the journey provided travelers with a great many new experiences. Yet in their reactions to hitherto unknown threats, theological and cultural differences emerge: French Jesuits resign themselves to God in the midst of a storm, while Puritan historiographers like Edward Johnson recount stories of safe passages that serve as signs of divine favor (see "Suggestions for Further Reading"). Similarly, Edward Taylor records instances of divine help: as the ship stalls, "it pleased the Lord . . . to answer our prayers as to cleare the aire . . . and to give us a fresh, gentle gale that made us slide on at a great pace." In addition to his observation of nautical phenomena and the sea, Taylor's entries correspond to those of other Puritan ministers who account for their spiritual lives and devotional activities: observing the Lord's Day, praying, and studying the Bible. Taylor also records the strange foods and animals that he encounters, thereby anticipating the marvelous descriptions in other exploration accounts, such as John Josselyn's *Account of Two Voyages to New England* (1675). In contrast, Sauer uses another common strategy to mediate the American experience, comparing the climate and plants that he finds in America to those in Europe.

Apart from the voyage, Sauer embraces the religious freedom and multiethnic conditions of Pennsylvania, but he also records the exploitation of Native Americans by colonial traders and settlers. With great respect for their morality and peacefulness, as well as a lively interest in their customs and religion, Sauer remarks that the Native Americans "are putting most Europeans to shame by their behavior." He is also acutely aware of Pennsylvania's unique position among the North American settlements of the time, in that it is based on religious freedom, a welcome departure from the kind of persecution that he and other radical Protestants suffered in their native Europe. While the Americas are divided into English, Spanish, French, and Dutch territories, Pennsylvania's tolerant religious policies make it a multi-faith community of "French, Welsh, Swedes, Dutch and Germans." Throughout Sauer's account, Pennsylvania emerges as a land of opportunity. He outlines the need for skilled workers and describes how he was welcomed upon his arrival and embraced by the German-speaking community; strangers immediately offered money and a job. Both Taylor and Sauer wrote during a period in which letters and journals were circulated among friends and copied—a time when the modern distinction between public and private spheres did not exist (Hewitt 2004). Sauer, for example, communicates with his "[d]ear Brothers and Friends" as a group, "[s]ince it is not possible to make a special report to each one [and] many may make shift with one account." These public letters served as a primary source of information about the New World and also as advertisements to promote emigration to America. Sauer's letter, for example, contains both specific and general advice about coming to Pennsylvania—practical information about farming and living conditions, prices for commodities and food, and occupations that were particularly sought after.

Anthony Thacher's letter to his brother Peter in England was copied by a number of New Englanders and has survived in the Mather papers. As the news of his shipwreck spread throughout the colony, it was recorded, for example, in John Winthrop's diary of 1635, which also circulated as a manuscript until 1790 (Winthrop 1996, 153). When collecting "wonders of Divine goodness" roughly fifty years later, Increase Mather quotes the account of the storm and shipwreck from Thacher's letter. Its various uses and transfer into print indicate that individual experience can always be related to the community as a whole. Thus, John Winthrop subsumes Thacher into an account written from the perspective of the colony at large. In Mather's *Illustrious Providences* (1684), however, the letter becomes the source for a historical event that illustrates God's unbroken care for the New England Protestants.

In contrast to the Atlantic voyage in "The Remarkable Deliverance of Major Gibbon," first published by James Janeway in England (1674) and most likely based on John Winthrop's journal (see "Suggestions for Further Reading"), Anthony Thacher's shipwreck actually did take place during a journey along the New England coast. A comparison of publication histories reveals the different uses to which a narrative can be put, ranging from personal information to the establishment of a communal history and evidence of divine interventions. Protestant reports counter the danger and chaos of sea journeys with patterns of providential history or divine favor, while Carlos de Sigüenza y Góngora records the experience of Alonso Ramírez as a series of misfortunes and hazards that kept him away from home for fifteen years, during which he traveled around the world as a sailor, slave, and captive. Ramírez's eyewitness account embodies the Atlantic and Pacific struggle of Spanish America against English, Dutch, and French colonial powers. Often regarded as a foundational text of South American literature, *The Misfortunes of Alonso Ramírez* (1690) raises a number of issues related to life writing in the seventeenth century and the construction of a subject in the position of both teller and writer. While English providential collections, such as Increase Mather's *Illustrious Providences*, are based primarily on written sources, Alonso Ramírez introduces himself as the subject of his account, even though it is transcribed by Carlos de Sigüenza y Góngora, a mathematician and astronomer as well as a member of the Creole elite of Mexico City. Sigüenza's historical account consists of a complex network of three entities: Ramírez's experience, Sigüenza's penmanship, and the censorship of the King's Royal Convent of Jesus and Mary in Mexico City (Lázaro 2011, 103–4). *Misfortunes* marks a transition from historiography to the articulation of a specific voice of a Creole intellectual culture "that is strategically negotiating his position towards the European within the framework of what is for the first time a view of the World that, if very problematic, is realistic, organized, and comprehensive" (Buscaglia-Salgado 2005, n.p.; cf. Boyer 2010, 26–28). Distinct from Spanish genres like the picaresque, in whose tradition many critics have tried to place the text, *Misfortunes* unfolds a unique cultural, legal, and maritime history about colonial Spanish America.

Similar to the selections in Part III, "The Circum-Atlantic World," the narrative situates Ramírez's journey in an economy based on trade and slavery and the colonial contest for power and territory among European nations. Like a modern autobiography, it starts with the situation of the Ramírez family in

Puerto Rico, which has been reduced to poverty level because the country's main exports—gold and cacao—have dwindled over the years. On his journey Ramírez travels the Spanish and Portuguese empires and is also held captive for two years by British pirates in the Philippines. Against this background of shifting roles and ambiguous identities, *Misfortunes* evolves as an amalgamation of voices and intentions that mirrors the complexity of colonial communication networks and economic relationships.

Similarly, the confessions of convicted money forger John Syllavan (alias Owen Syllavan) and rapist Thomas Powers provide evidence of the hardships experienced by marginal groups in the colonial economy—many of which are still present in today's society—and of the desire to keep the social order intact. The Irishman John Syllavan arrived in Boston as an indentured servant, as did many others who were too poor to fund the journey or were convicts seeking their freedom. Syllavan worked for seven years clearing land for a farmer in upper Massachusetts and as a soldier in the British army. After his term of indenture was complete, he stayed on with the army. As chief armorer, he developed skills at engraving and became a successful money forger, eventually heading a "club" of associates that operated throughout New England. Though he evaded or escaped imprisonment multiple times, he was finally captured and executed in 1756. Thomas Powers, an African American born into servitude in Connecticut, was executed in 1792 for raping a woman in New Hampshire. Before their executions, both Syllavan and Powers wrote their confessions, which were then published as small octavos of twelve pages; Syllavan's account was reprinted in 1802, but without the woodcut of an execution that was inserted on the second page of the 1756 version. The frontispiece of Powers's confession highlights both his ethnicity and his crime, featuring a woodcut image of a skull and bones and establishing a visual connection through the capitalization of both "Negro" and "Rape."

The confession—a typical genre of the seventeenth and eighteenth centuries and the precursor of the crime and detective literature of the nineteenth—presents a trajectory opposite to that of the spiritual autobiography. In contrast to a retrospective account of conversion and serving God, the confession recounts the life stories of convicts as a series of moral infractions that led to the crimes for which they faced execution. The typical plot of the confession therefore establishes a story of moral decline that originates in the convict's childhood (Williams 1993, 220). It is exemplified by Syllavan's running away from home, his emigration to America, and an early infatuation with sexuality.

Surveying narratives of the lives and executions of criminals in books, sermons, dying verses, and final speeches—typically circulated as broadsides—one finds sustained reader interest throughout two centuries and across social spheres, as indicated by the reprint of Syllavan's account and the collections of similar cases in periodicals and crime gazettes such as *The American Bloody Register* (1784) and *The Malfactors' Register* (1813).

Both confessions also highlight the prejudices and social functions behind much of the genre that associate specific crimes with specific ethnicities. While the convicts' fate acted as a warning to would-be malefactors, local ministers accompanied the condemned to the gallows and delivered a sermon explaining the negative consequences of sin in an attempt to shape social behavior. Publication of the sermons and confessions carried the social impact even further, addressing the audience in general, and sometimes even admonishing specific groups to return to God's ways. Yet the confessions also created a moral and racial Other against which colonial society could define itself amid a constant flow of multiethnic immigration. Syllavan's and Powers's confessions thus reinforce "racism as an interpretative strategy," as their repeated offenses and designs are exposed along with their weakness in being unable to resist temptation.[2]

Through the texts of this chapter, diverse perspectives on the Americas emerge at the intersection of personal writing, literary conventions, and the themes of exploration and travel. Syllavan's and Powers's confessions present lives as a series of vices that culminate in execution; they are thus stigmatized and positioned outside of social norms and publicly accepted behavior. Taylor's and Sauer's texts, which are either private or directed at only a small audience of friends, depict them as members of transatlantic religious communities. As Puritans and radical pietists, they experienced persecution in Europe, while the publication of the Ramírez narrative and the convictions of Syllavan and Powers reflect the social hierarchy and prejudices of colonial society. These narratives also represent the diversity of life writing produced during this period, ranging from retrospective texts that reveal a clear trajectory and conventional plot to that of Taylor, who writes his diary unaware of the outcome. Thus, instead of a plot, Taylor's diary contains chronological entries held together by the geographical and temporal movement of his journey, which only in hindsight are endowed with a fixed beginning and end. Sauer's texts—a considerable number of letters, travelogues, and promotional tracts that made the journey back across the Atlantic—compare and contrast the old and new worlds to advertise and inform about living conditions on the new continent. Among the authors in this section, only Powers was born in North America, and while his roots are African, the "routes" that go along with them represent the multiple narratives behind a circum-Atlantic world and its flow of people, commodities, and stories.

TRAVEL

PAUL LE JEUNE

*Relation of What Occurred in New France in the Year 1633 (1634)**

On the 4th, another council was held; I was present with Father Brebeuf, because the embarkation of our Fathers was to be talked over. Sieur de Champlain made his presents, which corresponded in value to those that the Hurons had made him.[3] To accept presents from the Savages is to bind oneself to return an equivalent. A great many things were spoken of in this council; among others, the Hurons asked for the liberation of the Savage prisoner who had recently killed a Frenchman, as I stated above. Sieur de Champlain sought earnestly to make the Hurons understand that it was not right to restore him to liberty; and that, having killed a Frenchman who had done him no harm, he deserved death. The Hurons were satisfied with the reason given them. They spoke also of the friendship contracted between them and the French, saying that it would be greatly strengthened by the Fathers going into their country.

The Hurons were the happiest people in the world. Those who were to embark and to carry the Fathers in their canoes had already received pay for their future trouble; we had placed in their hands the parcels or little baggage of the Fathers. We had gone to the Storehouse to sleep, Father de Nouë and I,[4]

* SOURCE: From Le Jeune, Paul. (1634) 1898. *Relation de ce qui s'est passé en La Novelle France, en l'année 1633*. In *The Jesuit Relations and Allied Documents: Travels and Explorations of the Jesuit Missionaries in New France, 1610–1791*, edited by Ruben Gold Thwaites. Vol. 6, 7–15. Cleveland: Burrows Brothers.

PUBLICATION HISTORY: *The Jesuit Relations* comprises annual reports from the Canadian mission of the Society of Jesus to its Paris office, in the years 1632 to 1672. They were written by missionaries in the field, then sent to Québec, where they were edited by the church superior to be printed in France by Sébastien Cramoisy. As ethnographic and travel accounts they were read for a long time and considered important documents of the French presence in North America. Reuben Gold Thwaites edited the original texts, written in French, Latin, and Italian, in 73 volumes from 1896 to 1901.

with our three Fathers, that we might see them off early the next morning in their little canoes, and might say to them our last farewell, when all at once our joy was changed into sadness. At about ten or eleven o'clock that night, a one-eyed Savage, belonging to the Island tribe, closely allied to the tribe of the prisoner, went among the cabins of all the Savages crying out that they should be careful not to take any Frenchmen in their canoes, and that the relatives of the prisoner were on the watch along the river to kill the Frenchmen, if they could catch them during the passage. On the previous Sunday some Savages of the same tribe as the prisoner had held a council with the captains of the Montagnaits,[5] of the island Savages, and of the Hurons, to determine how they might secure the pardon of this prisoner. The Hurons were besought to ask it. They refused, and this Island Savage, whose tribe was allied to the tribe of the murderer, raised this general cry among the cabins, warning every one not to give passage to a Frenchman, unless they wished to place him in evident danger of his life. Having heard the cry, and Father Brebeuf, who was listening, having interpreted its meaning to me, I went with Father de Nouë to the fort to give information of the same to sieur de Champlain.

We had been sleeping in the storehouse of the French, around which the Savages were encamped. The Fort was opened to us; and, after having made known the object of our night visit, we returned to the place whence we had departed. Upon the way we found the Captains of the Savages in council, to whom the Interpreter, according to the order of sieur de Champlain, declared that he desired to talk to them once more before their departure. The next morning, at daybreak, a Savage passed through the camp proclaiming that they were not to depart that day; and that the young men should keep the peace, and that those who had not sold all their merchandise should sell it. About eight or nine in the morning, sieur de Champlain again assembled the Captains of the Hurons, the Island Savages who had made this outcry, and the Captain of the Montagnaits. He asked the Savage why he had aroused that opposition; he answered that the whole country was in a state of alarm, and that it would be lost if the French were embarked to be taken to the Hurons, for the relatives of the prisoner would not fail to kill some of the party and that thereupon war would be declared; that the Hurons even would be dragged into it; for, if they defended the French, they would be attacked, and that thus the whole country would be lost; that he had not aroused any opposition, but had merely made known the wicked designs of the murderer's relatives; that, if the prisoner were released, these troubles would immediately be ended, and that the river and the whole country would be free.

The Hurons were asked if they still adhered to their wish to take us to their country. They answered that the river was not theirs, and that great caution must be observed in regard to those other tribes, if they were to pass by in security. As far as they were concerned, they asked nothing better than to furnish passage to the French. I observed the discretion of these Savages, for they gave evidence of their affection for us, in such manner as not to offend the tribes through which they must pass in coming to Kebec.[6] One of them, addressing the Island Savage, said: "Now listen; when we shall be up there in thy country, do not say that we have not spoken in behalf of the prisoner; we have done all that we could, but what answer wouldst thou have us make to the reasons given by sieur de Champlain? The French are the friends of all of us; if it depended only upon us, we should embark them." It must be confessed that the Hurons showed a strong inclination to take our Fathers with them. Sieur de Champlain, seeing this so sudden change, did all in his power, and gave us liberty to advance all the reasons we could, to the end that our fathers might be set on their way. He urged very strong and very pertinent reasons; he used threats; he proposed peace and war; in short nothing more could be desired. But to all this the Savage answered that they could not restrain their young men; that he had given warning of their wicked intentions, and that the French ought to postpone their departure for this year; that they would vent their anger upon the Hiroquois,[7] their enemies, and then the river would be free. "Do not blame us," said he, "if misfortune overtakes you; for we could not restore order." Thereupon, in order to win over this Savage, I asked for the pardon of the prisoner, having previously agreed upon this with sieur de Champlain, who replied to me that it was a matter of life and death with him, and that our great King would ask him to give an account of the man who had been killed. I begged him to suspend the execution of the death sentence, until the King might be spoken to, and his will learned. And thereupon, following my point, I addressed the Savages, representing our affection for them; saying that we had never sought the death of any one; that we everywhere tried to promote peace.

Sieur de Champlain did admirably on his part, saying that we talked to God; that we were loved by all who knew us, that he wanted no other witnesses of this than the Hurons themselves, who had cherished us so dearly; that we were going to teach them great things. The Hurons answered that it was very well, that we had proposed a good expedient; that of postponing the death of this Savage until we should have news from our great King. I then importuned the Island Savage, asking him whether the prisoner's kindred, if they knew that we were pleading

HVRONVM EXPLICATA TABVLA
OENTARONK LACVS
TIONONTATE
LACVS SVPERIOR
MARE DVLCE
ONTARIO
SANCTI LVDOVICI
NOVVM BELGIVM
NOVA SVECIA
VIR GI NIA
Concilium

FIG. 1: Map Depicting French Indian Encounters in the Northern and Great Lake region, including the martyrdom of French Jesuits Jean de Brébeuf and Gabriel Lalemant. Francesco Bressani, *Novae Franciae Accurata Delineatio*, 1657. Bibliothèque nationale de France.

for him, would not allow us to pass if they encountered us. "What dost thou wish me to say?" he answered, "they are furious. If the prisoner is not liberated, there is no safety; they will pardon no one." Thereupon the Interpreter replied: "If they act the part of devils, so will we." In a word, Sieur de Champlain intimidated them, saying they must look out for themselves; that if a Savage was seen with arms, he would give permission to his men to fire upon him and kill him; that they [the savages] had threatened him himself, because he went about alone; but hereafter he would not go around like a child, but like a soldier. "I am a friend to all, you are my friends," said he to the Hurons; "I love you; I have risked my life for you, I will risk it again; I will protect you; but I am the enemy of evil-doers."

EDWARD TAYLOR

*An Atlantic Voyage (1668)**

[Anno D]omini. 1668. April 26, being Lord's [day, a]t between 10-11 at night, I came [for s]ea, taking [a] bote at Execution Dock, Wa[pping], with another, [a] Gentlewoman, and had a smoo[th] tide, a gentle Gale of Winde and a prosporous [fa]re to Gravesend about 4 on the 2nd day; and then the winde arose [and the w]ater was rough and so continued that [tide. A]bout 9 of [the] clocke we being dispatcht we waited for passengers till almost night. [A]t night we removed about a league.

[Tue]sday, 28, in the morning, haveing a fair [s]ail, on we went, and about eight of the cloc[k] we were over against Chatham, and the winde being somewhat contrary, we cast a[nchor] and continued till towards 6 of [the] clock at night, and th[en] striking saile we came to the Downs and there [dis]mist our Pilot, and some of our company went to [Deal?] and there continued til the next day, the winde being con[trary].

Wednesday, 29, In the Morning the ship were blown so th[at] the Boy of the Anchor were under the Rudder of the S[hip]; the winde was still contrary and

* SOURCE: Taylor, Edward. 1964. "An Atlantic Voyage." In *The Diary of Edward Taylor*, edited and with a short introduction by Francis Murphy, 25–36. Springfield, MA: Connecticut Valley Historical Museum. Copyright 1964 by Springfield Library and Museums Association. Reprinted by permission of the Springfield Museums Association, formerly the Springfield Library and Museums Association. Original manuscript held by Redwood Library and Athenaeum, Newport, Rhode Island, USA.
PUBLICATION HISTORY: The handwritten manuscript of Taylor's diary was believed to be lost, but was kept by Henry W. Taylor, a descendant of the author, who gave it to the Massachusetts Historical Society, which printed it in a modernized version: "The Diary of Edward Taylor." 1880. *Proceedings of the Massachusetts Historical Society* 18: 5–15.

somewhat high. [At] noon the Shipmaster went ashore, and came no [more] that day. At evening his bote had liked [to] hav[e been] lost, the winds being still high and contrary.

Thursday, 30, we are forced to tarry, the winds remaining contrary. On friday,

May 1, We are forced to tarry, for the winds we[re still c]ontrary, lying in the west. Then there came a [*torn*] of Marchant that were bound for Bar[badoes] [*torn*] with the Shipmasters, then also [*torn*] London and another to Sketchly.[8] [At nigh]t the winds were high. But on Satur[day, May 2 . . .] In the morning we were set upon [with a vio]lent storm, insomuch that the seamen beg[an to ap]prehend the ship to be in great danger, and [in th]eir looking to their Cables and tacklings were wet through to the skin. The waves flashed over the sh[ip. The] Mate in his hastening to his business would [oft] hasten the men with this motive, that if [the] cable should breake it were as much as a[ll our liv] es were worth. The fore Castle of the ship wa[s fi]lled ankle deep [and] flowed with water, and he said he were there till the water run out [of the] wast of his breeches. But about ten of the [cloc]k the storm was over, and in the evening the sun [set] very cleare. I being on the Decke heard a trum[pe]t play, most curiously in one of the King's [m]en of war. I also then saw a Porpus swiming [a]long the water. On the Lord's day,

May 3, I had a sad forenoone but towards evening [th]e shipmaster sent for me and injoined me to go [to] prayer with them. On Munday,

[May 4], the winde still remained in the North-west, co[ntrary] to us, but it was a comfortable day. On Tuesday, May 5, We had fare weather but a West winde [s]til. About four in the afternoone two of the King's men of war came and fired, w[h]ere before the report of the gun [t]here first gave a flash like li[ghtning, t]hen arose a thick smoke, like as a [*torn*] after that the burst. Wednesda[y],

May 6, Was a fair day but the [*torn*]. [At] night about one of [the] clock [*torn* . . . wa]ter, [cryi]ng out for healp, who with much ado was [sav]ed though almost drowned before. He belo[ngs to] the Man of war called the Admirall, and affirms [that] there came one out before him to swim [a]way, but what was become of him, whether drowned or not, he knew not. On Thirsday,

May 7, In the morning the winde was fair for us, and [t]herefore we hoisted up saile, and on forward; and when the master called [us] to prayer the mate was backward, saying that our course was so shor[t] that we should turn before half an hour, insomuch that tarrying till we had passed that place. And so we were put off, but when he had sayled about three Leagues as was supposed, and come over against the South Point, the winde turned and was South-west, just against us, insomuch that we and many more other ships was fain to fall saile, and so were drove back to the Downs again, about two Leagues and an ha[lf], and there we cast anchor, the winde being somewhat high. But in the evening it was very com[fort]able weather, but a contrary winde. Friday,

May 8, was a cleare day but windy. Saturday,

May 9, was a calm, cleare morning but cloudy and stormy in the afternoone. On Lord's day,

May 10, In the morning it were very wet, and when it gave over raining the winde rose and was high all day.

May 11, The winde was very high, but the weather =[clear?] [a]nd in the afternoon it raind. At night I saw [the] light that was set up upon the South foreland [to] give light to passengers. Tuesday,

[M]ay 12, the winde was still contrary.

[Ma]y 13, was a comfortable day, but the winde contra[ry] [*torn*] [and t]herefore served right to bring in the Straits flig[ht], [for] then they came in. About noon I saw three Porpoises [like] hogs, swimming southward. On Thursday,

May 14, The winde was North-East and then we prepared to weigh Anchor and hoile [i.e. *hoist*] up Sayle, and in the meanetime the Lieutenant of the King's man of war, called the "Princess," came to search for a man that had made his escape, but he were not with us. This were about noon. About four [of] the clocke we came over against Dover. There went a great flight, consisting of about [5]o saile, as is supposed. But we were interested, what by the King's officer and the sayler's business [so t]hat we were put off from our morning duty [of] prayer. The winde was very calme so that we [did] but drill along very slily and sloly. The day was [v]ery comfortable. I sent a letter to my brother [R]ichard. About 11 a Clock at night we came over in sight of Farelee, and about six in the morning, May 15, on Friday, we came over against the [Be]ache, and had a fair easterly winde and a comfor[ta]ble morning. About one of [the] clock in the afternoon we came in sight of the Ile of White [i.e. *Wight*]. About four, Captain South, his ship bound for Barbadoes, overtooke us, we lowering our sails for him, and he received Letters tied in the [*blank*] Cord, and sent a pot of about two pounds of butter to our ship in the same [*word crossed out*] Cord, and told us that the man tha[t] had made his escape from the "Princess" was caught again in his ship by them. About eig[ht] of [the] clock we came over against the Ile of W[ight]. We sailed amain, having a fair winde, and cle[ar w]eather. On Saturday,

May 16, The winde was down and would not fill our sails in the morning, and the morning was cleare; bu[t] about noon that winde as were was South-we[st, the] sun hid with white clouds, and so it was till ni[ght]. [A]bout four a clock the wind was just agains[t] us, so that we did lower sails, and make a stand, but between five and six, I being on the quarter [d]eck, looking to see land, saw two birds call W[ills] [i.e. *sea-gulls*] swimming along the sea and the winde that were was Northward and so served for us again; and then [it] rose till we went on with it, being a side win[d] a good pace. Lord's Day,

May 17, We were constrained to drive on by angling in and out. About twelve of [the] clock I saw a fish rise out of the water with a back and should[ers] like a Hog, and a thing went from between his shoulders like a thick oxe horn, and they ca[ll it a] Grampus. On Munday,

May 18, We was constrained to drive on our voyage by angles also, but towards night [the] west threatened us with storms insomuch [that] we went aside to Plymouth. But being beni[gh]ted, we cast anchor in Plymouth Sound about [a] mile off of Plymouth Bay, just before St. F[ran]ces' Island. On Tuesday,

May 19, We continued on the Sound til toward night, and then we weighed anchor, and went to Catwater because the winde continued wes[ter]lie, and we judging that a safer harbour to lie in. But on Wednesday,

May 20, in the morning the Winde being Easterly, [we] weighed anchor againe to set forward on o[ur v]oyage about ten a clock. About three in the after[n]oon we came over against Deadman's Hea[d] [*now Dodman's point*]; [ab]out 4 we came against Weymouth;[9] about [fi]ve we came over against the Lizard, and the clou[ds driz]zled small rain. When we went from [Pl]ymouth we was forced to tarry on the Sound [for so]me of our company who were gone ashore, and [t]here we fired twice before they came. On

[M]ay 21, Thirsday morning, it rained, but the wind [w]as right with [us]; then we came into the sea [be]yond the Land's end; about 3 a clocke it cease[d] [r]aining, but was thick still. At evening the skie [t]hreatened us with stormes. We sailed about 6 [l]eagues a watch In the night we spied a ship [whi]ch we knew not, and somewhat mistrusted it, [bu]t it proved a Merchant. On Friday,

May 22, winde North-East, the morning cloudy and [da]rke, yet sometimes the sun did show himselfe. [Y]et after[ward] it rained, but before night it was some[wh]at comfortable weather. I vometed up both my [b]reakfast, dinner, and supper. We saw two ships at [n]ight on the lure [i.e. *leeward*] of ours. Saturday,

May 23, winde north, weather comfortable, we [st]eared South-west by west. About ten of [the] clock [we] received a cask of Rum from Captain Hunt's ship, who were our consort to New England. At night [th]e winde was down, and there rose a thick cloud [which colo]red the skie towards sunsetting. Lord's day,

May 24, the winde in the morning was very low, yet a rig[ht no]rth-East winde; afterwards it was higher but more Northerly. I then being put to exercise spake [f]rom John 3.3. In the morning watch we sailed 2 lea[gues and] 2 miles in a watch; at night 5 knots a glasse.

May 25, Munday, winde north-east; we sailed 4 knot[s a g]lass. We had a strange dish at dinner: a leg of [m]utton boiled and cut in gobbits, and powdered with sa[lt and] pepper, then some of the broth put into a dish [with so]me Claret wine and the gobbits put into it; then [t]hey broke some egges, and [added] viniger and [boiled?] them on a Cafing dish of Coals; after this [we mu]st have a second dish, i.e., Eggs backed in C[lar]et wine, and butter and pepper put therein; and w[hen] they boiled they melted the Dish bottom out, and th[en] in hast putting the mess into another dish they brake the eggs, and meddled them together and put [s]uggar in it, and so eat it as a meddley with spoo[ns]. We saw a great company of Porpoises swimming and playing at the head of our ship; and a ship, wh[ere] it were [from], or whither [bound], we know not. I saw a bir[d] flying over the waters. Tuesday,

May 26, Winde south-westward. We sailed 2 knots, in the forenoon watch, a glasse, and went one while Western by North, one while Western by Sou[th].

May 27, Wednesday, wind South East. Our ship went so awry that one could scarce stand without holding. The seas were very rough, so that the ship's roaling made me very much out of order. We sailed 8 leagues, 2 miles a watch; at night abo[ut] 6 leagues. I saw two Birds called Sheerwater skimi[ng] over the water, which I saw almost every day. Thirsday,

May 28, we had a fair North-East winde and sayled South-West by South. We were by this time well nigh 240 leagu[es] from England. Friday,

May 29, about 3 a clock in the morning the men were rallied in all hast, for the winde was turned. In the day it settled just in the west against us, so that w[e] were forced to take a cross course, one while sailing North-West by North, another South-West by South. Saturday,

May 30, Winde West by North. We sailed in [the] morning South-west by South; about 12 of the clock we went on of another tack and sailed North-west by west; the weather comfortable though the winde contrary. A black cloude lies towards sun set.

May 31, Lord's Day, Winde west. I was very sick so that [I co]uld not perform the Duties of the day. At night the winde [wa]s North and very high, insomuch that it served our [pu]rpose. We sailed amain South-West by West, having put [up a] new sail. Munday,

[Ju]ne 1, Winde North by West. I was crazy, yet retained [*illegible*] till supper, m[y di]nner being of fried liver and sweetbreads. The winde [fla]shed the waves over the ship, and those that were in the way were wet as if they were dipt in water. Tuesday,

June 2, Winde North by West; we sailed West; had a c[om]fortable day, a low winde. I saw a fish called a Carvil, and was indifferently well all day. Wednesd[ay],

June 3, Winde South, weather good. I was well and free [f]rom distemper, but towards night the winde rose and [t]hen I was not so perfect in health. I saw several Carvails, a fish called Boneta [i.e. *tuna*] and a huge flock of Porpoises and Albit[r]oses. At night we had such a fresh gale of winde that we sailed 11 leagues in a watch. Thirsday,

June 4, Winde South by West; we sailed West and Northward, at night North-west; had good weather. My health not so good as it was the day before. I saw an old [tr]ee swimming on the sea. Friday,

[Ju]ne 5, We had a fair winde and somewhat fresh, [b]eing North; we sailed West somewhat Northerly, [s]ometimes 6, sometimes 7 knots a glasse; at [n]ight we saw a company of Porpoises; in the even[i]ng there came a whale swimming by, but I being between decks, he was out of sight, before I came abaft.[10] Our Latitude were 44 [degrees] 23 minutes. Saturday,

[J]une 6, Winde North-East, a fresh gale, we [s]aild West by North, sometimes 6, sometimes 5 [knots] a glasse. Towards night we lowered sail and tarried about 2 glasses, i.e., an hour, for Captain Hunt our Consort, who was on the stern of us a league or more. Lord's day,

June 7, Winde North by East, somewhat fresh. We saild We[st]; Our latitude is 43 [degrees]. These three last [days] we sailed well nigh[11] 150 [leagues]. [A]bout noon we saw a drift of Porpoises. I being some [b]etter in health than before did exercise and apply the [do]ctrine that before I proved. I saw a little black [bird] called a Pickrill [i.e. *stormy petrel*] about as big as a Pie, fly along the water, and the seamen said it was [a] sign of a storm.

June 8, Monday, winde was faire in the morning, but low; at noone it whistled up and down, and at last settled in the North-west so that we sailed South by West. Tuesday,

June 9, about 2 a clock in the morning the winde was North and so served our purpose. Then I saw an old piece of wood swimming on the water; the pole was elevated; latitude 42 degrees, 14 [minutes]. We were on the south of Newfoundland and sounded with a line, sot for ground, but found none. Wednesday,

June 10, Winde West by North. We sailed South-West by West; the winde still, sea calm, and the day cleare. Our Master sent his bote for Captain Hunt to his ship to dine with us, and some of our passengers went back with him to his ship and there over dranke themselves, some of them.

June 11, Thirsday, winde calme so that we lay and could not go on all the afternoon. About 10 of [the] clock before noon in [*sic*] [we] saw a piece of wood about halfe a mile off on the water, and firewood beginning to ware, we saild to it, and it was a piece of White Firwood full of barnicles, which are things like due to worms skins about 2 inches long hanging to the wood, and the other end that did not stick to the wood had little shels on them, and that which is in the shels is the meate of them. We had a dish of them; and also there were many black fishes swimming by the wood and our Master with a fisgig [i.e., *harpoon*] caught a dish of them; and after we had tooke up the wood the fishes law [*sic*] [lay] by hundreds, (I believe), swimming about the ship all day after. We also saw a sharke which they said wer[e] 9 or 10 foot long, but could not catch him. At night we had one on the hook but he shattered and got off again. After we had been at prayer it pleased the Lord to answer us so far as to give us a right wind, which continued till about 8 of [the] clock on Fryday. Fryday,

June 12, Winde North by East but low; about 8 of [the] clock quite down, but when we had been at prayer, the winde came fresh [f]rom the East by South. We sailed North-West by West; the wea[ther] very hot. We made but slow motion. Saturday,

June 13, Winde East by South; we saild West by South; at night we lay by 2 hours and an halfe to tarry for our consort Captain Hunt, who held not sail with us. In the meantime we sounded with a line 180 fathoms[12] long for ground, but found none. Lord's day,

June 14, In the morning and at evening a thick fog, so that we could not see far; wherefore we discharged a Musket in the morning to give notice to our Consort where abou[t] we were. The winde low East by South; we steered West by South. It were exceeding hot when the fog were broke up. I exercised from Isiah 3, 11. Munday,

June 15, A thick fog, low winde, North-West. We steered South-West by

West in the morning; when the fog brake up we saw our Consort's ship. The winde quite down insomuch as we were calmed from 10 to 3 of [the] clock or there about; in which time we sounded for groun[d] a line about 250 fathoms but found none. Tuesd[ay],

June 16, Winde East by South; we sailed West by North; the day w[as] thick with fogs. In the morning we discharged tw[o] Muskets that our consort might know by their report where about we were. About 8 a clock we saw him about two or three leagues side-slip us [i.e. *on the larboard or left-hand side*]. We saw after noon a green branch of a tree swimming on the water. Several shark fishes swam by our ship, but we could catch none of them. At length there came a dead butterfly swimming on the water, whereupon we judged we were nigh lande and therefore we sounded again 250 fathoms of cords for land, but found none. We saw many seafowls as Gulls, Noddies, Sherewaters, etc. In the morning we sailed 6 leagues a watch; before night not over one.

June 17, Wednesday, winde somewhat fresh in the morning from South-East; after, it were down, so that we could scarce make any progress, and were much whis[t]ling, one while South-east, another North-East; yet we steered our course West by North. The day was foggy so that we could not discern far; onely we saw straw, feathers, rockweed, etc., that made us judge we were not far from land. Thirsday,

June 18, Morning foggy and misty; the Winde South-East but low; many whales were heard in the morning about 3 a clock, but not seen for the fog. About 8, I being between decks at study against Lord's day, was called to see one, for they heard one coming towards the ship, and when I got above deck I only heard his voice (which was a rough, hoarse noise blothering [i.e., *making a great noise to little purpose*] in the water), but could not see him by reason of the misty fog. The fog being of continuance from Lord's day, we could not well see any further than we went; but it pleased the Lord so far to answer our prayers as to cleare the aire in the afternoon, and to give us a fresh, gentle gale that made us slide on a great pace. We had a tide now againe which when we came to it they called the Rippling, because the water by the running of the stream curled and rippled the top of the waves. [*A line of short-hand is inserted here.*]

June 19, Friday, was cleare, the winde South by West; we sailed North-West about 4 leagues a watch. We were much expecting to see lan[d] but it proved a fog bank; we also sounded to finde ground, but found not. We took up a pie[ce] of wood out of the sea for firewood; our latitude 41 [degrees] and 55 [minutes]. After dinner, I reading the 4[th chapter of] John in greek, was so sleepy that when I had done, I lay down, and dropping into a sleep, and dreaming of my brethren, was so oppressed with sorrow that I had much to do to forbea[r] weeping out, but being over-pressed with this passion, I awakened and was almost down-right sick.

June 20, Saturday, cleare, the Winde South by West; we saild North-West, some watches 9, some 8 leagues. In the afternoon I[t] rained a great pace and when it gave over, the winde fell and was down. I was very ill this day. Lord's day,

June 21, Winde North-West, westerly; we saild South-West by West. I applyed the doctrine I delevird Lord's day before.

June 22, Winde West by North; we saild one while South-West by West, another, North-West by West. We saw a scoure of Mackrils swimming by our ship. Munday,

June 22 [*sic*, 23, Tuesday], Winde West, and low; we saild North-East and North by West. We saw a pair of sunfish lie flapping on the Water. They say that this kind of fish is thus, that it cannot sinke while the sun shines. At night the winde got more South, so that we came nearer our Course. But in the night it served our turn so that we saild a pace West by North.

June 24, Wednesday, Winde South by East, and fresh; we sail[ed] West by North, our right course. We saw a great fis[h] called a Dubartas, with a head like a notted [i.e., *shorn*] boare, his back like a great scalded Hogs, his colour like a pilled [i.e., *peeled*] oake; his length (I suppose) was fo[ur] yards. When we saw him first we took it to hav[e] been a piece of a tree and made to him to get it for firewood. Thursday,

June 25, Winde high in the North; a great rough sea, weather cleare; we saild West-North-West 5 or 6 knots a glasse.

June 26, Friday, Winde fresh in the South; but at night it w[as] North-West; we saild till night North by West, but then West by South. [We] sounded but foun[d] no ground. At night I was much troubled in a dreame of my brother Joseph, for I dreamed that he was dead. Saturday,

June 27, winde low, North-West; the day cleare. Saturday we sounded but found no ground. Lord's day,

June 28, Winde South by West; we saild West by North. I exercised from these words: for the reward of their [*sic*] hands shall be given him. Isiah 3, ii.

June 29, Monday, it rained, thundred, and lighten[ed] in the morning, beginning about 3 a clock; it continued raining very sore till 12, which time w[e] lay by the Lee, and the winde whistled up and down. But then the day cleared up and the winde settl[ed] in the South by West. I saw a Dubartas much bigg[er] than the former. Tuesday,

June 30, Winde North-East; we sailed West-North-West and West by North. We sounded but met with no ground. We saw our Consort today again on the head of our ship, about a league. In the afternoon about 4 [o']Clock we saw a ship we tooke for a New English fishing vessell, and when we came to it, the Master of it told us that Bridges[13] in Barbados was Burned down about two months and an halfe [ago] by a Negers blowing his Tobacco pipe so as it lighted in Cotton woole. We saw another vessell about 6 a clock; we were about 100 Leagues from Boston. Wedn[esday],

July 1, Day darke and drizlie; Winde fresh and North-easterly; we sailed west and northerly. There was a blew Pidgeon came and settled on the main top saile yard, which the Bote Swain shot, but as it fell it hat against the main saile yard and so was struck overboard. We saw a Ganet, and after, some New England Rockweed on the water, which was like yellow mareblobs [i.e., *marsh marigolds*]. The winde was very high towards night, insomuch that we tooke down all our sailes and lay by, lest we should be drove upon the shore before we were aware, and so suffer dammage. About sunset we saw a fish rise spouting water out, and leaping out of the water, as big as a huge horse; some took it for a young whale, some for a Grampoise; our Master, f[or] a Thresher. Thursday,

July 2, weather fare, winde low in the South by Ea[st], but afterwards it rose and was high again. Fryda[y],

July 3, weather good, winde South by East. We much looked for land, but spied none. We saw man[y] Ganets swimming like geese, and some Ducks on the [s]ea. I saw two Whales spout water a great w[ay off], but could not descern them. We cought so [m]any Mackrils as that we breakfasted, dine[d and s]upt with them, and left for another meale. There [a]rose a thick fog at night, so that we put the he[lm a] lee[14] and sounded and found 50 fathom water. We ha[d l]et a Cod-hook down with the line [and] halled up a great [fish with] the line; but at night, perceiving we were neerer shore than we were aware, and not knowing where well we were, nor se[eing] for the fog, we struck saile back some 4 leagues and coursed for two watch[es] time up and down. Saturday,

July 4, Winde East by South; the day thick with fogs. We saw our Consort on the head on us and spake with him in the afternoon. We saild faintly on because the d[ay] was so foggy; we sounded and had some 45 or 40 fathoms water; and we saw many Whale Spouts. Af[ter] the day clearing up, we saw land on both hands, Plymoth on the Left and Salem on the Right towards su[n] setting. About five a clock we saw the Ilands in our passage up to Boston; about 8 I saw a flying crea[ture] like a sparke of red fire (about the bignesse of a[n] Humblebee) fly by the side of the Ship; and presentl[y] after there flew another by. The men said they were fire flies. About 11 or 12 a clock I went to lie down to sleep on my Cabbin (for none went [to bed] because we were nigh our Harbour and waited to go [a]shore as soon as we cast Anchor); but when I w[as d]ropt in a slumber, there was a sad outcry mad[e], insomuch that I was wakened with it in a fright, th[ink]ing the Ship had been cast upon some rock. But th[e c]ause were this: there were a Ketch [i.e., *small vessel*] at anchor, [and c]oming to it, our men did so hoe the Ship (for that is [their] word when they call to any in another ship), and the[re] being a Horse aboard, he leapt overboard into the S[ea]. [It was that] that they hooted at so. About three a clock on the Lord's [day],

July 5, In the morning, we came ashoar, and I lay in Mr. Ti[?–]er's house, who was brother to one Mrs. Allen, th[at w]ent into New England in our ship with us. In the mo[rning], going to delevir a letter to Mr. Mayo, Minister of [God's] word to his people that meet in the New Meeting House, I dined with him and lodged at Mr. Mather's in the two following nights. This Gentleman Married Mr. Cotton's daughter, lives where Mr. Cotton lived and died, and is the other Minister of God's word in the Meeting house.

July 7, I delivered a letter from Mr. Clerke, and another from his Brother Meadwel, to their Kinsma[n] Mr. Hull,[15] who invited mee to his house till I had dispatched my Businesse and were settled in the Colledge, and also to bring my Chest to his wearhouse. This Gentleman would not be said nay, therefore I was with him, and received much Kindnesse from him. I continued with him till I settled at Cambridge. About

July 14, I went to Cambridge to speake with the President, who gave me incouragement. At night it Thundred and lightened very dreadfully, insomuch that I had little rest for the flashes of lightening. Now about Mr. Staughten had his Miller wound in by the Cogs and Rounds till they squeeze his Extas [i.e. *bowels*] out. About

July 22, I went to Cambridge again, and lay at the President's. At night it thundred, lightened and rained very mu[ch], and as his son Elnathan and I were going to bed, about 1[0] or 11 a clock in the night, as it rained, there cam[e] a white peckled [i.e. *speckled*] Dove Pidgeon and flew against the Casement of our Chamber window, and there sat. And I onely being in bed when I heard it were a Pidgeon got up, and so we opened the Casement upon the Dove so far as that we took him in, and when he wa[s] in we would have caught him, and he run from us and Cooed and brissled at us. In the morning he was let [out] againe. The President, when he heard it, said he would not (of any good) he should be hurt; for on[e s]hould not heare of the like, it was omenous surely.

[J]uly 23, I was admitted into the Colledge.

CHRISTOPHER SAUER

*An Early Description of Pennsylvania and the Sea Voyage from Europe (1724)**

Germantown, Dec. 1, 1724.
Dear brothers and friends,
Since I left all of you, dear friends, and promised to write how we arrived here in America and how we lived, many have desired in addition that I should report somewhat more in detail on the quality of this country. Since it is not possible to make a special report to each one, many may make shift with one account.

The sea voyage has been reported upon. I, therefore, pass it over and will say in short that we sailed in 16 hours from Holland to England and arrived there, at Dover, where our ship was cleared. We were, however, obliged to wait there about 3 weeks for a favorable wind. We were out 6 weeks and 3 days from land to land and had neither hot nor cold weather, also little storm, but as pleasant weather as in the month of May. During the greatest storm we were all, my wife and children, on deck by the fire, and baking cookies. Nor did we hear of any man that was afraid of the sea and the storm. The Palatines had their fun with it. When our ship would sometimes roll or pitch, they said: "The lion has fetched another mouthful of water." My wife said: "I thought people would be afraid if they saw nothing but sky and water" Our troubles were only: 1. That we had not taken an extra ration of water along, instead of believing the captain so fully that he would give us as much as we wanted. There were 3 liters of water per 5 persons per day, which to be sure would have sufficed for extra cooking, but the beer was used up too soon. 2. The meat was over salted. 3. The cod-fish

* SOURCE: Sauer, Johann Christoph. 1921. "An Early Description of Pennsylvania. Letter of Christopher Sower, Written in 1724, Describing Conditions in Philadelphia and Vicinity, and the Sea Voyage from Europe." *The Pennsylvania Magazine of History and Biography* 45 (3): 243–54. PUBLICATION HISTORY: The original German letter is in the library of the University of Göttingen, Germany, and can be accessed by the library's digital archive. An English translation was made available by the Historical Society of Pennsylvania in 1921.

was soaked in fresh water, to be sure, but cooked in the same water in which it was soaked. 4. All people on shipboard got lice. 5. The greatest trouble was that there were too many people, so that quarters were restricted, and with many there was not a little stench. Yet we did not suffer from it because we three families had larger accommodations than the others.

During this voyage, of 6 weeks and 3 days, we lacked only the necessary east wind, and were obliged to sail with nothing but tack and head-winds, and it was wonderful that the sailors knew so exactly in what part of the sea they were. It is 1100 leagues[16] from England to this coast, and yet the head helmsman, though he is a young man and had never made this voyage before, hit it within three hours when we should see land. Because we had a strong wind, we got, however, a distance of 23 leagues to the left side of the river called Delaware. God, however, sent us a south wind which carried us in one day into the river. When evening came all were full of joy because we saw—the river. When almost everybody had gone to bed the helmsman begged the captain, since they were close to a sandbank which barred the river, to cast anchor until daybreak; otherwise they would be in danger, as there were only 12 feet of water at that place. The captain, however, was not willing, but thought of still getting into the river. While the captain was still consulting with the sailors, the prow of the ship struck the sandbank although they had scarcely advanced a stone's throw after they had cast the plummet and still found 7 fathoms. And because the bank was hilly, the ship struck ground as many as 18 times, so that we thought it would go to pieces. Then the people came running out in their night-shirts. Simultaneously there were heard cries of distress from young and old, but I and 2 other men were without fear. My wife lay quite still and our child slept and did not wake up. In the meantime I remained firm in the hope that none of us would come into danger. The captain cried aloud and grew quite pale. Because, however, all sails were still set, the wind lifted the ship from one hill to the other. Then they wished to cut the mast. The head helmsman wished to have the three boats lowered and the people taken ashore, for we were scarcely half a league away from it. The captain forbade it because he was afraid everybody might desire to be first and therefore they might get drowned sooner than in the ship. When this distress had lasted a quarter of an hour, we were in deep water again. There we rode at anchor until daybreak and got a favorable wind.

Now we were still 100 miles from the boundary of Pennsylvania and instead of taking 8 to 10 days, as many do in getting up the river, we, with an extraordinarily good wind, arrived at Philadelphia Sunday noon, October first, and while they were casting anchor in the river they fired 22 guns. Then a great crowd of people came running to see the new comers. Then people came and brought apples to divide among the people [passengers], others brought fresh bread and the like, and when I went ashore a man came up to me and asked whether I was free and did not owe anything. I said I did not owe the captain anything, but I had to pay something to a Palatine for brandy. The man went to get 20 Florins[17] with which I was to pay and make my start. N. N. are now free. They are living together and have their place free from debt this winter and they have been offered, if they desired an allotment for pastures and fields, to get as much as they wanted; they might also cut wood free of charge. There have also been made considerable contributions for them. N. is also free and his friends in Holland have raised 288 Florins for him. I myself, however, who had not been suffering any want, was given 10 Florins by some one without my desire. Then I bought some tin because earthenware was said to be very high here. Thus the Lord has taken us safely to this country. His name be praised.

Scarcely had I arrived here when I was offered a vocation, as a foundry was to be constructed. I was to superintend it and, in order to be all the more faithful, I was to have an interest in the foundry and its returns. But because I said that I felt no special inclination and besides had no money for the construction, they wanted to advance me up to 1000 Thaler[18] and compensate me for losses. I said however that I felt no inclination and did not aspire to great things in this world and went away, rented a house and moved in. Then there came one good friend after another and they brought me very many apples, whole baskets full, also nuts, wine, spelt, wheat, bread, eggs, turnips, cabbage, dried pears, buckwheat, chickens, pork and beef, of which I have salted 120 pounds, and presents are coming from a distance of 20 leagues [i.e. 60 miles] for the newly arrived Schwartzenau people.[19] For the rest we have nearly all been ill and those who had been well on shipboard have become ill here, also people with the strongest constitutions. Those however who come here weakly and sickly generally grow strong again and live to old age, the doctors say. Because they make a change of sky and earth, water and air, food and drink, they generally grow strong and their whole constitution changes.

Because one may hold here as much property as one wishes, also pay for it when one desires, everybody hurries to take up some property. One may choose where one pleases. The farther one goes, the better it is. This continent, as may be seen on the map, is almost as large as the other three continents together and has south of New England, say Spain, Virginia, Negroland,[20] Pennsylvania; north of New England, New Holland, the borders of York, New France, unto the region lying beyond us, which cannot be inhabited on account of the cold. The farther the Germans and English cultivate this country, the farther the Indians retreat. They are our nearest neighbors and quite agreeable and peaceable. They would rather harm their own king than a German; they have very simple clothing. They do not gather more than they expect to eat. If a man's wife dies between seed-time and harvest, he gathers only for himself; the remainder is left standing. The traders take a few pounds of powder and lead and fetch for them whole wagon loads of ox-hides, deer-skins and bear-skins. There is also an excellent method of leather dressing known here, such that a tawer[21] with his own hand may completely dress 20 deer-skins in about 2 or 3 days so that they may be wrought by the tailor. Hence leather is very cheap and is worn much, and an honest old friend told me that in summer on warm days one may shoot a deer, dress the skin, and wear a pair of pants from it on the body within 24 hours.

As for the savages, they are dark yellow, believe that there is a God who has created everything and are very much afraid to commit a sin. They believe God does not like it and is looking on. If one has committed a fornication, they stone him to death by the roadside right away and anyone who within 20 years passes by where the malefactor lies, seeks a rock and increases the pile to show the All-seeing that he has a horror of such uncleanliness. They also believe that, when they are dead, and have lived such a life that the Pure One was not pleased with it, they will go to the North where it is very cold; in that land there is a bad ruler who torments them and lets them suffer from the cold. On the other hand the good go to the South where it is nice and warm, and a good ruler receives them kindly. They think more of a hen that is laying eggs than of some ducats. They make baskets and brooms and bring them here or to Philadelphia and accept blue blankets and red stockings, knives, etc., in exchange. The wise know full well the meaning of the godhead and call God in their language "Acs" and speak of him with fear, saying that the Acs sees it. Other simple minded ones say that the Acs at first made only one man and woman. At that time the garden in which he placed them was only small. But now that men had become many, the garden also has grown larger; and similar simple minded talk. They are putting most Europeans to shame by their behavior.

The Pennsylvania borders lie between other well settled countries, most of them belonging to the King of England. This country also is pretty well settled and is said to have over 100,000 inhabitants, consisting of French, Welsh, Swedes, Dutch and Germans. There are some companies in this country that have bought it of William Penn, to whom the king and his heirs have granted it. Here may one select a piece [of land] where one desires, near or far. All inhabitants of this country are free to live quietly and piously by themselves and everybody may believe what he chooses.

Whether the land be good or bad is seen by the trees. Where there are many chestnuts and alder trees growing, the soil is somewhat poor, but where there are many cedars, walnut trees, white and black oaks, sassafras, poplars, beeches and the like, there it is better. In short, this country is a very good and blessed land before many other countries and must be called, as it were, an earthly paradise. Also everything is growing nice, straight, high and fast. Many people make a living by planting fruit trees and selling the young trees so that, when somebody chooses a farm, he may at once have fruit trees and plant them and gather from them the first year. But if one sows seeds himself, he may have fruit from them in 5 years. The land is not really dear. One takes up 200 acres, promises to pay, by installments, within 10 years, and instead clears off his debt in 5 years. According as the land is near or far from the city [prices vary]. Near the city it is high. An acre of woodland is purchased for 1 Florin, perhaps also for 2, 3, 4, or more, according as it may furnish good pasture. I scarcely know of any tree, any herb, any animal which is with you that is not here; any thorn, any thistles, any toads, any cuckoo. On the other hand there are a thousand things more than with you, which do not just occur to me, as sassafras, aloe, myrrhs, Brazilwood, precious stones, white coral, lode-stone in large quantities. Many a man has bought a property for 100 Florins and found 1000 Florins in gold, silver, copper ore, and people only lack smelters. They gladly give a third part to him who can smelt. A false rumor went out that I could smelt. I have therefore been pestered much by the poor people who were gold and silver struck. There is also much copper ore here. Iron stone occurs in such great quantities that it lies often for a space of some miles only knee-deep in the ground, and is rich in iron. They say 100 pounds of stone contains 70–80 pounds of iron. Up to the present time the iron is not even melted, but they carry the iron-stone right away to the forge and bake bars. As far as one buys land by the water, so far also the water is his. He may fish, dig, hunt there what he wishes and is able to do. Neither in the country nor in the city are any imposts known, no duty, no excise, no contribution, in short nothing but a ground-rent of about 20 Kreuzer[22] on 100 acres and twice a year the neighbors congregate to repair the roads. There are people who have been living here for 40 years and have not seen a beggar in Philadelphia. The land yields spelt, barley, wheat, oats, buckwheat, tobacco, Indian corn, also all your garden vegetables in great abundance. I cannot describe all the fruit. There are seven kinds of peaches. Many a man drinks cherry-wine and cider the whole year; also brandy is made of them. There is also plenty of domesticated cattle. A fat ox of 5-600 pounds is worth 10-12 Thaler, a cow for 7-8 Thaler, a sheep 2 Florins, horses as with you, a quart of wine 30, 40, 50 Kreuzer, the strong beer 3 Batzen,[23] the weak 6 Pfennig.[24]

Artisan's work is dear. The English carpenters are usually joiners at the same time and receive a Florin a day and board. The carpenters who work on the ships—for there are many ships building here—get 1 Thaler 1 Groschen[25] per day. Turner's work is very dear, a spinning wheel 5 Florins. There are no stocking weavers at all in this country. Stockings are therefore dear. A Thaler is paid to knit a pair of stockings and the knitters have plenty to do. The linen-weavers have three times as high wages as with you. An industrious spinning-girl earns 5 Groschen per day. Four Groschen are paid for carding a pound of wool. A day laborer gets 10, 12, 15 Groschen per day, and 21 times a week meat with his board; in winter 8 Groschen and his board and nobody works longer than while the sun is shining. The day, however, is in summer 2 hours shorter and in winter 2 hours longer. There is also a special lack of rope makers here. The hemp which is raised here has therefore to be exported elsewhere in order to make the ropes needed for shipbuilding here. A quart of fish oil is 6 Groschen, honey 10 Groschen a quart, a pound of soap 4 Groschen, a pound of feathers 10 Groschen. There is no lack of chickens, geese, ducks and the like. A pound of butter is 2 or 2? Groschen, occasionally 3 Groschen; 12 eggs 1 Groschen. All spices are twice as high as with you except that which grows in this country and looks like pepper. A pound of steel is 8 Groschen, a quire of paper 8 Groschen,—the poor kind that is made here, 5 Groschen. As for mills there are no more than 100 in this country. The miller takes the tenth part and has it run through only once. He who wants the bran has to separate it from the flour himself. There are also bolters in this country so that one may have the flour as fine as one desires. I know of 5 fulling mills. A farm hand gets 100 Florins a year, a girl 50 Florins. There is a lack of all artisans, for, when an artisan has collected a sum of money in 3 or 4 years, maybe even in 1 or 2 years, he buys a farm and moves into the country.

There are found few stables and barns here, for they put the grain up in round piles and thresh it in good weather on the ground and because there are scarcely 3 or 4 days of really cold weather when ice appears, they let their cattle run summer and winter in their inclosed woodlands. They either fell the large trees or take young stems and place them one upon another to the height of 6 feet and then let all cattle go where they please. They provide all the large cattle with bells of different tones in order to be able to find them among the many in case the farm is large, for everybody reserves woodland and firewood for himself. A teamster asks 5 Florins to drive a cart of wood to which he hitches 5 little horses.

House rent is high because the houses are all built of bricks. The city has already 2000 houses occupied chiefly by English Quakers and merchants; it is situated right on the river Delaware, as Mainz or Cologne on the Rhine, and has 2 fairs a year. According to appearances, plainness is vanishing pretty much. The dear old folks, most of whom are dead by this time, may have spoken to their children a good deal about plainness. It is still noticeable in the clothes except that the material is very costly, or is even velvet. Anything may be had at Philadelphia, but everything is twice as dear. A bottle of Cologne water of 15 Pfennig is here 5 Groschen, an ivory comb 1 Groschen [Florin?], a dozen brass buttons, which cost 5, 6-7 Kreutzer with you, 6-10 Groschen. The wholesale trade is very brisk on account of the adjoining countries. The Palatines have brought very many goods with them so that many a man has made up to 600 Florins by this trip, for everything was free because it was not examined in England. There were among the people some who to my knowledge had 40,000 sewing needles, a hundred of which cost in Holland up to 10 Groschen, here 2 Thaler. One had sold 300 scythes here at 20 Groschen each Gunpowder is 4 Groschen a pound in Holland, here 17 Groschen, a scythe-stone 1 Groschen, here 8 Groschen, and one had several hundred stones etc., etc.

P. S. I wrote you, when the first vessel left here, by what means a poor man, who has not even 5, 6, 7 Thaler, may come over here. Now if God wishes to have you come here, he will also give you ways and means to do so. In case Mr. Kuster, as he desires, should obtain free passage from the king, see to it that, apart from the ship's fare, you provide yourself with such food as you are accustomed to, dried bread, sausages, flour, butter, dried fruit, and something to move the bowels, because one easily gets constipated on shipboard. And if you, dear friends, should be expelled from a place and God should desire to lead you here, cling then firmly to the arm of God, as children are wont to

do, and do not worry, for where a father goes, who has plenty of everything, the children may easily follow. In all your doings let this be your touch-stone, whether your heart is earthly. Seek only heavenly things, otherwise earthly things may flee away, or you may have to leave them. May God guide you according to His will! I greet you all and remain,
Yours affectionately,
Joh. Christoph Sauer
Germantown, 2 leagues from Philadelphia, Dec. 1, 1724.

MISADVENTURE

ANTHONY THACHER

*The Shipwreck of Anthony Thacher (1684)**

I must turn my drowned Pen and shaking Hand to Indite the Story of such sad News as never before this hapned in *New-England*. There was a League of perpetual Friendship between my Cousin *Avery* (note that this Mr. *Avery* was a precious holy Minister who came out of *England* with Mr. *Anthony Thacher*) and myself never to forsake each other to the Death, but to be partakers of each others misery or welfare, as also of habitation in the same place. Now upon our Arrival in *New-England*, there was an offer made unto us. My cousin *Avery* was invited to *Marble-head* to be their Pastor in due time; there being no Church planted there as yet, but a Town appointed to set up the Trade of Fishing. Because many there (the most being Fishermen) were something loose and remiss in their behaviour; my Cousin *Avery* was unwilling to go thither, and so refusing we went to *Newbery*, intending there to sit down. But being solicited so often both by the Men of the place, and by the Magistrates, and by Mr. *Cotton*, and most of the Ministers, who alledged what a benefit we might be

* SOURCE: Mather, Increase. 1684. *An Essay for the Recording of Illustrious Providences. Wherein an Account is Given of Many Remarkable and Very Memorable Events, which Have Happened in this Last Age; Especially in New-England*. 1–14. London.
PUBLICATION HISTORY: As Increase Mather notes, he reprinted the account from a letter sent by Anthony Thacher to his brother Peter in England nearly fifty years earlier, in 1635. As an example for the practice of scribal publication, copies of the letter have survived in the Mather papers as well as in Simon Bradstreet's collection; Thacher's shipwreck has been mentioned by John Winthrop in his *Journal*, and subsequent historians of New England recorded Thacher's case. A modern edition of the letter can be found in Emerson, Everett, ed. 1976. *Letters from New England: The Massachusetts Bay Colony, 1629–38*, 168–74. Amherst: Univ. of Massachusetts Press.

to the People there, and also to the Countrey and Common-wealth; at length we embraced it, and thither consented to go. They of *Marble-head*[26] forthwith sent a Pinnace[27] for us and our Goods. We Embarqued at *Ipswich*, *August* 11. 1635. with our Families and Substance, bound for *Marbel-head*, we being in all twenty three Souls, *viz.* eleven in my Cousin's Family, seven in mine, and one Mr. *William Eliot* sometimes of *New Sarum*, and four Mariners.

The next morning having commended ourselves to God, with chearful hearts, we hoised Sail; but the Lord suddenly turned our chearfulness into mourning and lamentations. For on the fourteenth of this *August* 1635. about ten at night, having a fresh Gale of wind, our Sails being old and done were split. The Mariners because that it was night, would not put to new Sails, but resolved to cast Anchor till the Morning. But before daylight, it pleased the Lord to send so mighty a Storm, as the like was never known in *New-England* since the *English* came, nor in the memory of any of the *Indians*. It was so furious that our Anchor came home. Whereupon the Mariners let out more Cable, which at last slipt away. Then our Sailers knew not what to do, but we were driven before the wind and waves. My Cousin and I perceived our danger, solemnly recommended ourselves to God the Lord both of Earth and Seas, expecting with every wave to be swallowed up and drenched in the Deeps. And as my Cousin, his Wife, and my tender Babes sat comforting and chearing one the other in the Lord against ghastly Death, which every moment stared us in the face, and sat triumphing upon each ones Forehead, we were by the violence of the Waves and fury of the winds, (by the Lords permission) lifted up upon a Rock between two high Rocks, yet all was one Rock, but it raged with the stroke which came into the Pinnace, so as we were presently up to our middles in water as we sat. The Waves came furiously and violently over us, and against us, but by reason of the Rocks proportion could not lift us off, but beat her all to pieces. Now look with me upon our distress, and consider of my misery, who beheld the Ship broken, the water in her, and violently overwhelming us, my Goods, and Provisions swimming in the Seas, my Friends almost drowned, and mine own poor Children so untimely (if I may so term it without offence) before mine eyes drowned, and ready to be swallowed up and dashed to pieces against the Rocks by the merciless waves, and myself ready to accompany them. But I must go on to an end of this woeful Relation. In the same room whereas he sat, the Master of the Pinnace not knowing what to do, our fore-Mast was cut down, our main-Mast broken in three pieces, the fore part of the Pinnace beat away, our Goods swimming about the Seas, my Children bewailing me, as not pittying themselves, and myself bemoaning them; poor Souls, whom I had occasioned to such an end in their tender years, whenas they could scarce be sensible of death. And so likewise my Cousin, his Wife, and his Children, and both of us bewailing each other, in our Lord and only Saviour Jesus Christ, in whom only we had comfort and cheerfulness, insomuch that from the greatest to the least of us, there was not one scriech or out-cry made, but all as silent sheep were contentedly resolved to die together lovingly, as since our acquaintance we had lived together friendly. Now as I was sitting in the Cabbin room-door with my body in the room, when lo one of the Sailers by a wave being washed out of the Pinnace was gotten in again, and coming into the Cabbinroom over my back, cried out, we are all cast away, the Lord have mercy upon us, I have been washed over-board into the Sea, and am gotten in again.

His speeches made me look forth. And looking towards the Sea, and seeing how we were, I turned myself to my Cousin and the rest, and spake these words, Oh Cousin, it hath pleased God to cast us here between two Rocks, the shoar not far off from us, for I saw the tops of Trees when I looked forth. Whereupon the Master of the Pinnace looking up at the Scuttle hole of the quarter Deck, went out at it, but I never saw him afterwards. Then he that had been in the Sea, went out again by me, and leapt overboard towards the Rocks, whom afterwards also I could not see. Now none were left in the Barque that I knew or saw, but my Cousin, his Wife and Children, myself and mine, and his maidservant. But my Cousin thought I would have fled from him, and said unto me, Oh Cousin leave us not, let us die together, and reached forth his hand unto me. Then I letting go my Son *Peter*'s hand took him by the hand, and said, Cousin, I purpose it not, whither shall I go? I am willing and ready here to die with you and my poor Children. God be merciful to us, and receive us to himself, adding these words, the Lord is able to help and deliver us. He replied, saying, truth Cousin, but what his pleasure is we know not; I fear we have been too unthankful for former deliverances, but he hath promised to deliver us from sin and condemnation, and to bring us safe to heaven through the alsufficent satisfaction of Jesus Christ, *this therefore we may challenge of him*. To which I replying said, that is all the deliverance I now desire and expect. Which words I had no sooner spoken, but by a mighty wave I was with the piece of the Barque washed out upon part of the Rock, where the wave left me almost drowned, but recovering my feet I saw above me on the Rock my daughter *Mary*, to whom I had no sooner gotten, but my Cousin *Avery*, and his eldest Son came to us, being all four of us washed out by one and the same Wave, we went all into a small hole on the top of the Rock, whence we called to those in the Pinnace to come unto us, supposing we had been in more safety than they were in.

My Wife seeing us there was crept up into the scuttle of the Quarter Deck to come unto us, but presently came another wave and dashing the Pinnace all to pieces, carried my Wife away in the Scuttle, as she was with the greater part of the quarter Deck unto the Shoar; where she was, cast safely, but her Legs were something bruised, and much Timber of the Vessel being there also cast, she was sometime before she could get away being washed by the Waves. All the rest that were in the Barque were drowned in the merciless Seas. We four by that wave were clean swept away from off the Rock also, into the Sea; the Lord in one instant of time disposing of fifteen Souls of us, according to his good pleasure and will, His pleasure and wonderful great mercy to me was thus. Standing on the Rock as before you heard, with my eldest Daughter, my Cousin and his eldest Son, looking upon, and talking to them in the Barque, whenas we were by that merciless wave washed off the Rock, as before you heard. God in his mercy caused me to fall by the stroke of the wave flat on my face, for my face was toward the Sea, insomuch that as I was sliding off the Rock into the Sea, the Lord directed my toes into a joynt in the Rocks side, as also the tops of some of my fingers with my right hand, by means whereof, the wave leaving me, I remained so, having in the Rock only my head above the water. When on the left hand I espied a Board or Plank of the Pinnace. And as I was reaching out my left hand to lay hold on it, by another coming over the top of the Rock, I was washed away from the Rock, and by the violence of the waves was driven hither and thither in the Seas a great while, and had many dashes against the Rocks.

At length past hopes of Life, and wearied in body and spirits, I even gave over to nature, and being ready to receive in the waters of Death, I lifted up both my heart and hands to the God of Heaven. For note, I had my senses remaining perfect with me all the time that I was under and in water, who at that instant lifted my head above the top of the water, that so I might breathe without any hindrance by the waters. I stood bolt upright as if I had stood upon my feet, but I felt no bottom, nor had any footing for to stand upon, but the waters. While I was thus above the water, I saw by me a piece of the Mast, as I suppose about three foot long, which I laboured to catch into my arms. But suddenly I was overwhelmed with water, and driven to and fro again, and at last I felt the ground with my right foot. When immediately whilest I was thus groveling on my face, I presently recovering my feet, was in the water up to my Breast, and through Gods great mercy had my face unto the shoar, and not to the Sea. I made hast to get out, but was thrown down on my hands with the waves, and so with safety crept to the dry shoar. Where blessing God, I turned about to look for my Children and Friends, but saw neither, nor any part of the Pinnace, where I left them as I supposed. But I saw my Wife about a Butt length from me getting herself forth from amongst the Timber of the broken Barque: but before I could get unto her, she was gotten to the shoar: I was in the water after I was washed from the Rock, before I came to the shoar a quarter of an hour at least. When we were come each to other, we went and sat under the Bank. But fear of the Seas roaring and our coldness would not suffer us there to remain. But we went up into the Land and sat us down under a Cedar Tree which the wind had thrown down, where we sat about an hour almost dead with cold. But now the Storm was broken up, and the wind was calm, but the Sea remained rough and fearful to us.

My Legs were much bruised, and so was my head, other hurt had I none, neither had I taken in much quantity of water: but my heart would not let me sit still any longer, but I would go to see if any more were gotten to the Land in safety, especially hoping to have met with some of my own poor Children, but I could find none, neither dead nor yet living. You condole with me my miseries, who now began to consider of my losses. Now came to my remembrance the time and manner, how and when I last saw and left my Children and Friends. One was severed from me sitting on the Rock at my feet, the other three in the Pinnace: my little Babe (Ah poor *Peter*) sitting in his sister *Ediths* arms, who to the uttermost of her power sheltred him from the waters, my poor *William* standing close unto them, all three of them looking ruefully on me on the Rock; their very Countenances calling unto me to help them, whom I could not go unto, neither could they come at me, neither would the merciless waves afford me space or time to use any means at all, either to help them or myself. Oh I yet see their cheeks, poor silent Lambs, pleading pity and help at my hands. Then on the other side to consider the loss of my dear Friends, with the spoiling and loss of all our Goods and Provisions, myself cast upon an unknown Land, in a Wilderness, I knew not where, nor how to get thence. Then it came to my mind how I had occasioned the Death of my Children, who caused them to leave their native Land, who might have left them there, yea, and might have sent some of them back again and cost me nothing: these and such like thought do press down my heavy heart very much. But I must let this pass, and will proceed on in the Relation of Gods goodness unto me in that desolate Island, on which I was cast. I and my Wife were almost naked both of us, and wet and cold even unto death. I found a Snapsack[28] cast on the shoar, in which I had a

Steel and Flint and Powder-horn. Going further I found a drowned Goat, then I found a Hat, and my Son *William*'s Coat, both which I put on. My Wife found one of her Petticoats which she put on. I found also two Cheeses and some Butter driven ashoar. Thus the Lord sent us some clothes to put on, and food to sustain our new lives which we had lately given unto us; and means also to make fire, for in an Horn I had some Gun-powder, which to mine own (and since to other mens) admiration was dry. So taking a piece of my Wives Neck-cloth, which I dried in the Sun, I struck fire, and so dried and warmed our wet Bodies, and then skinned the Goat, and having found a small Brass-pot, we boyled some of her. Our Drink was brackish water; Bread we had none. There we remained until the Monday following, when about three of the Clock in the afternoon, in a Boat that came that way, we went off that desolate island; which I named after my name, *Thachers Woe*, and the Rock *Avery his fall*; to the end that their fall and loss, and mine own might be had in perpetual remembrance. In the Isle lieth buried the body of my Cousins eldest Daughter, whom I found dead on the shoar. On the Tuesday following in the afternoon we arrived at *Marble-Head*. Thus far is Mr. *Thachers* Relation of this memorable Providence.

CARLOS DE SIGÜENZA Y GÓNGORA

*The Misfortunes of Alonso Ramírez (1690)**

Chapter I

The Motives He Had for Leaving His Country. Work and Travel Through New Spain, His Presence in Mexico until Leaving for the Philippines

I hope that the curious who read this book may entertain themselves for a few hours with the incidents which caused me mortal anguish for many years. And

* SOURCE: Translation from Sigüenza y Góngora, Carlos de. (1690) 1902. *Infortunios de Alonso Ramírez descríbelos D. Carlos de Sigüenza y Góngora*, 27–49. Colección de libros raros y curiosos que tratan de America 20. Madrid.
PUBLICATION HISTORY: The Spanish librarian Pedro Vindel Álvarez published Ramírez's account in 1902, together with a facsimile reproduction of the original title page. The adventures of the Puerto Rican carpenter who became a captive of the English pirate William Dampier and then voyaged with his crew on a global thieving tour appeared as a quarto volume in Mexico City in 1690. For a long time considered a fictional character, Ramírez is actually a historical character whose eyewitness account was embellished and molded by Carlos de Sigüenza y Góngora, who was commissioned by the Spanish viceroy to write a useful piece of propaganda against the enemies of Spain and their allied pirates in the western hemisphere. Another Spanish edition was published in 1951, an English translation appeared in 1962, and a modern English critical edition in 2011.

although we are concerned only with events which subsisted in the mind of a man who invented them, maxims and aphorisms may be deduced which together with the pleasures of the narrative may cultivate the reason of those persons who occupy themselves here. However, this will not be my main intention but rather to arouse sympathy, even though long after my ordeals, which will make their memory tolerable, thus coupling the reader's feelings with those which vexed me at that time. Not for the reason that I am so close to my pain would I fall into the error of vacilation[29] and thus omit details which from a less unfortunate person would be the cause of many complaints. I will say first what seems most notable in this series of events.

My name is Alonso Ramirez and my homeland the city of San Juan in Puerto Rico, the capital of the island, known by this name now as in olden times it was called Borriquen[30] and which lies between the Mexican mainland and the Atlantic Seas. It has become famous as a delightful watering place for those who for long times past suffered thirst in navigating to New Spain; for the beauty of her bay and the invincible Morro Castle which defends her; the walls and bulwarks crowned by artillery assuring her safety. Thus she is protected from the hostilities of pirates as are other lands in the Indies, her defenses supporting the spirit which the genius of that land of plenty gives to its sons.

The natives are now hard pressed in their fidelity and honor since the wealthy gold veins which gave the island its name are no longer worked because the original inhabitants who provided the labor have died off. Also the vehemence of fearful hurricanes whipped the cacao trees that provided for their owners a substitute for gold. As a result the rest of the islanders became poor. Among those who suffered from this situation were my parents who had it forced on them since their way of life deserved something better; but now it is an annoyance in the Indies that life is so hard. My father's name was Lúcas de Villanueva, and although I do not know the place of his birth it is clear to me from what people heard him say that he was Andalucian, and I know very well that my mother was born in the same city of Puerto Rico and her name is Ana Ramirez, to whose Christianity I owed in my childhood the only thing which the poor can give their children: advice which inclines them toward virtue. My father was a ship-carpenter who, when my age permitted, put me to work at his vocation, but recognizing that construction work was irregular and realizing that I would not live forever, for that reason, together with the inconveniences they forced on me even as a child, I determined to flee from my native land to seek out more convenient localities in other climes.

I took advantage of the opportunity which Captain Juan del Corcho's bargue offered me to become a page and to leave that port for Habana. It was the year 1675 and I was thirteen years old. The position did not seem laborious to me considering myself free and without the obligation of cutting wood; but I confess that perhaps foreseeing the future I doubted if it could promise me anything worthwhile, having begun my fortune on a cork at sea. But who can deny that my doubts were well founded noting the events that followed that beginning? From the port of Habana (famous among those which the Windward Islands enjoy, both for the favor of nature and the fortresses which art and work provided for its protection), we went on to that of San Juan de Ulva, on the mainland of New Spain where I left my ship's master and went up to the city of Puebla de los Angeles, not without much discomfort along the way due to the rough paths that run from Xalapa to Perote and also bemuse of the cold which seemed intense to a person unaccustomed to it. Those that inhabit this city declare it to be next to Mexico City in size, in the width of her streets, in the magnificence of her temples and in every other way which makes her comparable to the capital. So it occurred to me (not having seen until then a larger one) that in such a large city it would be easy for me to find a more favorable life. I determined, without more thought than this, to remain there earning a living in the service of a carpenter until I should discover some other way to become rich.

During the period of six months which I lost there I experienced more hunger than in Puerto Rico. Despising the indiscrete resolution to abandon my country for a land where one does not always receive a welcome for generous liberality, increasing the number of muleteers, I reached Mexico City without considerable trouble. It is a great pity that the greatness and magnificence of such a superb city should not spread through the world engraved by a glazier's diamond on plates of gold. What I had learned about the size of Puebla was erased from my memory from the moment I tread the causeway over the great lagoon which is open to strangers at the southern approach. And since one of the greatest compliments due this metropolis is the magnanimity of those that inhabit it, aided as it is by the abundance of everything needed to spend a restful life; I attribute to the fatality of my star the necessity of having to exercise my vocation in order to sustain myself. Cristobal de Medina, a master in building and architecture, employed me at a competent salary in what work he set forth, and I was to spend at this position about a year.

The reason I had for leaving Mexico City for Huasaca [Oaxaca] was the news that Don Luis Ramirez lived there, a relative of my mother, with the honorable title and duties of alderman. I felt sure that I would find a helping hand there even if not an ascent disproportionate to what the situation seemed to represent. After a trip of eighty leagues he denied the relationship in unpleasant language and I was obliged to turn to strangers so as not to suffer the world's asperity which was all the more painful being unexpected. Thus I came to serve a merchant carrier by the name of Juan Lopez. The latter bartered with the Míxe, Chontal, and Cuicateca Indians merchandise from Castille which they lacked, for the products of their lands which consist of cotton, blankets, vanilla, cacao, and cochineal. To secure these items one passes over rough mountains fearful at every moment of falling off cliffs lining the paths, of deep ravines, annoyed by continuous rain and many swamps, and to which are added small humid valleys full of mosquitoes and everywhere vermin abominable to every living creature because of their poison.

My longing for wealth stumbled over all of this. I went along accompanied by my master, persuaded that the recompense would be in proportion to the effort required. We made a trip to Chiapa and from there to different places in the provinces of Soconusco and Guatemala, but as it is the lot of mankind to mingle with a joyful and prosperous day a sad and tasteless night, on our return to Huaxaca, my master became ill in the village of Talistaca to such an extreme that they administered the last sacrament for the dying. I regretted his suffering and equally my own, passing the tune thinking up ways of living less laboriously, but when Juan Lopez had a turn for the better my depression disappeared to be followed by a tranquility which proved to be temporary since in the following journey he had the same attack in the village of Cuicatlan. No remedy could help him and he passed away. I collected from his heirs what they were willing to give me for my presence and despising myself and my fortune, I returned to Mexico City. Wanting to enter this city with a few reales, I sought work in Puebla without finding any master at all who welcomed me. Fearful of experiencing the same hunger as when I was there before, I hurried on my way.

Due to my application at work when I was with master Cristobal de Medina for a year, those who knew me tried to find me a location in Mexico City. I managed this through marriage with Francisca Xavier, a young girl who was the daughter of the widow Doña María de Poblete, sister of the venerable Doctor Don Juan de Poblete, Dean of the Cathedral, who had renounced the miter of Archbishop of Manila in order to die as a paragon in his native abode. He lived as an example to all those who might aspire to eternal memory by the rectitude of their ways. I know quite well that to mention his name is to summarize everything that one may find in the highest nobility and the most outstanding virtue, so I shall remain silent with reluctance concerning everything that gratitude suggests in order not to make my narrative long.

In my wife I found much virtue and affection but such good fortune was as if in a dream since it lasted but eleven months when she died in childbirth. Left without her after such an unexpected and sensitive blow, I decided to distract my mind by returning to Puebla. Entering the employ of Estevan Gutiérrez, a master carpenter, who sustained himself by extreme frugality, you can imagine how things would go with his assistant. I despaired then of ever being anything and finding myself in the tribunal of my own conscience, not only accused but useless, I planned to sentence myself for this deed as they do in Mexico City for delinquents by sending them into exile to the Philippines. Therefore I went there in the galleon *Santa Rosa*, which (under orders of General Antonio Nieto whose pilot was Admiral Leandro Coello) left the port of Acapulco for that of El Cavite in the year 1682. This port is at latitude sixteen degrees and forty minutes north and whatever it has which is beautiful and secure for ships that enter, is matched by the trials of those that inhabit it. The population is sparse because of its poor climate, the sterility of the countryside, the lack of sweet water and even food which drives people away. Add to this ravines and precipices along the roads with their intolerable heat and every condition begs release from the port.

Chapter II

His Departure from Acapulco for the Philippines. The Route of this Voyage and how He Passed the Time until Capture by the English

Ships leave the port with strong winds from the west northwest or northwest which arise about eleven in the morning; but, since it is more usual to have winds from the southwest, if a ship leaves toward the south or south southwest, it must wait until three in the afternoon to avoid racking (this being true because in the afternoon the winds come up blowing toward the west northwest and northwest and a ship can leave without tacking). They navigated from there toward the south with the winds mentioned above (without noticing very much the changes of the points of the compass or that the ship was moving away somewhat from the Meridian), until she was at twelve degrees or somewhat less. Here the winds began to change from northeast to north and as soon as they noticed winds from the east northeast and east causing the route to be west southwest and west and toward the northwest, they had departed from that meridian five hundred leagues at thirteen degrees longitude.

From here the needles begin to move to the northeast. On reaching eighteen degrees they will have navigated (without the five hundred above mentioned) one thousand one hundred leagues,[31] and without moving from the thirteenth parallel, when the needle moves toward the northeast only ten degrees (which will be one thousand seven hundred and five leagues from the meridian of Acapulco), with a single day's run of twenty leagues or a little more, you will come upon one of the Mariana Islands named Guan running from thirteen degrees and five minutes to thirteen and twenty-five. Once past a tiny island which is near-by, the sounding line must be dropped to a depth of about a hundred feet to reach the bottom of the bay of Humata which is the closest. A single cannon ball shot away the reef which extends westward from the island and you know there are twenty fathoms for casting anchor where the bottom is clean and good.

In order to look for the channel mouth of San Benardino from here, one has to proceed west and southwest and after navigating two hundred and ninety-five leagues (being careful to follow the route indicated by the compass) you reach the Espíritu Santo Cape, which is at twelve degrees and forty-five minutes, and if one could seek out a more southerly route that would be better, because if the violent sea winds come up and enter from the south southwest or from the southwest, it is extremely important here to be to the wind ward and sheltered by the island of Palapa and the same Cape.

If the breezes are blowing one will navigate along the coast of this same island a matter of twenty leagues with the bow to the west north west lurching to the west and passing along the eastern side of the small island of San Bernardino you head for the island of Capul which is four leagues to the southwest from here it is west six leagues to the island of Ticao, and moving along the coast the five leagues to the northeast to the northern end you veer to the west southwest seeking out the straits between Burias and Masbate Islands. The distance between the two is not quite a league, Burias lying to the north. These straits are about four leagues from the head of Ticao.

When these narrows have been passed you steer to the west northwest toward the passage between the islands of Marinduque and Banton, the latter being three fourths of a league to the south of the former and sixteen from Burias. From here the isles of Mindoro, Lobo, and Galván are northwest and west. Then through the straights of Isla Verde and Mindoro you head west eleven or twelve leagues until you are near the Island of Ambil and the fourteen leagues beyond to Marivelez (which is at fourteen degrees and thirty minutes), then north northeast, and finally north, and northeast. From Marivelez you head for Cavite toward the northeast, east northeast, and east about five leagues to avoid the shallows which are to the east northeast of Marivelez with four fathoms and a half of water covering the bottom.

Disabused in the course of my voyage that I would ever escape from my sphere and thinking about those who with fewer qualities had managed to improve their lot, I dismissed from my mind those ideas which had been perplexing my imagination for several years. Much abundance is to be found in those islands and especially that which the city of Manila enjoys in the extreme. Whatever one needs in the way of sustenance and clothing is to be found there at a moderate price due to the competition among the Chinese and Japanese merchants to enrich themselves in their Parían, which is a place outside the walls where they have been given permission to settle by the Spanish. This, together with the beauty and fortified security of the city helped by the amenity of its river and gardens and other attractions, make it famous among the colonies which the Europeans have in the orient, and permits those who live there to pass their time pleasantly. What is ordinarily traded there is imported and because of that there is continuous navigation from place to place, so taking up the work of a sailor, I settled in Cavite.

I managed by this means not only to trade in goods which brought me a profit and promised me a future but to see various cities and ports in India on several trips. I was in Madrastapatan, called of old Calamina or Meliapor, where the apostle Saint Thomas died, a large city when the Portuguese owned it, but today a mound of ruins caused by the struggle between the French and Dutch to possess her. I was in Malaca, the key to all India and her trade because of its location in the strait of Syncapura [Singapore] and whose governor receives anchorage fees from all navigators passing through. The Dutch are her owners as they are of many other places, under whose yoke groan the destitute Catholics that have remained there and are not permitted the exercise of the true religion even though Moors and gentiles who are Dutch vassals are not disturbed in carrying out their ritual sacrifices.

I was in the very celebrated city of Batavia which the same Dutch possess in Greater Java and where the Governor and Captain General of the States of Holland dwells. Its walls, bastions, and fortresses are admirable. Here are seen ships without number owned by Malayans, Macassares, Bugises, Siamese, Chinese, Armenians, French, English, Danish, Portuguese, and Castilians. In these markets are found all the handiwork there is in Europe and what Asia sends in return. Excellent arms are manufactured there for those who may wish to buy them. Macán [Macao] I also visited. It is fortified by the Portuguese owners but is nevertheless subject to the treachery of the Tartars, who dominate a large part of China.

Even more for convenience than for pleasure I kept busy in these matters, but carrying out orders did not always spare me trouble and one occasion caused me the ill-fortune in which I find myself today and which began as you will hear. By orders of General Don Gabriel de Cuzalaegui, who governed the Philippine Islands, a one-deck frigate was dispatched to the province of Ilocos to bring supplies to the presidio at Cavite as had been done before. Those who embarked were all men of the sea and I was placed in charge of the ship and its twenty-five seamen. *Four pikes and two muskets* were taken from the royal storehouse and given to me to defend the vessel, but since the serpentines were broken we needed to keep the fuses constantly lit to be able to shoot the muskets: They also gave me a *few bullets and five pounds of powder.*

With this supply of arms and munitions but without artillery or even a stone mortar (in spite of the fact that we had portholes for six pieces), I set sail. It took six days to reach Ilocos and about nine or ten were spent in the barter and loading of supplies. On the fifth day we were on our way back plying to the windward in order to enter the mouth of Marivelez and the port when, at four in the afternoon, two ships were discovered toward land. Presuming, not only myself, but those that were with me, that they were ships in charge of Captains Juan Bautista and Juan de Caravallo which had gone to Pangasinan and Panay to get rice and other things needed in the presidio at Cavite and other nearby places, I proceeded (although to the leeward) without any suspicions because there was no reason for them.

Then, within a short while two canoes came toward me at full speed and I became disturbed. My surprise was extreme when I recognized close up that they were enemies. Prepared for the defense as best I could be with my two muskets and four pikes, they rained shots upon us but without boarding us. The muskets responded striking one of the canoes and setting fire to the other. Meanwhile we split the balls with a knife to double the ammunition so that with more shots we might continue for a longer time our ridiculous resistance. The two large ships from which we had seen the canoes leave, bore down on us immediately. Taking in the main-topsail, asking quarter, and being boarded by fifty Englishmen with cutlasses in their hands was all a matter of a moment. They seized the round-house, drove us into the bow and mocked us with loud laughter at the sight of the arms we had and even more when they discovered that the frigate belonged to the king and that the arms had been taken out of the royal storehouse. It was then six o'clock in the afternoon of Tuesday the fourth of March in the year 1687.

CONFESSIONS

OWEN SYLLAVAN

*A Short ACCOUNT of the Life of John—Alias Owen Syllavan (1756)**

I WAS bred and born in the County of *Waxford* in *Ireland*, of English Parents near the Town of *Fedard*,[32] and from my youth I was always in all kind of Mischief; so that I never minded Father nor Mother, Sister nor Brother; but went on in all Manner of Vice, till I came to the Age of eleven Years, or there-abouts; I was confined by my Parents in a Room, and fed upon Bread and Water for a considerable Time, and then I seemed to humble myself; till I again obtained my Liberty, and after that I was ten Times, worse than I was before; so that my Parents was obliged to send me to another Place, some Distance from home to a School-Master, who my Parents gave strict charge to keep me from Vice, and keep to my Learning.

And the first Night that I lodged there, I was called by an evil Spirit by my Christian Name; *John*, *John*, *John*, *John*, and that for several Minutes together, to the Surprise of myself, and all the Family: and so continued for three or four Nights together, before there was any Notice taken of it; but the fourth Night my Master set up, and Read by me till Eleven o'Clock; and then the Spirit began to call again, *John*, *John*, *John*, and that every Minute, for sixty Times together by my Master's Watch; and that lasted so for three Months together. The Ministers from sundry Parishes came to set with me; as also sundry Persons, who always pray'd by me, and giving me all good Advice in their Power, begging and praying of me, to Repent. Then I began to fear GOD; and finding so many

* SOURCE: Syllavan, Owen. 1756. *A Short Account of the Life of John—, Alias Owen Syllavan . . . Taken from His Own Mouth: To which is Added HIS Dying Speech at the Place of Execution*. New York/Boston.

PUBLICATION HISTORY: A reprint appeared under a slightly changed title in Leominster, Massachusetts, 1802. This version excludes the illustration on the second page of the original version, which resembles a woodcut of an execution scene that was widely used in colonial broadsides like *An Address to the Inhabitants of Boston*, published on the execution of Levi Ames in Boston, 1773.

Hundreds of People that came to see me from far and near, who took pitty upon me. At last some of them concluded to take me to one of their Houses, which they did; as soon as it was eleven o'Clock, the Spirit began to call again, *why John! Why John! Why John!* it called so loud that the Windows shook, and every one in the House trembled for Fear, except myself. I was taken Sick about five or six Days, before the Spirit had done calling, and during my Sickness it called louder than before; and as I laid in Bed, there was something that seem'd to press me between my Shoulders with a Hand, but saw nothing.

So this continued till I was Removed to my Parents, who then took Compassion upon me; and to the best of my Knowledge I lay Sick, for about the same Time as the Spirit had called me before, but not troubled with any more of that evil Spirit. So it pleased GOD to restore me to my former Health, and I went to School again; but fell from Good to Evil, by provoking my Parents and giving ill Advice to others, such as my Playmates, &c. And when my Parents chastised me for my Faults, I look'd upon it as Tyranny, and told them several Times to exercise their Tyranny upon me. And when I was about thirteen Years of Age I deserted from my Parents, and stroll'd away to a Place called *Bellaback*, near the Passage of *Waterford*, so coming down to the Water Side, there was a small Boat ready to push off, and I desired of them to take me aboard, which they refused and told me they was not going over the Ferry; but told me they was going to *Waterford*, I asked of them to give me a Passage there, for I wanted to see my Aunt; so they asked my Name, and I told my Name was *Owen Syllavan* which was a Lye, for it was there I changed my Name, and so they gave me my Passage to *Waterford*, and I strol'd from Place to Place, till I came to the County of *Limerick*. There was a Gentleman Riding along, asked me whose Son I was, I made answer I was born in *Dublin* and of poor Parentage, and that they were Dead, and I told him I was going to *Cork*, expecting to find some Relations, and told him my Name was *Owen Syllavan*.

The Gentleman told me if I would go and live with him, he would be my Friend and Relation too, with that I consented and went with him to his Country-Seat, his Lady looking out of the Window, he with a smiling Countenance said, I have brought you a pretty Boy to wait upon you, the Lady seemed to like me very well, and I gave them an Indenture[33] to serve for seven Years, and so become my Lady's running Foot-Page. And was train'd up to running, and served them almost six Years, which pleased me better than Schooling; and in the sixth Year of my Servitude, I seemed to be home sick; and set a Resolution if I should be sent of an Errand that way, I would make the best of my Way Home, which was about one 100 Miles: And soon after my Master wanted me to carry a Letter to a Gentleman, about twenty Miles distance. I embrac'd that Opportunity, delivered my Letter, but did not wait for any Answer; but went direct for *Waterford*, where I arrived the same Day, about four o'Clock in the Afternoon, which was seventy Miles. When I came to *Waterford*, I drank a Tumbler full of Wine, and being very Hot, I was taken with a Pluratick Pain, and lay Sick there for some Time; although I was then about thirty Miles from my Father's House, I would not let myself be known; but told the People, that my Errand was as far as *Waxford* Town. After I got well I went down to the Wharf, where I saw several Passengers going on Board of a Vessel bound for *Boston*, in *New-England*; so I goes up to the Captain, and agrees with him for my Passage; and Bound myself for four Years, and in a few Days set Sail for *Boston*; where we arrived in about nine Weeks: but having many Souls on Board, we was very scant of Provision. I agreed with the Captain to serve him three Years more, for as many Biscuit as I could Eat, during the running of three Glasses, which caused the Captain burst into a Laughter, and so consented to it: but I was to have no Water during the Time. After our arrival at *Boston*, I told the Captain I would a soon be sold for seven Years, as for a Day; since I must be Sold, and to get for me as much as he could. And he Sold me to one Captain *Gillmore*, living about twenty-four Hours Sail to the Eastward of *Boston*, to a Place called St. *George's River*. I served that Gentleman two Years and an half, in chopping of Wood and clearing of Land; and hearing of a *French* War, my Master and all the Family Removed to *Boston*, except myself; my Master Sold the Remainder of my Time to Captain *Bradbery*, who I served two Years, as a Soldier, and proved faithful to my King and Country.

And after that, contrary to my Master's Will, I listed under Captain *Waldo*, in General *Shirley's* Regiment of Foot, for *Cape-Breton*,[34] and after that, I was Drafted into Captain *Gordon's* Company of Grenadiers, and took great Delight in the Discipline, which pleased my Officers exceedingly, and they was pleased to put me chief Armourer[35] of the Regiment; and some Time after, they thought proper that I should Number and Engrave the Arms of the Regiment belonging to Governor *Shirley*,[36] as also Sir *William Pepperrell's* Regiment's Arms, and so continued as Armourer for two Years; then I unhappily Married a Wife, which proved a Torment to me, and made my Life uncomfortable; and she was given to take a Cup too much, and I for my Part took to the same; and through her aggravating Tongue, neglecting my Business, I was turned out, and was obliged to do private duty again as a common Soldier. And after I was off Duty,

I took and set myself up as a Silversmith, and followed Engraving and Seal-Cutting; and as I was Moulding, I cast a *Spanish* Dollar[37] amongst the rest of my Work and laid it down on the Work-Bench, so that I did not care who saw it; and by an ill-minded Man who made it his Business to inform against me, I was taken up for the same and Try'd by a General Court-Marshal; I pleaded Guilty, and by the Dollar's being good Silver was acquitted, and some Time after, I quarrel'd with a brother Soldier, and he complain'd to his Officer about it, and for that Crime I receiv'd Fifty Stripes;[38] and in a short Time after the Regiment was broke, I came to *Boston*, and sat up to Engraving; and in that Time there came two Men who persuaded me to Engrave them a Plate for *New-Hampshire* Money, which I did, and they Rewarded me well for it. I thought it was an easy Way of getting Money, so I Counterfeited the *Boston* Bills of Credit; but never made none above *Forty Shillings*.[39] Soon after, my Wife and I having differed together, she cry'd out Hey, you Forty Thousand Money-Maker, which was heard by some of the Neighbours, who made a complaint against me; for which I was Apprehended, and stood Tryal, and was acquitted, by Reason they had no Law for that Money: The Attorney-General desired that I should be continued in Custody till next Court, or give Bail for my Appearance; the next Sessions they found a Bill against me for Forgery, and was found Guilty, for which I stood two Hours in the Pillory and received Twenty Lashes at the public Whipping-Post; during my Confinement, I engraved three sorts of Plates, two of *New-Hampshire* money, and one for *Boston* Currency, and for want of a Rolling Press, struck it off by Hand, sign'd it in Goal and gave it out by Quantities to my Accomplices, and some Time afterwards, being in low Circumstances, two Gentlemen came and paid my Bill of Costs, and took me out of Goal; soon after I came out of Confinement, the *New-Hampshire* Money was found to be false, (that is the first Money that I Engraved for the Gentlemen,) one of them turned King's Evidence[40] and swore against me for engraving the Plate, and against his Confederate; but both got clear by Swearing it upon me; for my Part I made my Escape and got into *Rhode-Island* Government, where I met with a Man who I had known in *Cape-Breton*, where I laid concealed for some Time; he and sundry more came to me, and desired of me, and intreated of me to cut them a Plate, which I did and struck off *Twelve Thousand Pounds*, and divided the Money amongst them, as I thought proper; and in one Day I changed and past about *Sixteen Hundred Pounds*, and got good Money for it; and coming through the Town of *Providence* one of my Accomplices Wives was taken up for Counterfeiting Money. I told her before she should Swear, that she might say she had the Money from me; and she would never have been taken up, if she had not taken a Bill clandestinely and Sign'd it herself.

My Partner *Nicholas Stephens* and I, rid about three Miles out of Town, and divided the good Money we had by us, and then parted; he Rid in Town and there gave himself up as an Evidence, in behalf of King and Country, and they confin'd him to Goal; and he brought in seven or eight more, who all pleaded not Guilty and swore they had the Money of me, and received it for good Money in Trading; and in about a Week after, I was taken and confin'd to Goal: I was brought to Examination and pleaded Guilty, and said that those People that was in Goal I had Cheated in Trading. I had hid about *Four Thousand Pounds*, which the Authority demanded of me; I told them that I would not deliver the Money till they would deliver, and Discharge the Innocent now Confin'd; and after they were Discharged, I was brought out under a Guard and delivered up the Money; soon after that, I was brought to Tryal and found Guilty; and was Branded in both Cheeks with the Letter R. and Cropt in both my Ears, so I was returned to Custody again. I broke out of Goal and saw *Nicholas Stephens* Cropt and Branded, the High Sheriff of *Providence* came to me, and desired of me to return to Prison, for he said he should loose his Place; with that I went very quietly, and soon after, on a Monday I broke out of Goal and went to a Husking Frolick[41] about three Miles out of Town, and differ'd with the Company, and got almost Kill'd, and the next Morning returned to my old Prison again, then I was put in strong Irons and confined very close; but I soon found Means to break out again; although they pursu'd me very close, sent Post haste after me, and did all they could to Apprehend me; but all in vain, till I came to *Dutchess* County, in the Province of *New-York*; and going from House to House, there was a Person that knew me, and asked if my Name was not *Syllavan*? No, said I, you are mistaken in the Person my Friend; and so I went off for fear he would betray me; which he did, by describing my Visage and Apparel, and said, he was sure it was *Syllavan* the Money-Maker.

Then I provided myself with a secret retreating Place, at the Side of a Swamp; in a large unfrequented Wood: but hearing that some of my Accomplices were taken, and expecting they would betray me, or discover my Habitation. I therefore abandoned it, and fled to the Mountains, where I concealed myself seven Days; till being compel'd by Hunger, I ventured to a House of my Acquaintance, hoping they would favour my Concealment; and having cut a Plank in the Floor of the House, I dig'd a Cavity under the Hearth, and had a Fire-place, the Smoke of which issu'd by a Vent into the Chimney above; I had not been long conceal'd there, before the House was surrounded by several Men: so I suffer'd myself to be taken, and surrender'd to them. First I was carried to *New-Haven* Goal, and afterwards removed to *New-York*.

During my stay in *Dutchess* County, I made large Sums of *Rhode-Island* Money, of six Assortments, and of the *New-Hampshire* Currency *ten or twelve Thousand Pounds*, and left the Plates with my Accomplices; of *Connecticut* Money, I made three Sorts, and printed off about *three Thousand Pounds*, and left the Plates with my Accomplices; of *New-York* Currency four Sorts, and had four different Sets of Accomplices; and there was four Sorts Counterfeited by my Accomplices, which I had no Hand in at all; and all of the new Currency, with the following Signers Names to it, viz. *De Lancey*, *Depuyster*, and *Livington*. All my Accomplices deserv'd the Gallows, as well as myself; but I will not betray them, or be guilty of shedding their Blood.

And then turning to the Spectators, said, well Gentlemen, *You may all take Warning by me, and look out for the King of Terrors; and told the Sheriff that he must needs confess, that he was not willing to die. Then looking about him, said, I see none of my Accomplices here; but I hope they will burn and destroy all the Money, Plates and Accoutrements, that they have by them, and that they may not die on a Tree as I do. Then call'd to the Executioner and said, don't pull the Rope so tight, it is hard for a Man to die in cold Blood: after which he cried out* O good GOD! O good God! *Have Mercy on my Soul I then said the Lord's Prayer. Just as he was turn'd off the Cart, he cry'd,* LORD have Mercy on my Soul.

THOMAS POWERS

*The Narrative and Confession of Thomas Powers, A Negro (1796)**

I THOMAS POWERS, was born in Wallingford, in Connecticut, September 15th, 1796. My father's name is Thomas Powers; and my mother before mar-

* SOURCE: Powers, Thomas. 1796. *The Narrative and Confession of Thomas Powers, a Negro, Formerly of Norwich in Connecticut, Who Was in the 20th Year of His Age. He Was Executed at Haverhill, in the State of New Hampshire, on the 28th July, 1796, for Committing a Rape*. Norwich. PUBLICATION HISTORY: Numerous local newspapers recorded Powers's execution. The Philadelphia-based *Claypoole's American Advertiser* informed its readers in June 1796 that Thomas Powers, "a mulatto" and "resident in Lebanon, was convicted of a most barbarous rape, committed on Sally Messer, on the evening of the 7th of December last." Besides these short reports, there is only one longer text, a sermon by Noah Worcester, who uses Powers's execution as a warning case to address the "rising generation." Published sermons served as news and were frequently used by other ministers for their services. It became known as *A Sermon Delivered at Haverhill, New Hampshire, July 28, 1796, at the execution of Thomas Powers, who was executed for a rape, committed at Lebanon, on the 7th of December, 1795*.

riage was Prudy Waterman. I was the second and youngest Son of my father, with whom I lived, till I was two years old. He then put me out to live with Mr. Moses Tharp, of Norwich (Conn.) where I resided one year, and then returned to my father, who, being a very pious man, endeavored to instruct me in several duties, to God, to my parents, and to all mankind; as far as my young and tender mind was capable of receiving any virtuous impressions. But I was naturally too much inclined to vice, to profit by his precepts or example; for I was very apt to pilfer and tell lies, if I thought there was any occasion.

When I was nine years old, I was put out to live with Isaac Johnson, of Lebanon (Conn.) where I lived two years, and very early began the practice of villainy and debauchery. It was here I began my career in the gratification of that corrupt and lawless passion, which has now brought me to the threshold of eternity, before my years were half numbered.

Being one Sunday at home from meeting, with nobody but a young Negro woman, who lived in the house, she, enticing me to her bed, where she was lying, soon taught me the practice of that awful sin, which now costs me my life; for which together with disobedience to my master, and many other villaneous tricks which I used to play upon him, he often corrected me, but to so little purpose that he dismissed me from his service.

Then I returned once more to my father, where I lived a few months, till he, not liking my behaviour, bound me out to Mr. Oliver Hayde, of Norwich, (Conn.) Dating my residence with him, who as a pretty kind master, I was taught to read and write a tolerable good hand; but being naturally vicious I improved my talents, (or rather misimproved them) to very bad purposes. I used to make a point of pilfering whenever I could; for when I saw an opportunity, the devil, or some other evil spirit, always gave me a strong inclination. I suppose it was because I was naturally inclined to be light-fingered; for I never hesitated to touch anything that came in my way. Here too I played my pranks, with the young black girls about the streets; and indulged myself as freely as I could without discovery.

In the year 1789, I broke open a store in Norwich, (Conn.) owned by Mr.— took a few articles of goods and fifteen dollars in Cash. In the next place, knowing my present master, Oliver Lathrop, to have on hand a large sum of money, I supposed that I might take about twenty dollars and neither of us fare the worse. I, however, soon repented of this bargain; for being discovered, I was forced to return the money, and take a few stripes on my back; but if I had received my just deserts I might possibly have escaped the fate, which now awaits me.

In the year 1793 I moved with my master from Norwich, in Connecticut, to Lebanon, in New Hampshire, where I soon run the length of my chain, and compleated my villainy, committing a number of crimes, which black as I am, I should blush to repeat.

Before I removed from Norwich, (Conn.) I attempted to ravish a young girl, who was visiting in the neighborhood. For this purpose, I took an old sword, and went into the woods where I supposed she would return in the evening, and concealed myself in the bushes, where I waited till 12 o'clock; but as providence ordered it, she did not go home that night, and so escaped the snare I had laid for her.

On the 7th day of Dec. 1795, being at work with Mr. Gordon Lathrop, I agreed to meet him in the evening, at Thomas Rowels, to wrestle. Accordingly a little after sundown I sat out, without any evil intentions. I overtook a young woman, whom I knew to be——I passed on by her, a pretty good jog, till after a little querying with myself, and finding nothing to oppose, but rather the devil to assist me, I determined to make an attempt on her virgin chastity.—So I waylaid her, and as she came up, seized her with one hand, and her horse's bridle with t'other, she ask'd me what I wanted?—I told her to dismount and I would tell her. At the same time taking her from her horse, I threw her on the ground, and in spite of her cries and entreaties, succeeded in my hellish design. Then left her, and went to the place proposed, where I found my antagonist; but the evening being far spent, I returned to my master's house and sat down, as usual, to play chequers[42] with the children.

It was not long before I heard people round the house, and was afterwards informed they were after me; but seeing me so lively at play, says the Esq. "It can't be Tom"—so they went away. I soon went to bed; but in about two hours, I was awaked from sleep by a number of people who entered my room, and called me their "prisoner."

I was confined, till next day, when I had my trial before Esq. Hough, who sentenced me to prison; accordingly I was immediately secured in Haverhill jail, on the 10th day of Dec. As we were passing by the place where the crime was committed I was questioned concerning the fact; but, I, like a hardened villain, as I was, denied every syllable of the truth, and had but little sense of my situation, till the key of the prison was turned upon me, when my feelings were such as no pen or tongue, can describe. On the fifth of April, after 4 months confinement, with the help of two of my companions we broke goal after three hours hard work. We went to the river, stole a boat, ran three miles down, and sent her adrift. One of my comrades, by the name of Bayley, went to his father's, where he procured some refreshment for us.—

From thence, we went to Capt. Frye Baley's in Newbury, where we stole a horse, and went fifteen miles to Ryegate. On Sunday evening we arrived at St. Johnsbury, & took up lodgings in a barn. At twelve we took up our line of march, and returned to Barnet, where I parted with my companions; It being my object to go to Portland, and ship myself aboard of a vessel. I, however, missed my road and came back to Littleton where I enquired for Lake Champlain, and as I was going quite the other way, I was suspected of being a rogue, and I confess they had some grounds for their suspicion, as one of them was acquainted with me. I was, of consequence, immediately returned to my old lodgings in Haverhill. Here I was now hand-cuffed, and my arms pinioned;[43] and put into the upper loft of the Prison: but on Sunday, the 4th day after my last commitment, I sawed of my pinions across the grates of the prison; and with the help of a knife, I got a piece of board, with which I pryed off the grate. I then went to work to cut up my blanket, into strips, and tying them together from the grate, I descended from the upper loft. As I passed by the grate of the lower room, I called to the prisoners below telling them, of my liberty but desired them to say nothing till I had got off; but Holmes swore he would stop me; if in his power, and immediately raised the Jailor.—I ran as fast as I could, after being almost spent with fatigue, in getting my liberty, and descending from the upper loft, with hand-cuffs on; and while they were looking for me in the most obscure places, near the Goal, supposing me to be there concealed; but I made my escape into the river road, and at break of day, I found myself at Capt. John Mann's in Orford. I then thought it prudent, to avoid discovery, to go back into the woods, where I lay till night.

I then proceeded on to Lyme, and broke into a blacksmith shop, to rid myself of my Hand cuff's which in my travels, I found rather uncomfortable companions, and I suspected, in case of being seen and noticed, they would prove but a poor recommendation. However I could not succeed; so I went on to Gould's Tavern, and took a horse, which I rode about three miles; but not being able to get him any farther, I attempted to drown him to get my revenge; but could not easily succeed, and I left him to shirk.[44] I then proceeded on to a smith's shop on College Plain, where I made another fruitless attempt to get my hands at liberty. When I got into the edge of Lebanon, it was daylight; so I wandered about in the woods till evening, when I went to Mr. Quimbe's shop in Lebanon and sawed, and twisted my hand-cuffs about two hours, and gave out being quite overcome for want of food. I then went to my master's house, looked in at the window, but guilt being my companion, I dared not enter. I then gained some distance from the house and sawed my cuffs across a rock, till by the help of a file, I liberated my hands, and went to Mr. T. Rowel's, whom I supposed to be a friend; But he, like most friends, in adversity, forsook me, and turned my enemy. For upon seeing how cold and hungry I was, he seemed to pity me, and told me to go to a certain barn, and he would bring me some refreshment; but instead of victuals, he mustered all the force he could to take me. Being however, aware of his treachery, when day light appeared, I fled to the woods, and lay there, where I suffered extremely with the cold. Upon seeing them come into the woods I lay down under a log, and as they passed along one of them trod on me, but did not perceive me. I then thought best to shift my course, and taking a cross lot, one of them saw me, as I ascended a little rise of ground, and hailed me. I pointed to a barn at some distance, and said, "he has just gone by the barn.—" which turned the attention of the whole that way; he then supposed me to be one of their party, as it was between day light and dark.

This gave me a little breath again, and I thought of trying to get some refreshment by milk, from a cow of my master's, as I had not eat or drank for nigh 4 days, but could not find her, where I expected. I however found some raw potatoes and eat of them freely. At last I took up a resolution to use my hand-cuff bolt, for my defence, and to go into the house; which I did, but found none but children round the tea-table, who were exceedingly frightened, and run away, all but a boy, who told me to take what I wanted, if I was hungry. I seized half a cheese, and half a loaf of bread, which was on the table, and ran off. I soon met a Mr. Colburn, who knew me, and told me to go with him, and nobody should hurt me adding that I should have any refreshment I wanted. I followed him home, and no sooner had we got there, than he sent to inform my pursuers. I stept to the door, and saw them coming over the hill—I started to run and Colburn struck at me, but I escaped and ran till I fainted and fell. His dog followed me, however, and barked till they came up and took me, as their prisoner.

The time of my trial was now come on, and instead of carrying me to Haverhill, I was carried to Plymouth, where I immediately had my trial before the Hon. Superior Court, and was sentenced, very justly, to death. At first, upon hearing my sentence, it had no impression on my mind—for my heart was hardened beyond description. After a little reflection, however, I fainted, and could not speak for some time.—At length I came to myself, and desired to see the young Lady, whom I had injured. This she refused, but said she, would receive any message I wished to send to her. I then set down and wrote a confession of my crime, and of the justness of my punishment. I begged pardon, most sincerely for the injury, I had done her. She sent me for answer, that she could forgive me, and hoped that God would do the same. I was then conducted to prison and bound with irons. During my residence here under sentence of death, I have not been wholly insensible of my pitiable situation; as my master as well as the divines who have attended me, have ever endeavored to impress me with a sense of a state of future happiness or misery to which I was destined; but the secret hope of making my escape, and, the jollity of countenance that appeared in most of my spectators; did in some measure banish the idea of death from my mind. The ninth of June, a number of Doctors made application to me for my BODY, for DISSECTION, after my execution; to which I readily consented for the small sum of ten dollars, thinking it might afford me a comfortable subsistence while here, and my BONES be of service to mankind after the separation of soul and body, which must shortly take place, and at which time may I receive forgiveness of all mankind, and of my God, before whom I must appear through the merits of a Redeemer.

Notes

1. Smith and Watson (2010, 4) assert that "the oral performance of self-narrative has existed in many indigenous cultures prior to literacy" and—together with evidence from other countries such as India and China—contradict the idea that "autobiography is a uniquely Western form and a specific achievement of Western culture" that can be reduced to a form of writing (103–4). With its concentration on the autobiography—a genre that developed in Enlightenment Europe—and its representation of a "sovereign self," life writing has only recently started to include other self-referential forms and media as well as marginal experiences; see Lanzendörfer and Scheiding, forthcoming.

2. Surveying extant confession narratives, Babb (1998, 79) states that most offenders were young and were not elite members of society, while the majority of murders were charged to Irishmen or African Americans in the 1780s and 1790s, thus linking crime to ethnicity. Like Syllavan, who forged and thereby stole money, all robbers in collections of criminal cases like *The American Bloody Register* were Irish, whereas the majority of extant rape narratives feature African American convicts. The stereotype of the "oversexed" or "sexually degenerate" African American is exemplified by the shocking image of Powers raping a white virgin; he violated not only racial borders, such as laws against miscegenation, but also the "sacred" female body, defying both "social and sexual codes" (Williams 1993, 216, 220). For Powers's relationship to female victims and his own "lack of control," see Sobel (2000, 143–44).

3. Samuel de Champlain (1567–1635) was a French explorer, and the founder and

first governor of New France. The Hurons, actually called Wyandot after their shared language, were indigenous people living around present-day Lake Ontario and the Georgian Bay, where the first encounter between them and Champlain took place.

4. Father Anne de Noüe accompanied Jean de Brébeuf to Lake Huron in a canoe. They took their residence at Ihonatiria, an Indian town near Georgian Bay, where they founded a mission. In Huronia, Jesuits were often regarded not as priests but as Frenchmen who helped secure the alliance between tribes and the colonial powers. Therefore, they were offered residence in native villages and towns.

5. The Montagnais, the French name for the Innu peoples, live in what is today northern Quebec and Labrador in Canada. Le Jeune's *Relation* of 1634 provides a first ethnographic account of their life and customs through several missionaries living among them for an extended period of time.

6. The Algonquin word *kébec* translates as "where the river narrows" and was used by Samuel de Champlain to name Québec in 1608, the seat of the French colony New France.

7. The Iroquois, living in northern New York, were a league of five nations that raided and fought against the Innu (Montagnais) as well as the Huron peoples. From 1609 onward, they also engaged in a war against the French and their Native allies and against other neighboring tribes and the English colonies. Subsequently, some of their nations became important trading partners for the Dutch colonies, exchanging furs for weapons.

8. Taylor's birthplace.

9. Falmouth was the place intended.

10. Abaft: toward the stern.

11. Nigh: almost.

12. One fathom is equal to 6 feet.

13. Originally named "Indian Bridge," the Bridgetown burning occurred in the late 1660s.

14. To put the helm a lee: to move the tiller to the leeward side to make the vessel's bow cross the wind.

15. Mint-master and treasurer of the colony. Like Taylor himself, he was a native of Leicestershire.

16. Unit of length that corresponds to 3 nautical miles (4,828 m).

17. Florin: originally an Italian gold coin, here Rheingulden, worth approximately 200 modern U.S. dollars.

18. Thaler: silver coin used throughout Europe, also known as dollar in England; equivalent to 100 modern U.S. dollars.

19. The Brethren, a reform-seeking Protestant group influenced by Anabaptists and pietists.

20. The interior regions of West Africa.

21. A tanner, one who prepares leather.

22. Kreuzer: a copper coin used in the southern parts of Germany. 90 Kreuzer make a Thaler.

23. Batzen: a silver coin used in the southern parts of Germany and Austria; worth 4 Kreuzer.

24. Pfennig: old German coin of low value.

25. Groschen: Southern German penny, worth 3 Kreuzer.

26. Ipswich and Marblehead, two communities in Massachusetts on the Atlantic seaboard.

27. Pinnace: a small sailing ship.

28. Snapsack: similar to a rucksack.

29. Vacilation: wavering or uncertainty.

30. Taíno/Arawak name for the island of Puerto Rico.

31. For nautical measurement, see Taylor's diary.

32. Fethard: a village in South Tipperary in Ireland.

33. A common practice to recruit labor in North America; indentured servants sold their work for a specific time to pay for their passage to America.

34. At the outbreak of the French and Indian War (1754–63), British forces prepared to attack the French fortress of Louisbourg on Cape Breton Island, Nova Scotia.

35. Amourer: officer in charge of repairing or replacing the soldier's arms.

36. William Shirley (1694–1771) became governor of Massachusetts Bay twice and served for some time as commander-in-chief of North America.

37. Also known as a piece of eight, the Spanish dollar is a silver coin that was originally struck to correspond to the German Thaler; see Sauer's account on colonial coinage use.

38. Public punishment with lashes.

39. In British America, colonies issued their own paper money and used pounds, shillings, and pence for payment. Currency varied, but usually a shilling is one-twentieth of a pound. The bill of credit is state-issued money without an intrinsic value; it is used to pay debts.

40. Turned King's Evidence: to give information in a court of law about other people involved in the crime in order to have their own punishment reduced.

41. Husking Frolick: a gathering to help a neighbor with husking, or peeling, corn, usually combined with festivities.

42. Chequers: American English, a board game.

43. Pinioned: bound or shackled.

44. Shirk: to avoid responsibility.

Suggestions for Further Reading

Travel

Bradford, William, and Edward Winslow. 1622. *A Relation or Journall of the Beginning and Proceedings of the English Plantation Settled at Plimoth in New England.* 4–8. London.

Josselyn, John. 1674. *An Account of Two Voyages to New-England.* London.

Le Jeune, Paul. (1632) 1900. "Brief Relation of the Journey to New France." In *The Jesuit Relations and Allied Documents: Travels and Explorations of the Jesuit Missionaries in New France, 1610 to 1791*, edited by Ruben Gold Thwaites. Vol 5. 11–17. Cleveland: Burrows Brothers.

Winthrop, John. 1996. *The Journal of John Winthrop 1630–1649*, edited by Richard S. Dunn, James Savage, and Laetitia Yeandle. Cambridge: Belknap Press of Harvard Univ. Press.

Misadventure

Carey, Mathew. 1786. "The Shipwreck: A Fragment." *Columbian Magazine* 1 (Sept.): 6–8.

Marrant, John. 1785. *A Narrative of the Lord's Wonderful Dealings with John Marrant, a Black, with the assistance of Reverend William Aldridge*. London.

Mather, Cotton. 1711. "A Relation of a Remarkable Deliverance, . . . received by Captain John Dean and Company." In *Compassions Called For: An Essay of Profitable Reflections on Miserable Spectacles*, 50–60. Boston.

Mather, Increase. 1684. "[Remarkable Deliverance of Major Gibbons]." In *An Essay for the Recording of Illustrious Providences*, 14–17. Boston.

Confessions

Bradford, William. 1898. "[Thomas Granger's Sodomy]." *Bradford's History 'Of Plimoth Plantation,'* 474–78. Boston: Wright and Potter.

Mather, Cotton. 1699. "A Whoredom Unmasked." In *Pillars of Salt: An History of Some Criminals Executed in this Land, for Capital Crimes*, 60–62. Boston.

Moodey, Samuel. 1726. *Summary Account of the Life and Death of Joseph Quasson, Indian*. Boston.

PART II
FEMALE AGENCY

IN SPITE OF women's restricted legal status and political influence, female agency was an important cultural force in colonial and early national North America. The narratives in this section document the various ways in which women expressed their experience and views in a society that remained strictly patriarchal even after the American Revolution. Through their authorship and choice of subjects, they espouse a translocal perspective as they deal with the hardships of slavery, tenant farming in Europe, marginalized groups like German-speaking settlers, African Americans, and Native Americans, as well as changing political contexts from colonial warfare to the Jackson administration in the 1830s. The captivity narrative, for example, is often based on firsthand accounts by women in which the experience of a different culture allows for the exploration of different roles and ambiguous identities (Castiglia 1996). However, female voices in captivity narratives were tightly controlled by the men who published that material. Narratives written both by women and about them contributed to the formation of a religious community or regional identity, as in the local legends associated with the stories of Hannah Duston and Regina Leininger, or the image of the Republican mother who embodies and hands down virtue to the next generation of citizens (Weis 1998). Yet the Republic also saw an increase in female writing that attacked social ills, such as slavery, or revealed the hypocrisy of male assertions of intellectual or physical superiority, as in Margaretta Faugeres's rebuttal of Jefferson's racism. These writings combine stereotypical elements of sensibility with the construction of individual identity and social activism, and the sheer amount of female writing defies their social and legally marginalized position (Mulford, Vietto, and Winans 1999, xviii).

Reading fiction and even writing novels was regarded as a dubious pastime, yet women used literary forms to address a variety of political issues that emanated from their immediate concerns and educational tasks, and these writings also had a wider social impact. Women were highly regarded contributors to periodicals, as can be seen in the careers of Judith Sargent Murray, Susanna Rowson, and Ann Eliza Bleecker, and in the narrative output by countless anonymous or pseudonymous female authors. Women chose more accessible forms of expression than the classical models that governed poetry, drama, or even historiography, frequently writing essays, short fictions, novels, and advice pieces—the forms that were most popular at the time. They also built on earlier genres in which they were well versed: advice and conduct books, diaries, and letters (Harris 1996). Thus, novels like Hanna Webster Foster's *The Coquette* (1797) are written in an epistolary style or intended as lessons to an imaginary girls' school.

Since Mary Rowlandson's *The Soveraignty and Goodness of God* (1682), captivity narratives have often been considered a typical "American" genre, though they are predated by biblical and ancient examples and by accounts of British sailors held captive by Algerians or Moroccans in the Mediterranean (Allison [1995] 2000; Peskin 2009). Even its religious significance as a version of the spiritual autobiography seems less unusual when read alongside reports of French Jesuits or Quakers who were held captive by Natives in the early Americas (Voigt 2009). If not the first genre of print best sellers, captivity narratives were at least among the most popular publications, constituting three-quarters of the best sellers between 1680 and 1720. Published and read on both sides of the Atlantic, reprints of captivity narratives remained a "popular theme in fiction" (Ebersole 1995, 10) during the eighteenth and nineteenth centuries, even though the Indian Wars had ceased and captives were no longer being taken.

The situation on the Pennsylvania frontier in 1755 was very similar to the Native American raids in New England of the 1670s. England and France fought over the dominion of these territories and employed varying alliances with Native tribes that conducted raids and abductions, which resulted in a number of Pennsylvanian captivity narratives (Snyder 2010; Carocci 2012). In 1759 a German press in Philadelphia, formerly co-owned by Benjamin Franklin, published *Die Erzehlungen von Maria le Roy und Barbara Leininger*, a story about two women who successfully fled from their abductors and brought news from various other captives. The account contains many typical motifs and plot patterns of the genre, from a bloody scene of abduction to the lengthy stay in captivity and ending with a note to other survivors—reports that have frequently been identified with anti-Indian and anti-French propaganda. Yet the narrative is also the first German example of a genre that is not based on an English text, and it was the only one published before the American Revolution (Derounian-Stodola and Levernier 1993, 114–15).

In 1697 the story of Hannah Duston's captivity and violent escape sparked great interest in New England, and Cotton Mather's report was reprinted several times, forming the basis for subsequent treatments in local histories as well as poems and prose in nineteenth-century periodicals. The evolution of the captivity genre can best be traced in this example, since Hannah Duston was at once the most notorious and controversial captive (Ulrich 1982, 167). As James Levernier (1999, 107–11) argues, the voices of both Mather and Duston are present in the narrative. Mather's narrator relates Duston's killing of her Native captors to the biblical precedent of Jael, while Duston sees herself justified by the fact that her own life was not protected by any law as long as she remained in captivity. Hawthorne's rewriting of the story especially enunciates Mather's voice by constantly criticizing his "bigotry" in justifying and aggrandizing Duston's violence. Duston's narrative, probably a first-person account taken in an interview with Mather, served different purposes according to its publication context. First appended to a Fast-Day sermon, it shows how New England could act if it had God's support, and Duston's escape becomes a providential deliverance granted in response to the prayers of Mather's congregation. In the second publication, as part of Mather's history of King William's War (1689–97) titled "Decennium Luctuosum" (the sorrowful decade), Duston's resolution and violent effectiveness contrast with the ineptitude and cowardice of men (Toulouse 2007, 103). Hawthorne's version emphasizes the courage and sensibility of Mr. Duston—in line with the "benevolent paternity" of the Jackson administration—and accuses Hannah Duston of losing all motherly qualities in slaughtering a helpless Native family. This perspective also highlights the changing image of Native Americans, who, at the time, were diminished, relocated, and not posing any threat to the expansion of the United States. While threatening images of Native American raids were still present in literature side by side with Romantic conceptions of the vanishing but "noble savage," Native Americans also became ancestors to the modern nation and helped define its identity against the British (Silver 2008).

The narrative written by Marie le Roy and Barbara Leininger (1759) combines an account of their capture, their life among the Delaware Indians, and their escape with information on other living captives collected for the benefit of their families. Published by the German printing press in Philadelphia, the narrative was geared to the large audience of German and Swiss immigrant farmers who lived in rural Pennsylvania and were concerned with Native American attacks during the French and Indian War (1754–63). Consequently, the account combines Pennsylvania geography and the lifestyle and customs of the Delaware tribes with the motifs of attack, capture, and escape typical of earlier New England narratives. After being captured, Barbara Leininger was exposed to a severe beating as an initiation ritual, then adopted into the Native village of Kittany, where she participated in the typical tasks of Native women before her status was reduced to that of a servant. Both women, together with two Englishmen, escape to Fort Pitt, and frequently credit God for protecting them through His providence. The account ends with a long list that provides detailed information about captives whom they have met as "the chief reason why we have given the foregoing narrative to the public," loosely resembling the rhetorical figures of modesty employed in Puritan accounts of captivity.

Margaretta Faugeres's "Inhuman Treatment to a Negro Slave" (1791) portrays the suffering of a slave and his gratitude when he was bought and then freed by his new master. Her essay was originally titled "Fine Feelings Exemplified in the Conduct of a Negro Slave" in response to "eminent reasoner" Thomas Jefferson's claim that African Americans lacked the capability of "finer feelings," which were, according to the philosophy of sensibility, integral to their moral character. By illustrating—through a narrative—how her argument that "[the African American's] mental and external sensibilities are as acute as those of the people whose skin may be of a different colour," Faugeres follows not only the conventions of periodical essays like Sargent Murray's *Gleaner* (1798), but also the much older exempla in medieval religious literature. Faugeres's political activism is evident throughout her essays and poetry, which were published regularly in *The New York Magazine* under different pen names and revolve around "three important political movements" of the period: "the antislavery movement, support of the French Revolution, and opposition to capital punishment" (Harris 2005, 117; see also Part IV). In addition, Faugeres published poetry and prose written by her mother, Ann Eliza Bleecker, first in periodicals and eventually as a collection with some of her other works, as

The Posthumous Works of Ann Eliza Bleecker in Prose and Verse (1793). The volume also included the first fictitious and sentimental captivity narratives, "The History of Maria Kittle" (in Harris 2003, 3–35) and "Henry and Anne," which had first appeared in installments in *The New York Magazine* in 1790 and 1791 and was completed by Faugeres from her mother's unfinished version. "Henry and Anne" provides an early glimpse of German emigrants to America who were evicted from their land when they failed to produce the crops demanded by the landowner. They fled misfortune and poverty to the very village in which Bleecker lived. Yet another episode in "Henry and Anne"—one that involves the daughter of a baron—demonstrates how the privileged can be equally unhappy, reinforcing their resolve to "go to the land of simplicity . . . [because] pride and hypocrisy, and avarice, are stranger where luxury and titles are unknown."

A comparison of the original "Henry and Anne" manuscript with the version that was published in the magazine, however, reveals that the fulfillment of a wish for the "land of simplicity" and the settlement in Tomhanick were added by Margaretta Faugeres. In contrast to Ann Eliza Bleecker's less optimistic version, Faugeres's ending "reflects her alternative belief in an integrated new social order" that does away with class and property differences. At the same time, the different endings are also indicative of the artistic programs of both mother and daughter and correspond to the images they fashioned for themselves through their works. In a biographical sketch in *The Posthumous Works*, Margaretta Faugeres states that her mother destroyed lighter writings that did not fit her melancholy mood. Separated from the coastal literary and intellectual circle to which she belonged, living far away from her family and friends, and being under constant threat of Native American raids in her frontier community, Ann Eliza Bleecker suffered from serious bouts of depression (Giffen 1999). Most of her works are contained in letters she wrote to her network of female friends, as in the epistolary beginning of "The History of Maria Kittle," where she bemoans the loss of "Eden." Ironically, Tomhanick becomes the "new Eden" in her daughter's redaction of "Henry and Anne," and embodies the simplicity and freedom that contrasts so vividly with the class and tenant systems of Europe. The themes and language of sentimentality are characteristic for both mother and daughter, as is the effort to establish and fashion their images as literary artists—one melancholy and the other politically progressive—for which the periodical provided the space.

CAPTIVITIES

MARIE LE ROY AND BARBARA LEININGER

*The Narrative of Marie le Roy and Barbara Leininger, for Three Years Captives among the Indians (1759)**

Marie le Roy was born at Brondrut, in Switzerland. About five years ago she arrived, with her parents, in this country. They settled fifteen miles from Fort Schamockin. Half a mile from their plantation lived Barbara Leininger with her parents, who came to Pennsylvania from Reutlingen, about ten years ago.[1]

Early in the morning of the 16th of October, 1755, while le Roy's hired man went out to fetch the cows, he heard the Indians shooting six times. Soon after, eight of them came to the house, and killed Marie le Roy's father with tomahawks. Her brother defended himself desperately, for a time, but was, at last, overpowered. The Indians did not kill him, but took him prisoner, together with Marie le Roy and a little girl, who was staying with the family. Thereupon they plundered the homestead, and set it on fire. Into this fire they laid the body of the murdered father, feet foremost, until it was half consumed. The upper half was left lying on the ground, with the two tomahawks, with which they had killed him, sticking in his head. Then they kindled another fire, not far from the house. While sitting around it, a neighbour of le Roy, named Bastian, happened to pass by on horseback. He was immediately shot down and scalped.

Two of the Indians now went to the house of Barbara Leininger, where they found her father, her brother, and her sister Regina. Her mother had gone to the mill. They demanded rum; but there was none in the house. Then they called for tobacco, which was given them. Having filled and smoked a pipe, they said: "We are Alleghany Indians,[2] and your enemies. You must all die!" Thereupon they shot her father, tomahawked her brother, who was twenty

* SOURCE: Le Roy, Marie, and Barbara Leininger. (1759) 1905. "The Narrative of Marie le Roy and Barbara Leininger, for Three Years Captives among the Indians." *The Pennsylvania Magazine of History and Biography* 29 (4): 407–20.
PUBLICATION HISTORY: Originally, the account was printed in German as *Die Erzehlungen von Maria le Roy und Barbara Leininger*, published by Teutsche Buchdruckerey Miller und Weiß in Philadelphia in 1759. This print has been credited to Benjamin Franklin's press, but he ceased to collaborate with Anthony Armbrüster in 1759 and the German printing office passed into the hands of Peter Miller and Ludwig Weiss. Reverend Reuben Weiser wrote a mid-nineteenth-century biography of Regina Leininger, titled *Regina, the German Captive; or, True Piety among the Lowly.*

years of age, took Barbara and her sister Regina[3] prisoners, and conveyed them into the forest for about a mile. There they were soon joined by other Indians, with Marie le Roy and the little girl.

Not long after several of the Indians led the prisoners to the top of a high hill, near the two plantations. Toward evening the rest of the savages returned with six fresh and bloody scalps, which they threw at the feet of the poor captives, saying that they had a good hunt that day.

The next morning we were taken about two miles further into the forest, while the most of the Indians again went out to kill and plunder. Toward evening they returned with nine scalps and five prisoners.

On the third day the whole band came together and divided the spoils. In addition to large quantities of provisions, they had taken fourteen horses and ten prisoners, namely: One man, one woman, five girls, and three boys. We two girls, as also two of the horses, fell to the share of an Indian named Galasko.

We traveled with our new master for two days. He was tolerably kind, and allowed us to ride all the way, while he and the rest of the Indians walked. Of this circumstance Barbara Leininger took advantage, and tried to escape. But she was almost immediately recaptured, and condemned to be burned alive. The savages gave her a French Bible, which they had taken from le Roy's house, in order that she might prepare for death; and, when she told them that she could not understand it, they gave her a German Bible. Thereupon they made a large pile of wood and set it on fire, intending to put her into the midst of it. But a young Indian begged so earnestly for her life that she was pardoned, after having promised not to attempt to escape again, and to stop her crying. The next day the whole troop was divided into two bands, the one marching in the direction of the Ohio, the other, in which we were with Galasko, to Jenkiklamuhs,[4] a Delaware town on the West branch of the Susquehanna. There we staid ten days, and then proceeded to Puncksoto nay, or Eschentown. Marie le Roy's brother was forced to remain at Jenkiklamuhs.

After having rested for five days at Puncksotonay, we took our way to Kittanny.[5] As this was to be the place of our permanent abode, we here received our welcome, according to Indian custom. It consisted of three blows each, on the back. They were, however, administered with great mercy. Indeed, we concluded that we were beaten merely in order to keep up an ancient usage, and not with the intention of injuring us. The month of December was the time of our arrival, and we remained at Kittanny until the month of September, 1756.

The Indians gave us enough to do. We had to tan leather, to make shoes (mocasins), to clear land, to plant corn, to cut down trees and build huts, to wash and cook. The want of provisions, however, caused us the greatest sufferings. During all the time that we were at Kittanny we had neither lard nor salt; and, sometimes, we were forced to live on acorns, roots, grass, and bark. There was nothing in the world to make this new sort of food palatable, excepting hunger itself.

In the month of September Col. Armstrong arrived with his men, and attacked Kittanny Town. Both of us happened to be in that part of it which lies on the other (right) side of the river (Alleghany). We were immediately conveyed ten miles farther into the interior, in order that we might have no chance of trying, on this occasion, to escape. The savages threatened to kill us. If the English had advanced, this might have happened. For, at that time, the Indians were greatly in dread of Col. Armstrong's corps. After the English had withdrawn, we were again brought back to Kittanny, which town had been burned to the ground.

There we had the mournful opportunity of witnessing the cruel end of an English woman, who had attempted to flee out of her captivity and to return to the settlements with Col. Armstrong. Having been recaptured by the savages, and brought back to Kittanny, she was put to death in an unheard of way. First, they scalped her; next, they laid burning splinters of wood, here and there, upon her body; and then they cut off her ears and fingers, forcing them into her mouth so that she had to swallow them. Amidst such torments, this woman lived from nine o'clock in the morning until toward sunset, when a French officer took compassion on her, and put her out of her misery. An English soldier, on the contrary, named John . . . , who escaped from prison at Lancaster, and joined the French, had a piece of flesh cut from her body, and ate it. When she was dead, the Indians chopped her in two, through the middle, and let her lie until the dogs came and devoured her.

Three days later an Englishman was brought in, who had, likewise, attempted to escape with Col. Armstrong, and burned alive in the same village. His torments, however, continued only about three hours; but his screams were frightful to listen to. It rained that day very hard, so that the Indians could not keep up the fire. Hence they began to discharge gunpowder into his body. At last, amidst his worst pains, when the poor man called for a drink of water, they brought him melted lead, and poured it down his throat. This draught at once helped him out of the hands of the barbarians, for he died on the instant.

It is easy to imagine what an impression such fearful instances of cruelty make upon the mind of a poor captive. Does he attempt to escape from the savages, he knows in advance that, if retaken, he will be roasted alive. Hence he must compare two evils, namely, either to remain among them a prisoner forever, or to die a cruel death. Is he fully resolved to endure the latter, then he may run away with a brave heart.

Soon after these occurrences we were brought to Fort Duquesne,[6] where we remained for about two months. We worked for the French, and our Indian master drew our wages. In this place, thank God, we could again eat bread. Half a pound was given us daily. We might have had bacon, too, but we took none of it, for it was not good. In some respects we were better off than in the Indian towns; we could not, however, abide[7] the French. They tried hard to induce us to forsake the Indians and stay with them, making us various favourable offers. But we believed that it would be better for us to remain among the Indians, in as much as they would be more likely to make peace with the English than the French, and in as much as there would be more ways open for flight in the forest than in a fort. Consequently we declined the offers of the French, and accompanied our Indian master to Sackum, where we spent the winter, keeping house for the savages, who were continually on the hunt. In the spring we were taken to Kaschkaschkung, an Indian town on the Beaver Creek. There we again had to clear the plantations of the Indian nobles, after the German fashion, to plant corn, and to do other hard work of every kind. We remained at this place for about one year and a half.

After having, in the past three years, seen no one of our own flesh and blood, except those unhappy beings, who, like ourselves, were bearing the yoke of the heaviest slavery, we had the unexpected pleasure of meeting with a German, who was not a captive, but free, and who, as we heard, had been sent into this neighbourhood to negotiate a peace between the English and the natives. His name was Frederick Post.[8] We and all the other prisoners heartily wished him success and God's blessing upon his undertaking. We were, however, not allowed to speak with him. The Indians gave us plainly to understand that any attempt to do this would be taken amiss. He himself, by the reserve with which he treated us, let us see that this was not the time to talk over our afflictions. But we were greatly alarmed on his account. For the French told us that, if they [Indians] caught him, they would roast him alive for five days, and many Indians declared that it was impossible for him to get safely through, that he was destined for death.

Last summer the French and Indians were defeated by the English in a battle fought at Loyal-Hannon, or Fort Ligonier. This caused the utmost consternation among the natives. They brought their wives and children from Lockstown, Sackum, Schomingo, Mamalty, Kaschkaschkung, and other places in that neighbourhood, to Moschkingo, about one hundred and fifty miles farther west. Before leaving, however, they destroyed their crops, and burned everything which they could not carry with them. We had to go along, and staid at Moschkingo the whole winter.

In February, Barbara Leininger agreed with an English man, named David Breckenreach [Breckenridge], to escape, and gave her comrade, Marie le Roy, notice of their intentions. On account of the severe season of the year, and the long journey which lay before them, Marie strongly advised her to relinquish the project, suggesting that it should be postponed until spring, when the weather would be milder, and promising to accompany her at that time.

On the last day of February nearly all the Indians left Moschkingo, and proceeded to Pittsburg to sell pelts.[9] Meanwhile, their women traveled ten miles up the country to gather roots, and we accompanied them. Two men went along as a guard. It was our earnest hope that the opportunity for flight, so long desired, had now come. Accordingly, Barbara Leininger pretended to be sick, so that she might be allowed to put up a hut for herself alone. On the fourteenth of March, Marie le Roy was sent back to the town, in order to fetch two young dogs which had been left there; and, on the same day, Barbara Leininger came out of her hut and visited a German woman, ten miles from Moschkingo. This woman's name is Mary—, and she is the wife of a miller from the South Branch.[10] She had made every preparation to accompany us on our flight; but Barbara found that she had meanwhile become lame, and could not think of going along. She, however, gave Barbara the provisions which she had stored, namely, two pounds of dried meat, a quart of corn, and four pounds of sugar. Besides, she presented her with pelts for moccasins. Moreover, she advised a young Englishman, Owen Gibson, to flee with us two girls.

On the sixteenth of March, in the evening, Gibson reached Barbara Leininger's hut, and, at ten o'clock, our whole party, consisting of us two girls, Gibson, and David Breckenreach, left Moschkingo. This town lies on a river, in the country of the Dellamottinoes. We had to pass many huts inhabited by the savages, and knew that there were at least sixteen dogs with them. In the merciful providence of God not a single one of these dogs barked. Their barking would at once have betrayed us, and frustrated our design.

It is hard to describe the anxious fears of a poor woman under such circumstances. The extreme probability that the Indians would pursue, and recapture us, was as two to one compared with the dim hope that, perhaps, we would get through in safety. But, even if we escaped the Indians, how would we ever succeed in passing through the wilderness, unacquainted with a single path or trail, without a guide, and helpless, half naked, broken down by more than three years of hard slavery, hungry and scarcely any food, the season wet and cold, and many rivers and streams to cross? Under such circumstances, to depend upon one's own sagacity would be the worst of follies. If one could not believe that there is a God, who helps and saves from death, one had better let running away alone.

We safely reached the river [Muskingum]. Here the first thought in all our minds was: O! that we were safely across! And Barbara Leininger, in particular, recalling ejaculatory prayers[11] from an old hymn, which she had learned in her youth, put them together, to suit our present circumstances, something in the following style:

O bring us safely across this river!
In fear I cry, yea my soul doth quiver.
The worst afflictions are now before me,
Where'er I turn nought[12] but death do I see.
Alas, what great hardships are yet in store
In the wilderness wide, beyond that shore!
It has neither water, nor meat, nor bread,
But each new morning something new to dread.
Yet little sorrow would hunger me cost
If but I could flee from the savage host,
Which murders and fights and burns far and wide,
While Satan himself is array'd on its side.
Should on us fall one of its cruel bands,
Then help us, Great God, and stretch out Thy hands!
In Thee will we trust, be Thou ever near,
Art Thou our Joshua, we need not fear.

Presently we found a raft, left by the Indians. Thanking God that He had himself prepared a way for us across these first waters, we got on board and pushed off. But we were carried almost a mile down the river before we could reach the other side. There our journey began in good earnest. Full of anxiety and fear, we fairly ran that whole night and all the next day, when we lay down to rest without venturing to kindle a fire. Early the next morning, Owen Gibson fired at a bear. The animal fell, but, when he ran with his tomahawk to kill it, it jumped up and bit him in the feet, leaving three wounds. We all hastened to his assistance. The bear escaped into narrow holes among the rocks, where we could not follow. On the third day, however, Owen Gibson shot a deer. We cut off the hind-quarters, and roasted them at night. The next morning he again shot a deer, which furnished us with food for that day. In the evening we got to the Ohio at last, having made a circuit of over one hundred miles in order to reach it.

About midnight the two Englishmen rose and began to work at a raft, which was finished by morning. We got on board and safely crossed the river. From the signs which the Indians had there put up we saw that we were about one hundred and fifty miles from Fort Duquesne. After a brief consultation we resolved, heedless of path or trail, to travel straight toward the rising of the sun. This we did for seven days. On the seventh we found that we had reached the Little Beaver Creek, and were about fifty miles from Pittsburgh.

And now, that we imagined ourselves so near the end of all our troubles and misery, a whole host of mishaps came upon us. Our provisions were at an end; Barbara Leininger fell into the water and was nearly drowned; and, worst misfortune of all! Owen Gibson lost his flint and steel. Hence we had to spend four nights without fire, amidst rain and snow.

On the last day of March we came to a river, Alloquepy,[13] about three miles below Pittsburg. Here we made a raft, which, however, proved to be too light to carry us across. It threatened to sink, and Marie le Roy fell off, and narrowly escaped drowning. We had to put back, and let one of our men convey one of us across at a time. In this way we reached the Monongahella River, on the other side of Pittsburg, the same evening.

Upon our calling for help, Col. [Hugh] Mercer immediately sent out a boat to bring us to the Fort. At first, however, the crew created many difficulties about taking us on board. They thought we were Indians, and wanted us to spend the night where we were, saying they would fetch us in the morning. When we had succeeded in convincing them that we were English prisoners, who had escaped from the Indians, and that we were wet and cold and hungry, they brought us over. There was an Indian with the soldiers in the boat. He asked us whether we could speak good Indian? Marie le Roy said she could speak it. Thereupon he inquired, why she had run away? She replied, that her

Indian mother had been so cross and had scolded her so constantly, that she could not stay with her any longer.

This answer did not please him; nevertheless, doing as courtiers do, he said: He was very glad we had safely reached the Fort.

It was in the night from the last of March to the first of April that we came to Pittsburg. Most heartily did we thank God in heaven for all the mercy which he showed us, for His gracious support in our weary captivity, for the courage which he gave us to undertake our flight, and to surmount all the many hardships it brought us, for letting us find the road which we did not know, and of which He alone could know that on it we would meet neither danger nor enemy, and for finally bringing us to Pittsburgh to our countrymen in safety.

Colonel Mercer helped and aided us in every way which lay in his power. Whatever was on hand and calculated to refresh us was offered in the most friendly manner. The Colonel ordered for each of us a new chemise, a petticoat, a pair of stockings, garters, and a knife. After having spent a day at Pittsburg, we went, with a detachment under command of Lieutenant Mile, to Fort Ligonier. There the Lieutenant presented each of us with a blanket. On the fifteenth we left Fort Ligonier, under protection of Captain [Philip] Weiser[14] and Lieutenant Atly, for Fort Bedford, where we arrived in the evening of the sixteenth, and remained a week. Thence, provided with passports by Lieutenant [Henry] Geiger,[15] we traveled in wagons to Harris' Ferry, and from there, afoot, by way of Lancaster, to Philadelphia.

Owen Gibson remained at Fort Bedford, and David Breckenreach at Lancaster. We two girls arrived in Philadelphia on Sunday, the sixth of May.

And now we come to the chief reason why we have given the foregoing narrative to the public. It is not done in order to render our own sufferings and humble history famous, but rather in order to serve the inhabitants of this country, by making them acquainted with the names and circumstances of those prisoners whom we met, at the various places where we were, in the course of our captivity. Their parents, brothers, sisters, and other relations will, no doubt, be glad to hear that their nearest kith and kin are still in the land of the living, and that they may, hence, entertain some hope of seeing them again in their own homes, if God permit. . . . [What follows is a list of people that Marie Le Roy and Barbara Leininger met during their captivity, the place and circumstances they were in and ends with the following note.]

We became acquainted with many other captives, men, women, and children, in various Indian towns, but do not know, or cannot remember their names. We are, however, heartily willing to give all such as have, or believe to have, connections among the Indians, any further information which may lie within our power. We intend to go from here to Lancaster, where we may easily found.

COTTON MATHER

*A Narrative of a Notable Deliverance from Captivity (1697)**

On the fifteenth Day, of the Last *March*, *Hannah Dustan* of *Haverhil*, having Lain in about a Week,[16] attended with her Nurse, *Mary Neff*, a Widow, a Body of Terrible *Indians* drew near unto the House where she lay, with Designs to carry on the bloody Devastations, which they had begun upon the Neighbourhood.[17] Her Husband, hastened from his Employments abroad unto the Relief of his Distressed Family; and first bidding *Seven* of his *Eight* Children (which were from Two to *Seventeen* years of age,) to get away as fast as they could, unto some Garrison in the Town, he went in, to inform his Wife, of the horrible Distress now come upon them. E're she could get up, the fierce *Indians* were got so near, that utterly despairing to do her any Service, he ran out after his Children; Resolving, that on the Horse which he had with him, he would Ride away with *That*, which he should in this Extremity find his Affections to

* SOURCE: Mather, Cotton. 1697. "A Narrative of a Notable Deliverance from Captivity." In *Humiliations Follow'd with Deliverances*, 41–47. Boston.
PUBLICATION HISTORY: Mather, Cotton: 1699. "Article XXV: A Notable Exploit; Wherein, Dux Faemina Facti." In *Decennium Luctuosum*, 138–43. Boston. Reprinted in Mather, Cotton. 1702. *Magnalia Christi Americana*, 7: 90–91. London. The popularity of the story can be seen in a number of reprints and versions in magazines as well as historical records and fiction: [Cotton Mather]. 1795. "Heroic Exploit of Two Women.—From Mather's Magnalia." *The New York Magazine, or Literary Repository* 6 (5): 262; 1795. *The Rural Magazine; or Vermont Repository. Devoted to Literary Moral, Historical, and Political Improvement* (November 1): 577; "Hannah Duston." 1836. *Cincinnati Mirror, and Western Gazette of Literature, Science, and the Arts* 5 (10): 74; 1836. *The Every Body's Album: A Humorous Collection of Tales, Quips, Quirks, Anecdotes, and Facetiae* (September 1): 271.

Retellings can be found in nineteenth-century travel accounts: Dwight, Timothy. (1821) 1969. *Travels in New England and New York*, edited by Barbara Miller Solomon, 1:297–99. Boston: Belknap Press of Harvard Univ. Press; Thoreau, Henry David. (1849) 1868. *A Week on the Concord and Merrimack Rivers*, 330–42. Boston: Ticknor and Fields; Whittier, John Greenleaf. (1831) 1965. *Legends of New England*, 126–31. Gainesville, FL: Scholar's Facsimiles.

The story was altered and enhanced in numerous magazine pieces: "Heroic Exploit of Two Women in New England." 1809. *The American Magazine of Wonders and Marvellous Chronicle* 1:355–56; Knapp, Samuel L. 1834. "Female Biography: Sketches of American Women. Hannah Duston." *The New-York Mirror: A Weekly Gazette of Literature and the Fine Arts* 11 (44): 350; Anon. 1843. "Escape of the Duston Family." *The Rover: A Weekly Magazine of Tales, Poetry, and Engravings, Also Sketches of Travel, History and Biography* 1 (24): 382–83; Anon. 1864. "The Escape of Hannah Dustan." *Circular* 1 (11): 83–84.

pitch most upon, and leave the Rest, unto the care of the Divine Providence. He overtook his Children about Forty Rod, from his Door; but *then* such was the *Agony* of his Parental Affections, that he found it Impossible for him, to Distinguish any one of them from the Rest; wherefore he took up a Courageous Resolution, to Live & Dy with them All. A party of *Indians* came up with him; and now though they Fired at him, and he Fired at them, yet he manfully kept at the Reer of his *Little Army* of unarmed Children, while they March'd off, with the pace of a Child of Five years old; until, by the Singular Providence of God, he arrived safe with them all, unto a place of Safety about a Mile or two from his House. But his House must in the mean Time, have more dismal *Tragedies* acted at it. The Nurse, trying to Escape, with the New born Infant, fell into the hands of the formidable Salvages; & those furious Twanies, coming into the House, bid poor *Dustan*, to Rise immediately. Full of Astonishment, she did so; and Sitting down in the Chimney, with an heart full of most fearful Expectations, she saw the Raging Dragons rifle all that they could carry away: and set the House on Fire. About Nineteen or Twenty *Indians,* now led these away, with about Half a score other, English *Captives*: but e're they had gone many Steps, they dash'd out the Brains of the *Infant,* against a Tree, and several of the other *Captives*, as they begun to Tire in their sad Journey, were soon sent unto their long Home, but the Salvages would presently bury their Hatchets in their Brains, and leave their Carcases on the ground, for Birds & Beasts, to feed upon. [Christians, A *Joshua*[18] would have *Rent his Clothes & fallen to the Earth on his Face*, and have *Humbled* himself Exceedingly upon the falling out of such doleful Ruines upon his Neighbours!] However, *Dustan* (with her Nurse,) notwithstanding her present Condition, Travelled that Night, about a Dozen Miles; and then kept up with their New Masters, in a long Travel of an Hundred and fifty Miles, more or less, within a few Days Ensuing; without any sensible Damage, in their Health, from the Hardships, of their *Travel*, their *Lodging*, their *Diet*, and their many other Difficulties. These Two poor Women, were now in the Hands of those, *Whose Tender Mercies are Cruelty*:[19] but the Good God, who hath all *Hearts in his own Hands*, heard the Sighs of *these Prisoners* unto Him, and gave them to find unexpected Favour, from the *Master*, who Laid claim unto them. That *Indian Family* consisted of Twelve Persons, Two stout men, three women, and seven Children; and for the shame of many a *Prayerless Family* among our *English*, I must now publish what these poor women assure me, 'Tis *This*; In Obedience to the Instruction which the French have given them, they would have *Prayers* in their Family, no less than Thrice every Day; in the *Morning*, at

Noon, and in the *Evening*; nor would they ordinarily let so much as a Child, *Eat*, or *Sleep*, without first saying their *Prayers*. Indeed, these *Idolaters*, were, like the rest of their whiter Brethren *Persecutors*, and would not Endure that these poor *Women* should Retire to their *English Prayers*, if they could hinder them. Nevertheless, the poor Women, had nothing but fervent *Prayers*, to make their Lives comfortable or tolerable; and by being daily sent out, upon Business, they had opportunities together and asunder, to do like another *Hannah*, in *pouring out their Souls before the Lord*:[20] Nor did their Praying Friends among ourselves, forbear to *pour out* Supplications for them. Now, they could not observe it, without some wonder, that their Indian Master, sometimes, when he saw them Dejected, would say unto them; *What need you Trouble yourself? If your God will have you Delivered, you shall be so!* And it seems, our God, would have it so to be!

The Escape of the Duston Family.

FIG. 2: *The Escape of the Duston Family*. Engraving. In Samuel G. Goodrich, *Peter Parley's Method of Telling about the History of the World to Children*, 38. Hartford, CT: Huntington, 1836. Reprinted in *The American Magazine of Useful and Entertaining Knowledge* 2 (9): 395. Courtesy, American Antiquarian Society.

This Indian Family, was now Travelling with these two Captive women, (& an English Youth, taken from *Worcester*, last *September* was a Twelve month, unto a Rendezvouse of Salvages, which they call a *Town*, somewhere beyond *Penacook*; and they still told these poor women, that when they came to this Town, they must be Stript, & Scourg'd, and Run the *Gantlet*, through the whole Army of *Indians*. They said, This was the *Fashion*, when the Captives first came to a Town; and they derided, some of the fainthearted English, which, they said, fainted and swooned away under the *Torments* of this Discipline. [Syrs, can we hear of these things befalling our Neighbours, & not *Humble* ourselves before our God!] But on this Day Se'night, while they were yet it may be, about an hundred and fifty miles from the Indian Town, a little before Break of Day, when the whole Crew, was in a *Dead Sleep*, ('twill presently prove so!) One of these women took up a Resolution, to Imitate the Action of *Jael* upon *Sisera*,[21] and being where she had not her *own Life* secured by any *Law* unto her, she thought she was not forbidden by any *Law*, to take away the *Life*, of the *Murderers*, by whom her *Child* had been butchered. She heartened the *Nurse*, and the *Youth*, to assist her, in this Enterprise; & they all furnishing themselves with *Hatchets* for the purpose, they struck such Home Blowes upon the Heads of their *Sleeping Oppressors*, that e're they could any of them struggle into any effectual Resistance, *at the Feet* of those poor Prisoners, *They bowed, they fell, they lay down; at their feet they bowed, they fell; where they bowed, there they fell down Dead*. Only one *Squaw* Escaped sorely wounded from them, and one *Boy*, whom they Reserved Asleep, intending to bring him away with them, suddenly wak'd and stole away, from this Desolation. But cutting off the Scalps[22] of the *Ten Wretches*, who had Enslav'd 'em, they are come off; and I perceive, that newly arriving among us, they are in the Assembly at this Time, to give Thanks unto, *God their Saviour*.

ANONYMOUS [NATHANIEL HAWTHORNE]

*The Duston Family (1836)**

Goodman Duston and his wife, somewhat less than a century and a half ago, dwelt in Haverhill, at that time a small frontier settlement in the province of Massachusetts Bay. They had already added seven children to the King's liege

* SOURCE: [Hawthorne, Nathaniel?]. 1836. "The Duston Family." *The American Magazine of Useful and Entertaining Knowledge* 2 (9): 395–97. Although the story has been attributed to Hawthorne by many critics, it is not included in *The Centenary Edition of the Works of Nathaniel Hawthorne*.

subjects in America; and Mrs. Duston about a week before the period of our narrative, had blessed her husband with an eighth. One day in March, 1698, when Mr. Duston had gone forth about his ordinary business, there fell out an event, which had nearly left him a childless man, and a widower besides. An Indian war party, after traversing the trackless forest all the way from Canada, broke in upon their remote and defenceless town. Goodman Duston heard the war whoop and alarm, and, being on horseback, immediately set off full speed to look after the safety of his family. As he dashed along, he beheld dark wreaths of smoke eddying from the roofs of several dwellings near the road side; while the groans of dying men,—the shrieks of affrighted women, and the screams of children, pierced his ear, all mingled with the horrid yell of the raging savages. The poor man trembled yet spurred on so much the faster, dreading that he should find his own cottage in a blaze, his wife murdered in her bed, and his little ones tossed into the flames. But, drawing near the door, he saw his seven elder children, of all ages between two years and seventeen, issuing out together, and running down the road to meet him. The father only bade them make the best of their way to the nearest garrison, and, without a moment's pause, flung himself from his horse, and rushed into Mrs. Duston's bedchamber.

The good woman, as we have before hinted, had lately added an eighth to the seven former proofs of her conjugal affection; and she now lay with the infant in her arms, and her nurse, the widow Mary Neff, watching by her bedside. Such was Mrs. Duston's helpless state, when her pale and breathless husband burst into the chamber, bidding her instantly to rise and flee for her life. Scarcely were the words out of his mouth, when the Indian yell was heard: and staring wildly out of the window, Goodman Duston saw that the blood-thirsty foe was close at hand. At this terrible instant, it appears that the thought of his children's danger rushed so powerfully upon his heart, that he quite forgot the still more perilous situation of his wife; or, as is not improbable, he had such knowledge of the good lady's character, as afforded him a comfortable hope that she would hold her own, even in a contest with a whole tribe of Indians. However that might be, he seized his gun and rushed out of doors again, meaning to gallop after his seven children, and snatch up one of them in his flight, lest his whole race and generation should be blotted from the earth, in that fatal hour. With this idea, he rode up behind them, swift as the wind. They had, by this time, got about forty rods from the house, all pressing forward in a group; and though the younger children tripped and stumbled, yet the elder ones were not prevailed upon, by the fear of death, to take to their heels and leave these poor little souls to perish. Hearing the tramp of hoofs in their rear, they looked round, and espying Goodman Duston, all suddenly stopped. The little ones stretched out their arms; while the elder boys and girls, as it were, resigned their charge into his hands; and all the seven children seemed to say.—"Here is our father! Now we are safe!"

But if ever a poor mortal was in trouble, and perplexity, and anguish of spirit, that man was Mr. Duston! He felt his heart yearn towards these seven poor helpless children, as if each were singly possessed of his whole affections; for not one among them all, but had some peculiar claim to their dear father's love. There was his first-born; there, too, the little one who, till within a week past, had been the baby; there was a girl with her mother's features, and a boy, the picture of himself, and another in whom the looks of both parents were mingled; there was one child, whom he loved for his mild, quiet, and holy disposition, and destined him to be a minister; and another, whom he loved not less for his rough and fearless spirit, and who, could he live to be a man, would do a man's part against these bloody Indians. Goodman Duston looked at the poor things, one by one; and with yearning fondness, he looked at them all, together; then he gazed up to Heaven for a moment, and finally waved his hand to his seven beloved ones. "Go on, my children," said he, calmly. "We will live or die together!"

He reined in his horse, and caused him to walk behind the children, who, hand in hand, went onward, hushing their sobs and wailings, lest these sounds should bring the savages upon them. Nor was it long, before the fugitives had proof that the red devils had found their track. There was a curl of smoke from behind the huge trunk of a tree—a sudden and sharp report echoed through the woods—and a bullet hissed over Goodman Duston's shoulder, and passed above the children's heads. The father, turning half round on his horse, took aim and fired at the skulking foe, with such effect as to cause a momentary delay of the pursuit. Another shot—and another—whistled from the covert of the forest; but still the little band pressed on unharmed; and the stealthy nature of the Indians forbade them to rush boldly forward, in the face of so firm an enemy as Goodman Duston. Thus he and his seven children continued their retreat, creeping along, as Cotton Mather observes, "at the pace of a child of five years old," till the stockades of a little frontier fortress appeared in view, and the savages gave up the chase.

We must not forget Mrs. Duston, in her distress. Scarcely had her husband fled from the house, ere the chamber was thronged with the horrible visages of the wild Indians, bedaubed with paint and besmeared with blood, brandishing their tomahawks in her face and threatening to add her scalp to those that were already hanging at their girdles. It was, however, their interest to save her alive, if the thing might be, in order to exact a ransom. Our great-great-grandmothers, when taken captive in the old times of Indian warfare, appear, in nine cases out of ten, to have been in pretty much such a delicate situation as Mrs. Duston; notwithstanding which, they were wonderfully sustained through long, rough, and hurried marches, amid toil, weariness, and starvation, such as the Indians themselves could hardly endure. Seeing that there was no help for it, Mrs. Duston rose, and she and the widow Neff, with the infant in her arms, followed their captors out of doors. As they crossed the threshold, the poor babe set up a feeble wail; it was its death cry. In an instant, an Indian seized it by the heels, swung it in the air, dashed out its brains against the trunk of the nearest tree, and threw the little corpse at the mother's feet. Perhaps it was the remembrance of that moment, that hardened Hannah Duston's heart, when her time of vengeance came. But now, nothing could be done, but to stifle her grief and rage within her bosom, and follow the Indians into the dark gloom of the forest, hardly venturing to throw a parting glance at the blazing cottage, where she had dwelt happily with her husband, and had borne him eight children—the seven, of whose fate she knew nothing, and the infant, whom she had just seen murdered.

The first day's march was fifteen miles; and during that, and many succeeding days, Mrs. Duston kept pace with her captors; for, had she lagged behind, a tomahawk would at once have been sunk into her brains. More than one terrible warning was given her; more than one of her fellow captives,—of whom there were many,—after tottering feebly, at length sank upon the ground; the next moment, the death groan was breathed, and the scalp was reeking at an Indian's girdle. The unburied corpse was left in the forest, till the rites of sepulture should be performed by the autumnal gales, strewing the withered leaves upon the whitened bones. When out of danger of immediate pursuit, the prisoners, according to Indian custom, were divided among different parties of the savages, each of whom were to shift for themselves. Mrs. Duston, the widow Neff, and an English lad, fell to the lot of a family, consisting of two stout warriours, three squaws, and seven children. These Indians, like most with whom the French had held intercourse, were Catholics; and Cotton Mather affirms, on Mrs. Duston's authority, that they prayed at morning, noon, and night, nor ever partook of food without a prayer; nor suffered their children to sleep, till they had prayed to the christian's God. Mather, like an old hard-hearted, pedantic bigot, as he was, seems trebly to exult in the destruction of these poor wretches, on account of their Popish superstitions. Yet what can be more touching than to think of these wild Indians, in their loneliness and their wanderings, wherever they went among the dark, mysterious woods, still keeping up domestic worship, with all the regularity of a household at its peaceful fireside;

They were travelling to a rendezvous of the savages, somewhere in the north-east. One night, being now above a hundred miles from Haverhill, the red men and women, and the little red children, and the three pale faces, Mrs. Duston, the widow Neff, and the English lad, made their encampment, and kindled a fire beneath the gloomy old trees, on a small island in Contocook river. The barbarians sat down to what scanty food Providence had sent them, and shared it with their prisoners, as if they had all been the children of one wigwam, and had grown up together on the margin of the same river within the shadow of the forest. Then the Indians said their prayers—the prayers that the Romish priests had taught them—and made the sign of the cross upon their dusky breasts, and composed themselves to rest. But the three prisoners prayed apart; and when their petitions were ended, they likewise lay down, with their feet to the fire. The night wore on; and the light and cautious slumbers of the red men were often broken, by the rush and ripple of the stream, or the groaning and moaning of the forest, as if nature were wailing over her wild children; and sometimes, too, the little red skins cried in sleep, and the Indian mothers awoke to hush them. But, a little before break of day, a deep, dead slumber fell upon the Indians. "See," cries Cotton Mather, triumphantly, "if it prove not so!"

Uprose Mrs. Duston, holding her own breath, to listen to the long, deep breathing of her captors. Then she stirred the widow Neff, whose place was by her own, and likewise the English lad; and all three stood up, with the doubtful gleam of the decaying fire hovering upon their ghastly visages, as they stared round at the fated slumberers. The next instant, each of the three captives held a tomahawk. Hark! That low moan, as of one in a troubled dream—it told a warriour's death pang! Another!—Another!—And the third half-uttered groan was from a woman's lips. But, Oh, the children! Their skins are red; yet spare them, Hannah Duston; spare those seven little ones, for the sake of the seven that have fed at your own breast. "Seven," quoth Mrs. Duston to herself. "Eight children have I borne—and where are the seven, and where is the eighth!" The thought nerved her arm; and the copper coloured babes slept the same dead sleep with their Indian mothers. Of all that family, only one woman escaped, dreadfully wounded, and fled shrieking into the wilderness! and a boy, whom, it is said, Mrs. Duston had meant to save alive. But he did well to flee from the raging tigress! There was little safety for a red skin, when Hannah Duston's blood was up.

The work being finished, Mrs. Duston laid hold of the long black hair of the warriours, and the women, and the children, and took all their ten scalps, and left the island, which bears her name to this very day. According to our notion, it should be held accursed, for her sake. Would that the bloody old hag had been drowned in crossing the Contocook river, or that she had sunk over head and ears in a swamp, and been there buried, till summoned forth to confront her victims at the Day of Judgment; or that she had gone astray and been starved to death in the forest, and nothing ever seen of her again, save her skeleton, with the ten scalps twisted round it for a girdle! But, on the contrary, she and her companions came safe home, and received the bounty on the dead Indians, besides liberal presents from private gentlemen, and fifty pounds from the Governour of Maryland. In her old age, being sunk into decayed circumstances, she claimed, and we believe, received a pension, as a further price of blood.

This awful woman, and that tender hearted, yet valiant man, her husband, will be remembered as long as the deeds of old times are told round a New England fireside. But how different is her renown from his!

AUTHORSHIP

ANTONETTA [MARGARETTA V. FAUGERES]

*Inhuman Treatment to a Negro Slave (1791)**

For the NEW-YORK MAGAZINE.

Notwithstanding what the learned Mr. J——has said respecting the want of finer feelings in the blacks, I cannot help thinking that their sensations, mental and external, are as acute as those of the people whose skin may be of a differ-

* SOURCE: Antonetta [Margaretta V. Bleecker Faugeres]. 1791. "Inhuman Treatment to a Negro Slave." *The New-York Magazine, or Literary Repository* 2 (6): 338–39.
PUBLICATION HISTORY: Margaretta Faugeres reprinted her mother's work and some of her own in 1793. In the printed volume, the story appears as "Fine Feelings exemplified in the Conduct of a Negro Slave"; see Margaretta V. Faugeres. 1793. *The Posthumous Works of Ann Eliza Bleecker. To which is Added, A Collection of Essays, Prose, and Poetical, by Margaretta V. Faugeres*, 268–70. New York.

ent colour; such an assertion may seem bold, but facts are stubborn things, and had I not *them* to support me, it is probable I should not attempt to oppose the opinions of such an eminent reasoner.

In the interior parts of this state lived (a few years ago) a man of property, who owned a number of blacks; but formed in nature's most savage mould, his chief employment was inventing punishments for his unfortunate dependents, and his principal delight in practicing the tortures he had invented. Among the number of his slaves was an old Negro, who, in his younger days, had been a faithful servant; but captivity and sorrow had at length broken his spirit, and destroyed that ambition which actuates the free, and gives energy and life to all they perform. This was a proper subject for the cruelty of Mr. A——to act upon. Upon the commission of the smallest fault, or the most trifling neglect, he would himself tie Mingo, (as butchers do sheep intended for slaughter) and after having beaten him till the blood followed every stroke of the whip, he would retire, leaving the wretch weltering in his gore, exposed to the burning rays of summer or the gelid gales of winter. When rested he would return, and after a repetition of his amusement, would release the sufferer, lest a few more minutes of such extreme agonies should shorten the period of Mingo's woes, and—his master's felicity. However, this mode of punishment becoming a little troublesome to Mr. A——, he thought of another which he believed would answer nearly as well: he caused a large ox-chain to be made, and putting it to Mingo's waist, he brought it round his neck, and there fastened it again, leaving an end of about four yards, to which he nailed a piece of wood weighing upwards of forty weight. With this clog the slave was obliged to work—and this at night was placed in the master's chamber, (the chain passing through a hole in the door) while Mingo slept on the ground outside of the house, from which uncomfortable couch nothing but the most bitter cold excused him.

Seven long years did the miserable being groan under this load, when the captain of a vessel, hearing of his hard fate, out of pity bought him.

After having paid the money he went home, and sending for Mingo, told him he was free :—"You are your own master," said the humane sailor; "but you are old, and helpless—I will take care of you." Overpowered with joy, the old man clasped the captain's knees; he wept aloud—he raised his swimming eyes to heaven—he would have spoken his thanks;—but his frame was too feeble for the mighty conflict of his soul—he expired at his benefactor's feet!

ANTONETTA.

New York, June 17, 1791.

FIG. 3: Engraving, ornamental oval with panel, by Charles Tiebout (1773–1832), one of the first well-known American engravers. He also drew Ann Eliza Bleecker's portrait for *The Posthumous Works* (1793), edited by her daughter. *New York Magazine; or Literary Repository* 2 (4): n.p. Courtesy, American Antiquarian Society.

ANN ELIZA BLEECKER

STORY of HENRY and ANNE.[23]*—Founded on Fact [WITH AN ENGRAVING] (1791)**

Henry and Anne were born in Germany, in the Marquisate of Baden; their parents dwelt contiguous to each other, and the most sentimental friendship subsisted between the two families. Anne was graceful even in infancy—Henry tall and majestic, strong and active, tho' not regularly beautiful; their poverty early introduced them on the fields; their little hands were lacerated by the bearded grain, and their tender feet wounded by the asperities of a flinty soil. Anne's lovely complexion soon lost its delicate whiteness, but was amply recompenced by the bloom of luxuriant health. Whilst they toil'd together in gathering the stones from the green surface of a meadow, or weeding the vines, the courtly passenger would stop and gaze with pity to see so much elegance and beauty of form joined to the servility of unremitted labour. Henry redoubled his exertions constantly to lessen little Anne's fatigue, and when their task was done, they rejoined their companions, assisted them to complete their work, and with gleeful hearts sported themselves to sleep.

Nor were the old farmers displeased to see the growing affection between their children; "we shall soon be closer united," said they, "Henry and Anne (our only offspring) shall cement our friendship, and perpetuate our names to remotest centuries." Alas! in the midst of this inchanting vision, an officer, attended by a file of musqueteers, demanded Henry. He was now seventeen, full grown, and must enter his Lord's service. It was in vain to expostulate. Without a farewell sigh from Anne, or scarce an embrace from his distracted parents, he must depart. Being escorted to a distant town, he was there initiated into all the military maneuvers, and three weeks after joined his regiment, which left that part of Germany soon after. Henry's disappointed love sunk him into melancholy—he grew desperate, and negligent of life. In a very warm action, being engaged with the enemy in fight of the General, he ventured himself rashly, and fought without caution. It was called intrepidity, and he was advanced to the rank of sergeant. Having acquitted himself with honour, and the time of

* SOURCE: Ann Eliza Bleecker. 1791. "Story of Henry and Anne: Founded on Fact." *The New York Magazine; or, Literary Repository* 2 (4): 184–86; 2 (5): 263–67.
PUBLICATION HISTORY: The narrative is probably based on facts and retells the fate of two of Bleecker's neighbors at Tomhanick. It was reprinted in Margaretta V. Faugeres. 1793. *Posthumous Works of Ann Eliza Bleecker, in Prose and Verse. To which is added, A Collection of Essays, Prose, and Poetical, by Margaretta V. Faugeres*, 89–114. New York.

his service being elapsed, his Captain gave him his discharge, with previous offers of promotion if he would continue in his company. "I blush to decline my officer's generous proposal," said Henry; "but it is better to be virtuous than fortunate—I have left three broken hearts at home, I must hasten to heal them – the soft voice of my Anne calls me from the thunder of Bellona."[24]—"Go," said his commander in a softened tone, "I know what love is—my Henry can be happy, I only great;" then dropping a tear, "Go Henry—farewell—I know you deserve to be happier than I am."

The interview between the lovers was tender and romantic.—Anne, to console her Henry's parents, remitted not her assiduities to please them. She cultivated their garden; she cull'd the richest fruit and brightest flowers to amuse them: her active fingers extended an imperceptible thread of flax to provide them linen of finer texture than the product of Egyptian looms: she resisted the importunity of Henry's rivals heroically, while her old father, weeping for joy, commended her constancy. "My child," said he, "thou art no disgrace to thy lineage; Henry loves thee, he is worthy of thee, and worthy of every sacrifice thou canst make him; cheer up my little one, he will soon return."—"No, my father, some inexorable shot will cleave his brave heart." So saying, she rose agitated from weeding a bed of lupins, when a foot soldier approached. Scarce had the old man civilly accosted the stranger over the hedge when Anne screamed out, "Oh heaven! father, it is our Henry, our own Henry."—In an instant the family was convened; from tears they made abrupt transitions to mirth, which soon caught the ears of the good neighbours, who came in crouds to felicitate the soldier's arrival. His parents invited them to return the next day and share the general festivity, which they freely accepted, and assisted to slaughter the poultry and fattest lambs. The entertainment was truly pastoral. The tables were spread in the vineyard, beneath verdant arches that were empurpled by weighty clusters of grapes; a gushing fountain close by dispensed a delicious coolness, and baskets of flowers filled the air with balmy sweetness. To heighten the scene the silvery airs of music, from the violin, harp, and mellifluous flute, softly circled through the sky. In short, a priest was called and our lovers married.

For two years peace and plenty were their household gods; but then Henry seeing a family encreasing, began to reflect on the means of supporting them. He had no land, and had never been taught any mechanical branch of business; however, after taking advice, he purchased a small stock of merchandise, and prepared to follow the army. The good parents exhausted themselves to encrease his commodities. "Be frugal and cautious, son," said they; "remember Anne and her babe."—"Ah!" cried Henry, embracing them, "if I dishonour my parents, take Anne from my bosom, give my paradise to a stranger, and let me die the death of a villain!"

Henry visited his beloved friends frequently, but the army being stationed at a considerable distance from them, after an interval of three years, he sighed in absence near eleven months; he had accumulated eight hundred pounds in cash by extraordinary application, which compensated in some measure this painful separation, when he received a summons to return home. It seems his father-in-law had been dispossessed of his farm, through inability to discharge his rent. The good old man retired with his child to Henry's parents, where they were cordially received; but grief made insensible inroads on his constitution; in less than three weeks (having languished a few days) he died in Anne's arms.

Henry burst into tears at the news. "Cruel parent," said he, "you knew my happy situation—why did you let the canker of disappointment abridge your days? my treasure was your own—I am infinitely your debtor—I never yet earned my Rachel."[25]—Having paid a tribute of sincere drops of gratitude and love, he sighed and went to bed; he slumbered, and saw his Anne smile with joy at the gold and silver he poured at her feet—his little ones climbed his knees, and seemed to be delighted with the glitter of his treasures: his enamoured fancy called up every pleasing idea to sport round his innocent family, when he was suddenly awaked by four ruffians, who entered his tent well-armed; and, advancing to his bed, bade him be silent, at the peril of immediate destruction. Regardless of their menaces, he started up and demanded their business. Upon which they seized and bound him hand and foot, then fell to rummaging the tent. They soon discovered his money—what a glorious booty! In vain did he plead, soothe, and threaten. "Leave me a few pieces. Leave me but a little, a very little, to carry me to my poor wife and children." His rhetoric made no impression—they left him not a sous.

Being at some distance from the camp, his repeated calls for help were not heard; at length, in the silence of midnight, a centinel distinguished a mournful cry for assistance, and sent a couple of veterans to reconnoitre. Henry, now relieved from corporeal confinement, began to feel his heart contracted and shrunk by ideas of approaching beggary. He looked round him, the whole creation seemed comfortless and desolate. "How shall I behold my domestic blessings? How shall I look Anne in the face? would to God I had till'd some sterile spot of ground, we would have been content in indigence; nature would have been satisfied with herbs and lentils. Cursed ambition to be rich has ruined me, and I am a traitor to my family." With these bitter reflections the day broke, and having collected the little furniture of his tent, he disposed of it to advantage to the humane soldiery, who universally loved him and pitied his misfortune. Having secured his cash in a small bag, he set off with a reluctant step for home. In vain did the birds carol on the elms that shaded the road. In vain did the ploughman whistle gleefully, and the lambs wanton o'er the green hillocks. No enlivening scene could dissipate his melancholy.

He protracted his journey through fear of being too soon the messenger of ill tidings. On the second day at noon, having bought a loaf of bread, he sat down by a rivulet to eat; his tears flowed apace, and he began to deliberate whether he should return to Anne or not. He counted his little store, and fell listless on the grass through despondency. While thus he lay sadly ruminating, a handsome couple (thinking themselves unobserved) passed though the bushes. "Alas!" said the man, "for six years my Emma you have sustained the most bitter poverty with your unfortunate husband. My heart breaks under the oppression of your misery; I cannot bear it—return, I beseech you, to the Baron; ask his fatherly forgiveness; he will reinstate you to favour—and lovely Emma I shall die content."—"I smile," replied the fair one, "at your ignorance; gold and gems and banquets, have no charms for me—my heart was formed for social happiness—I love you, and deprived of your company I should languish and die, whereas I feel no uneasiness at the absence of riches; we have enough to subsist comfortably on, though it be coarse, so pray, my dear, drop this unwelcome delicacy."—Here they went out of hearing, and Henry, struck with the lady's sentiments, began to resume courage.—"I am ashamed," said he, "at my want of fortitude; here is voluntary poverty accepted in preference of an anxious mind—surely Anne will have as much philosophy in that article as the unfortunate Emma—what a destruction have I escaped; had I wandered away from my desolate family, we had all been miserable indeed." So thinking he took his pack on his shoulders and proceeded on the journey.

The fourth evening, passing leisurely by his deceased parent's door, he involuntarily turned back and walked in. Here his feelings received a new shock. Strange faces accosted him—rudeness and dirt had usurped the place where Anne once reigned the goddess of civility and neatness. The green inclosure, surrounded by jessamine, was trampled on by swine, and lean cattle browzed on the vines that mantled over Anne's window. He turned with grief and disgust from this mortifying scene, and had gone but a little farther, when Anne descrying him at a distance, flew like a bird across the meadow, and fell into his arms. After the first emotions of transport were subsided, Henry affectionately embraced his lovely babes and tender parents, who met him on the road. "I miss but one from this beloved company," said Henry.—Anne burst into tears. "My Henry, you will miss the chief of our good neighbourhood—our indulgent old Lord is dead; his tyrannical heir oppresses his tenants with heavy rents, and severe exactions, and they have unanimously agreed to shelter themselves from this great burden, by flying to the wilds of America."

After they were seated in the house, "What your spouse advances," said the old man, "is true; and your aged parents would have also been forced to venture their trembling limbs and grey hairs over the dangerous ocean, had not our blessed Henry's industry secured us a competency." This trial was too severe. Henry changed countenance, and cast his eyes around with an alarming wildness. "What is the matter with my child?" cried his mother. Alas! this encounter was too sudden. "Old and experienced as I am, I feel almost overcome with joy myself."—"Ah!" exclaimed her son (recollecting himself) "fain would I conceal from such endearing friends the motive of my distress; but I should expire in the effort—forgive and pity a wretch who brings home nothing but misery—who can see his family fall to ruin, and yet live."—All astonished they gazed at each other in silence, while Henry sobbed, unable to articulate a word. At length Anne, all shining through tears, drew nigh and kneeled before him—"Keep us not in suspence, my husband; pour your griefs into our bosoms, and wrong us not by reserve; you can never bring misery to us whilst you remain virtuous and loving as now."—Henry clasped the sad orator with passionate fondness in his arms; and after a little hesitation acquainted them with the particulars of his misfortune.

It was in vain to try to conceal their surprise and disappointment, though Henry's affliction forbad them to fall into repining, or any expression of discontent. By degrees their chagrin subsided. The poor acquiesce with greater resignation to calamity than the rich, who seldomer meet with disappointment. At last, by an insensible gradation, our pensive associates became blest and easy. A small repast was provided, and shutting out corrosive Care, they indulged the hour of festivity with as much glee as if the robbers had restored the money tenfold. (To be concluded next month.)

STORY of HENRY and ANNE.—Founded on Fact.

[Continued from page 186, and concluded.]

The story of Henry's robbery was soon known, and his parents concluded that their Lord would shew some lenity to them; but finding him invariably cruel and oppressive, they began to attend to the flattering informations about the New World—"At least," said Anne, "we shall go into a land of simplicity—the artless savages subsist not by rapine and deceit: pride and hypocrisy, and avarice, are strangers where luxury and titles are unknown."—The old man dissented from this opinion. "Wherever the print of human footsteps have appeared, there certainly, my child, all human vices follow, though often under different appellatives; however, we must hazard this adventure. As the Lepers said at Samaria,[26] if we stay here we shall certainly perish, and if we go away, at the worst, we can but die."

The ensuing week, as they were merrily chatting on the green before the door, a sudden cloud overspread the heavens with blackness, which soon fell in a torrent of rain, intermingled with thunder and lightning. The family retired in the house; but Henry hasted to drive the cattle and sheep to a place of security. All wet and dropping with rain he was returning to the house, when an elegant phaeton,[27] attended by a number of domestics, stopped at the gate. A gentleman handed out a lady, who seemed much affrighted with the storm, and conducted her, with a delicate tenderness, to the door. Henry opened it wide, and bowing to the ground, desired them to walk in, presenting them each with a chair. The noble air, and rich dresses of the new guests, awed our humble rustics, who scarcely durst lift up their eyes at them, until the gentleman, saluting the lady, enquired how his fair Emma did after her fright. Henry then instantly recollecting the lady's countenance—with a modest apology for his boldness recounted his adventure at the brook—"I presume," added he, "this lady is the very same lovely Emma whose noble disinterestedness made me blush at my want of fortitude, and in effect saved my family from ruin."—Here Emma, starting up, seized his hand—"I little thought, my kind friend, that our conversation had an auditor at that time; but since you have been a witness of my distress, rejoice with me in my present happy situation." Here resuming her seat, while her spouse hung enamoured over her chair, she favoured the attentive circle with an abridgment of her history.—

"I am the only child of the present Baron of Schauffhousen, who was particularly cautious that my education should render me up an accomplished lady to the world. On my first introduction into the *grande monde*, I found myself encompassed by admirers, whose addresses I permitted from vanity; but advancing to my twentieth year, my father grew solicitous that I should select a husband from the number. It was in vain to remonstrate to him that my heart was disengaged. He insisted on my accepting a partner for life.—"Chuse, my child," said he, "throughout all the empire; you can ennoble a peasant by our alliance with him, or cast a new lustre over the escutcheon of a prince."

"Seven months after this I became acquainted with my present husband; and not doubting but that the Baron would accede to our union, I permitted the most violent love to steal into my bosom. I acquainted him in a dutiful and affectionate manner of my attachment, to which he made no reply; but turning from me with a stern look (to my surprise) shut his closet door full in my face. In ten minutes I received his note—

"If you are determined, Miss, to debase the nobility of your birth, by a marriage with your present object, I renounce you forever. Take your jewels and clothes, and be miserable.

LODOVICUS STRELITZ."

"I wept incessantly on the perusal of this cruel billet. I wrote one to my lover, desiring him to forget me; but before I could dispatch it, my cousin Charlotte entered the room in great confusion. "Begone, Emma," said she, "your father is exasperated to a degree of madness. He bids me to give you this purse of pistoles,[28] and commands you to quit the castle instantly."—"Alas!" said I, sinking on the floor, "I sacrifice my love to my duty. My dear cousin, tell my old parent I am no longer a rebel to his will." Here I wept bitterly; but the cruel Charlotte called out, "Here, Joseph, if the chaise is ready, hand your young lady in. I am commissioned, dear Emma, to wait on you to another lodging. The angry Baron is from home, and I forfeit his favour if I do not oblige you to submit."—I then rose from my knees, and sullenly giving my hand to her, said faintly, "I see, Charlotte, you have supplanted me; your undermining arts have ruined me." She made no reply, and I suffered myself to be conducted to the chaise. In two hours we came to a neat farmhouse. Charlotte formally took leave of me, and I was shewn to a small, clean apartment, where, in a fit of agonizing despair, I threw myself upon a little bed. The woman of the house, coming in, informed me that Charlotte had advanced the pay for my year's board at her house; and concluding I was some refractory child, gave me long lecture on obedience to parents. I scarcely heard her.

"After a few days I wrote to my father. I begged the intercession of my relations, but in vain; Charlotte had stopped up every avenue to mercy. Finding myself rejected totally, I at length yielded to the emotions of a soft passion, and accepted the hand of my present husband. We lived happily during six years, when, being seized with a pleurisy, my physician made a report of my danger and poverty to my father. We had a small hut on the common. The Baron's coach drove up to the door. He stoop'd as he entered, and walked cautiously over the loose uneven floor of my poor bed-room. I rose up surprised to see him; and as I sat leaning against a pillow, the old man, in a gush of grief and remorse, fell on my bed sobbing and unable to speak. My two little ones, seeing me weep, came up with visible concern. The eldest kissed my hand and said, "Don't cry any more, mamma, Mrs. Morely has sent us bread and milk enough for two days." Here the Baron redoubled his sighs, and seemed nearly suffocated, when I feebly bent towards him. "O my father! Am I then forgiven?" But what he replied I know not—I fainted on the pillow. To be short, he took us all home. Charlotte's indiscretions drew the odium of the family on her, and a broken lieutenant carried her off to England. My father became excessively fond of my spouse and children, and we are now upon a visit to an old aunt, who lays a dying, and to whom I am sole heiress. "My friends," continued she, "I see by your looks my history is not impertinent, and I acknowledge myself yet indebted to Henry for his obliging partiality to me."

Anne, with pleased looks, immediately spread a table with a clean diaper cloth, and placed on it several earthen plates, filled with the most delicious fruits, some biscuits, a plate with honey-combs, and a flask of wine; while Henry, bowing low, thanked the lady for the honour she had done him. "I bless the Almighty," said Henry, "for so signally rewarding virtue. I even rejoice that the Baron's cruelty gave your excellent qualities an opportunity to shine out so philosophically in the test of poverty. Believe me, Madam, the lustre of many a soul lies hidden beneath the splendor of affluence, like the Grand Duke's gems in the green vault."[29] The gentleman smiled—"And many a sentimental mind, my Henry," said he, "is circumscribed by poverty, and is of little utility to mankind beyond the limits of his own family. I heartily wish you, my friend, a fortune equal to your merit; in the mean while accept this trifle," handing him a purse with twenty pistoles. Henry, amid the highest confusion of blushing gratitude, received the gift gracefully, and pressed his benefactors to accept his little regale. When they had eat, the sun began to shine out with new lustre after the rain, and Emma proposed to proceed on their journey. She took a tender leave of Henry, and kissing Anne, stept in the carriage, which instantly drove out of sight.

Soon after this agreeable interview, they prepared for their long voyage. The pensive neighbours assembled, and having delivered their cattle to the Marquis's steward, they all embarked in a small vessel on the Rhine. After a tedious sail down the river, they were taken aboard a ship bound for New-York, in America. A fair wind sprung up; they soon lost sight of the Imperial shores, and found themselves surrounded by a horizon of waters. The poor cottagers viewed the uncommon scene with pleasure, mixed with dread; but in a few days were accustomed to the prospect, and great agitation of the vessel. Henry, to lessen the expense, had conditioned to work out his passage; but he could procure only very indifferent accommodations for his family, the ship being so crowded. After a few weeks sail Anne's eldest son sickened and died, and the mournful parents, with agonizing hearts, committed the babe of their hopes, the darling of their bosoms, to the waves. "There sinks my child," cried Anne, weeping, "in the depth of the wild ocean, instead of slumbering in my arms: he is gone to be the food of sea monsters." Henry supported and comforted her. "We have another, my beloved; let us not sin away the only remaining little one by fruitless repinings; our son is ascended to his Creator; it is not him that welters in the deep: Oh! grieve not that he is taken from the evil to come, from evils which shall yet sorrow over. Wisely and mercifully has Providence proportioned our sufferings to our strength, and given the lenient hand of Time power to mollify those griefs he cannot cure." In a little space Anne's sorrows sunk into a languid serenity. She began to smile as usual, and Henry was happy.

They had a tedious passage; but at length, one moonshine night, the sailors cried out "land." In a moment they all crouded upon deck; it was very calm, and near day; a gentle south breeze arose soon after, and by sun-rise they clearly distinguished the little islands covered with verdure, and the white beach on the bold continent. As they sailed up the Narrows,[30] with a fair wind, the strangers admired the beauty of the country, which they little expected to find so well cultivated. When they were anchored in the harbour, Henry requested a scull-boat to go on shore; upon which an English sailor offered his assistance, rallying him a little, "Why, demme brother, these people can't understand your gibberish; they will set you in the stocks for a Jesuit." They got on shore, and the sailor procured for Henry's little family a decent apartment in Beaverstreet.[31] Henry expressed his acknowledgments to the generous sailor, for he really found he should never have been able, in his uncouth broken language, to make the people understand him.

Here Henry left his little family while he went to seek a spot on the vacant lands of this state where he might accommodate them. He sailed with a Dutch skipper to Albany, and being informed by him where he might find such a place as he wished for, he set off early the morning after his arrival on foot. As he walked along the clovery banks of the Hudson, the long beams of the rising sun glanced over its crumpled surface, and gilt the opposite shores with peculiar beauty; the tall pines of the adjacent forest waved in solemn grandeur; the thrush warbled in the thicket; and at every short distance a little fountain cast its silvery waves across the way, and supplied the thirsty traveller with a seasonable regale. Charmed with the scene, Henry often stopped. He surveyed each opening prospect with singular pleasure. The bright rays of Hope again dawned upon his soul, and diffused its enlivening influence through his late uncheery heart. "Yes," said he, "I feel that we shall, in the uncultivated forests of America, enjoy that tranquility which the inhospitable plains of Europe denied us." Here he was interrupted by the appearance of a traveller, who no sooner perceived him than he flew to him. "Oh my Henry!"—Oh my Frederick!" were all they could say for some time. They clasped each other in their arms. They wept and smiled alternately. It was a fellow soldier of Henry's, a very dear friend.

After their first transports were over Henry told him all that had passed since they parted, and the soldier, in return, told him, that soon after Henry quitted the army he left it too, and in hopes of settling happily in the village where he was born, had returned to it, after an absence of some years; but upon his arrival there, finding his parents dead, and the object of his sincerest affection married to another, in a fit of grief and rage he left his native country and came to America; "and here, my friend," continued he, "I am happily situated for life; I have married an amiable woman; my neighbours are all like brothers, and the acquisition of your dear family to our little circle will add new pleasure to it."

The sun was setting when they entered the beautiful village of Tomhanick.[32] The farmers had finished their daily talk, and were smoking by their doors, while the younger tribe gamboled on the green before them; the blush of health hung careless on every cheek, and content smoothed every brow. Frederick invited the cottagers home with him, and as they were seated round a table covered with fruits of the season, he related to them the history of Henry's life. The good people were affected by the recital of his misfortunes, and promised to assist him. "You have been unfortunate," said an old man, "but if you will live as we do, you shall be happy." The next day they assembled, and in the course of two days they finished a neat log-house for Henry, such as they themselves dwelt in.

With a heart filled with gratitude and joy, he returned to his Anne; he repeated the particulars of his journey and its happy issue, and proposed their removal to their new habitation as soon as possible. To this they all assented with pleasure; and having packed up their little effects, and paid their rent, they set out in a few days for Tomhanick. There they were received with the most hearty welcomes; and as they were much reduced, each of the neighbours contributed something to raise Henry's stock, and make him happy. There they reside still, beloved and respected by all, and find their industry rewarded by prosperity and contentment.

Notes

1. Marie Le Roy's parents arrived in Pennsylvania in 1752 and the Leiningers had arrived earlier in 1748. Sebastian Leininger and his son were killed in an Indian raid near Penn's Creek in 1755. His wife was not at home and so survived, but her two daughters, Barbara and Regina, were taken captive.

2. "Allegheny" evolved out of the various designations for the native tribes occupying the region from western Pennsylvania to the Ohio River.

3. While her sister managed to escape, Regina Leininger stayed in captivity until General Henry Bouquet's successful campaign in 1764. According to frequently quoted local legends, she had been brought up as a native and had forgotten her German; she was only identified among white captives by her mother as Regina sang along to an old German hymn.

4. The central point of the great "Chinklacamoose Path," on the present site of Clearfield.

5. On the great trail that connected Western native tribes and those in Susquehanna country.

6. Fort Duquesne was built by the French at the confluence of the Allegheny and Monongahela Rivers in 1754. As an important trading post of the Ohio valley region, the fort was destroyed by the British in 1758 and renamed Fort Pitt, then Pittsburgh.

7. Abide: stay with, submit to.

8. Christian Frederick Post (1710–85) was a Moravian missionary who came to Pennsylvania in 1742 and was well versed in Native languages.

9. Pelts: animal skins, either raw or with the hair still on them.

10. South Branch of the Potomac.

11. A spontaneous prayer or voicing of emotions; for example, part of Cotton Mather's devotional routine.

12. Nought: nothing.

13. The Allegheny River.

14. Philip Weiser (1722–61) was the son of John Conrad Weiser, who was well known in his time as a member of the colonial government and an Indian translator.

15. The names given here refer to Lancaster residents who served in the French and Indian War.

16. Hannah Duston was recovering from the birth of her eighth child.

17. Haverhill was a Massachusetts frontier town raided by French and Abenaki troops during King William's War in 1697.

18. The reference is here to Joshua 7:6 and the tokens of humiliation and sorrow in light of God's exposing His people to an unmerciful enemy.

19. Prov. 12:10.

20. Reference to Hannah's prayer (1 Samuel 1:15), the mother of the prophet Samuel.

21. According to Jewish legend (Judges 4), Jael killed the Canaanite general Sisera by hammering a tent peg into his temple.

22. Dustin received a reward of £25 for the ten scalps. The boy, Samuel Lennardson, and the nurse, Mary Neff, each received half this amount.

23. *[original footnote] This Tale was begun by the late Mrs. Ann E. Bleecker, but indisposition prevented her putting a finishing hand to it: that, however, has been accomplished by her daughter Miss Peggy V. [Margaretta] Bleecker. From the entertainment the productions of those pens have hitherto afforded the public through the medium of the *New-York Magazine*, we have no doubt but the story of Henry and Anne will meet with a cheerful acceptance.

24. Ancient Roman goddess of war, here probably a reference to the Seven Years' War (1756–63).

25. Rachel refers to Laban's second daughter for whom Jacob served numerous years, see Gen. 29:15–30.

26. Refers to the story of the four lepers in 2 Kings 7:3–11.

27. Phaeton: an open carriage.

28. A Spanish gold coin; sometimes that name also refers to the French louis d'or or guinea.

29. Green vault: one of the biggest collections of treasures at Dresden castle in Saxony.

30. The tidal strait or channel by which the Hudson River empties out into the Atlantic Ocean.

31. Street in the lower parts of New York City, named after the city's first major export, then New Amsterdam.

32. Town in the upstate New York frontier land twenty miles from Albany.

Suggestions for Further Reading

Captivities

"The Indians: A Tale." 1798. *The Philadelphia Monthly Magazine* 1 (1): 23–27; 1 (2): 74–77.

Mather, Cotton. 1697. "A Narrative Containing Wonderful Passages, Relating to My Captivity and Deliverances." In *Humiliations Follow'd by Deliverances*, 51–72. Boston.

"A Remarkable Instance of Courage and Address, in the Conduct of two Boys." 1790. *The Columbian Magazine* (January): 16–17.

St. John Crèvecoeur, J. Hector de. 1981. "The Frontier Woman." In *Letters from an American Farmer and Sketches of Eighteenth-Century America*, edited by Albert E. Stone, 402–6. Harmondsworth, UK: Penguin.

Authorship

Bleecker, Ann Eliza. 1790–91. "The History of Maria Kittle." *The New York Magazine, or Literary Repository* 1 (9): 512–16; 1 (10): 563–67; 1 (11): 633–38; 1 (12): 684–87; 2 (1): 12–17.

"The History of Henrietta." 1789. *The Gentlemen and Ladies' Town and Country Magazine* 1 (9): 429–33.

Lavinia. 1790. "Henry, or the Captive" and "Anna, or the Second Part of the Captive." *Massachusetts Magazine, or, Monthly Museum of Knowledge and Rational Entertainment* (Mar. 1): 178–79.

Murray, Judith Sargent. 1798. "The Gleaner, XCII." In *The Gleaner*, 3:224–34. Boston.

Rowson, Susanna. 1794. "The Happy Pair." *Monthly Miscellany or Vermont Magazine* 1 (7): 176–77.

PART III
THE CIRCUM-ATLANTIC WORLD

WITH ITS UNPRECEDENTED LENGTH and potential dangers, the Atlantic passage was a decisive experience for the first colonists and explorers. While the "old world," consisting of Europe and Africa, had been interacting economically and culturally for more than two millennia, trade relationships across the Atlantic started in the sixteenth century and developed into an expansive, well-connected Atlantic economy during the next two centuries. Driven by an "aggressive entrepreneurship" (Coclanis 2005, xii), merchants worked hand in hand with pirates, privateers, and smugglers to dodge the control of the empires involved in the Atlantic trade. Millions of African slaves suffered during the Middle Passage and were then forced to work on plantations and in mines to satisfy the European demand for such commodities as gold, silver, indigo, and sugarcane.

In his pioneering study *The Black Atlantic* (1993, 4), Paul Gilroy uses "the image of ships in motion across the spaces between Europe, America, Africa, and the Caribbean" as a basic metaphor for his cultural criticism and the dynamics it aims to describe; each ship represents "a living, micro-cultural, micro-political system in motion." Beginning with the first Portuguese and Spanish claims in 1493, the Caribbean islands attracted British, Dutch, and French interests, illustrating the shifting boundaries of the empires and the mingling of cultures. New and unlikely alliances emerged between pirates and traders, runaway slaves and indigenous tribes, as the moral, practical, and political issues of trade and slavery encompassed the nations active in the Atlantic region.

This critical focus on mobility and commerce also informs Stephen Shapiro's (2008) adaptation from Joseph Roach (1996) of the term "circum-Atlantic," to reach beyond the binary "transatlantic" relations and enunciate the colonial and commercial interactions along the Atlantic seaboard (Zahedieh 2010).

The first section of Part III revolves around the subject of slavery and the abolition of slavery from various perspectives. The selected narratives mirror the movement of slaves and goods across the Atlantic and along its seaboard; translated and transported across the ocean, these narratives were in due course published in American periodicals and magazines. The human toll of the circum-Atlantic capitalist system was not limited to slaves, but also affected the traders and seamen involved in human trafficking, as can be seen in both "Negro Trade, a Fragment" (1787) and "The Inexorable Captain" (1788). The choppy sentences and fragmented dialogue of "Negro Trade" contribute to the "striking effect" of the atrocities of the slave trade (Mayo 1962, 337–38). The scenes, more indicated than elaborated, demonstrate how "the cruelties incidental to the slave trade, were not confined to the unhappy negroes—but affected the instruments who carried it on" ("Negro Trade"). Printed first in the *American Museum or Repository* of 1787, and reprinted in John Wesley's *Arminian Magazine* of 1797 along with pastoral letters, sermons, and journals, the narrative aims to show that society at large is morally and physically compromised by basing its lifestyle on slave labor.

In a similar vein, Philip Frenau's "The Inexorable Captain" demonstrates how the crews and masters of ships were simply instruments and intermediaries who, like the slaves, suffered under a capitalist trade system. Through his experience as a captain on various trading ships in the Caribbean, Freneau was well aware of the hardships and capitalist underpinnings of trade in the Americas (Axelrad 1967; Walters 2011). His balanced portrayal thus reveals the predicament of both sides: starving people unable to pay for food meet the hard hand of necessity that requires the captain to turn the dangerous voyage into an economic success. "Negro Trade" and Freneau's story thus deal with the vicissitudes of the circum-Atlantic trade in which the constant danger of life is accompanied by great economic risks in a world that is ruled by chance rather than divine providence. Like the captains Peleg and Bildad in Melville's *Moby-Dick* (1851), the seafarers in these stories (written more than sixty years earlier) are tied into a larger system of capital circulation; the inexorable captain in "Negro Trade" must not only report to the ship's owners, but also consider his financial responsibility to his own family.

Indicating the international scope of the debate on slavery and its abolition, Jean-François de Saint-Lambert—French military officer, Enlightenment thinker, and poet—published "Zimeo: A Tale" in a French collection of poetry and prose in 1769 before it was reprinted by publishers of American magazines. Saint-Lambert draws on genres like the slave narrative to discuss both violent and peaceful ways to end or mitigate slavery. For example, the title character of "Zimeo" describes his life in Africa and his traumatic capture and transport in an embedded first-person narrative resembling Aphra Behn's *Oroonoko* (1688) and Olaudah Equiano's *Interesting Narrative* (1789). Hardened by his experience of the Middle Passage, which is described by Marcus Rediker (2007, 10) as a "ship factory" based on violence, Zimeo becomes the leader of a slave rebellion that, significantly, is set in Jamaica, where runaway slaves lived among the indigenous Taíno tribe and resisted the English colonizers (Zantop 1997, 149–52).[1] Zimeo's life story not only mirrors the conventions of the slave narrative, but also anticipates slave uprisings such as Nat Turner's 1831 Southampton insurrection. Turner's confessions exclude the pre-history of his mother's life and the enslavement of his family in Africa before being hanged for his role in the slave revolt (Carter 2010). The story also presents another alternative to the human exploitation and hardships of slavery in the character of the benevolent Quaker plantation owner Paul Wilmot, who treats his slaves with such respect that they continue to work for him even after being offered their freedom. In the sentimental ending, the fugitive slaves in the mountains live peacefully due to Paul Wilmot's liberality and Zimeo is reunited with his wife. "Zimeo" thus offers a balance of brutal and compassionate alternatives to the exploitative system of slavery that is representative of the contemporary discourse on the subject and ranges from advocating separate communities for former slaves to condoning their violent liberation to a renewal of the system through paternalistic slave ownership.

Travel across the Atlantic continues with "Memoirs of a Spy" (1798), which introduces various political actors and entrepreneurs of the circum-Atlantic world with the adventures of its protagonist Wimpfen through a number of European countries. Describing Wimpfen's changing alliances, the pseudonymous author unfolds the transatlantic theater of the Seven Years' War between France and Britain (1756–63). Antiphilus was a regular contributor to the debates—such as the social benefits of debtor prisons and theaters—that played out in the pages of *The Weekly Magazine*. The title of the story alludes to the genre of the memoir that typically relates the achievements of an eminent person. Like Tom Varien, another world-roaming character, Wimpfen was brought up by indulgent parents; but unlike Varien, who happily travels at his father's expense, Wimpfen runs away from home in reaction to his parents' first signs of disapproval. As the first spy story featured in an American magazine, "Memoirs of a Spy" does not adhere to the conventional patterns of journeys found in spiritual autobiographies, but psychologically traces the motivations and character of its protagonist. The various locations (depending upon the country he is spying for at the time) and turns of events are as much dictated by chance as they are by Wimpfen's decisions or talents; "accident" and "resolution" exist side by side in place of religious patterns of experience or providential guidance. From the beginning, Wimpfen appears "remarkably adventurous and inquisitive," yet he also becomes "dexterous and deceitful" to conceal his running away from home, a practice that leads to his occupation as a spy.

During his stay in Europe, and particularly while in Paris, Wimpfen acquires a great "subtlety and knowledge of the world"; unfortunately, "the same cannot be said of the firmness and integrity of his principles," which only deteriorate as he meets various political figures and becomes a double agent. When Wimpfen is confronted with the grief of his family in a sentimental scene, he resolves to return home to provide for them and "spend the remainder of his life . . . in the bosom of tranquility." The contrast between the corrupt Old World and the democratic, virtuous New World is one of the underpinnings of the narration, from Wimpfen's activity as a spy and double agent for England and France to his return to America. His career echoes that of other well-traveled schemers and profiteers, such as Welbeck in Charles Brockden Brown's *Arthur Mervyn: or, Memoirs of the Year 1793* (1799).

The narratives in this chapter mirror the global scale of trade and political relationships and their social and economic effects on individuals; they also reflect, however, the rise of global movement against this logic of exploitation, such as abolitionism. The worldly and skillful Wimpfen becomes a protagonist on various sides of a global conflict that stretches even to India, yet—as a moral alternative to European warfare and scheming—he is still loyal to the United States. Tales of slaves and traders are more explicit in voicing alternatives to this exploitative economic system through their use of form and emotional language. At the same time, "Memoirs of a Spy" and "Zimeo" use conventions of adventure and sentimental tales that could be read as answering the readers' demand for entertainment, exoticism, and adventure. In all of these cases, personal stories and developments emerge that reach wider audiences with their publication to replace—or at least balance—the conventions of spiritual autobiography and providence with those of individual agency or chance.

SLAVERY

ANONYMOUS

*Negro Trade. —A Fragment (1787)**

A Seafaring man made his appearance—

He was surrounded by a multitude of persons, who persecuted him with interrogatories.

This person was a captain of a ship in the negro trade.

From the conversation which passed between the captain and those who surrounded him, I discovered that the cruelties incidental to the slave trade, were not confined to the unhappy negroes—but affected the instruments who carried it on.

The captain before me had gone out mate[2]—the crew had been thirty—of whom only three returned.

He had a long scroll in his hand. It was a list of the original crew.

Where is my daddy? asked an infant.—Dead.

My husband? enquired a matron.—Dead.

My brother? interrogated a girl.—Dead.

In this manner he ran through the list.

One had died of a fever—another had been murdered on shore—several had been killed by slaves who had mutinied.

When the friends of the deceased had retired, the captain gave his employers an account of his voyage.

* SOURCE: "Negro Trade.—A Fragment." 1787. *The American Museum, or Repository of Ancient and Modern Fugitive Pieces* 1 (1): 45–46.

PUBLICATION HISTORY: The fragment was reprinted in an edition of "earlier numbers" of *The American Museum, or Repository* in 1790, probably an attempt by editor Matthew Carey to benefit from their popularity. The story further appeared on both sides of the Atlantic: 1794. *The Arminian Magazine* 17: 46; 1797. *The New-York Magazine, or Literary Repository* 2 (2): 96; 1797. *The American Moral and Sentimental Magazine* 1 (6): 181–82; 1814. *The Juvenile Port-Folio, and Literary Miscellany; Devoted to the Instruction and Amusement of Youth* 2 (9): 34.

Three ships had gone out together. They had each taken in their quantity of slaves, when a hard gale drove two of them on shore.

One was boarded by the negroes and the crew massacred.

On board the other, a similar attempt had been made. But the whites having got command of the small arms, fired into the hold, and made dreadful slaughter. Thus circumstanced, one of the negroes, who had discovered where the powder lay, rushed into the room, set fire to a powder barrel, and blew the vessel to pieces.

The captain ran over these occurrences of horror with a philosophic calmness: but it was not so with his employers: they frequently interrupted his detail with imprecations[3] against the damned blacks.

And why is this cruelty practiced?

That we may have sugar to sweeten tea that debilitates us—

Rum to make punch, to intoxicate us—

And indigo, to dye our clothes.

In short, thousands are made wretched—nations are dragged into slavery—to supply the luxuries of their fellow creatures!

[JEAN-FRANÇOIS DE SAINT-LAMBERT]

*ZIMEO.—A TALE (1789)**

SOME years ago, Paul Wilmot, a quaker,[4] native of Philadelphia, having settled in Jamaica, retired to a plantation beautifully situated on the declivity of a mountain near the centre of the island. His family consisted of a wife and three young children. He possessed a number of slaves, whose looks and whose appearance betokened that their servitude was not grievous. Indeed Wilmot was

* SOURCE: [Jean-François de Saint-Lambert]. 1789. "Zimeo: A Tale." *The American Museum, or, Universal Magazine* 6 (5): 371–73; 6 (6): 472–75.
PUBLICATION HISTORY: The French original appeared in the 1769 Amsterdam version of Jean-François de Saint-Lambert's *Les Saisons, Poëme*, under the title "Ziméo par George Filmer, *né primitif*." It was translated into German in *Des Herrn von Saint-Lambert Orientalische Fabeln: nebst drey* Erzählungen. 1772. Leipzig. 156–95, and also adapted by Johann Ernst Kolb's 1789 *Erzählungen von den Sitten und Schicksalen der Negersklaven*. Bern. The figure of Zimeo was used by the German poet Gottfried Herder in "Neger-Idyllen" (1797) and, as Zameo, in August von Kotzebue's tragedy *Die Negersklaven* (1796); the story was reprinted in England after 1800 as well. As there is no previous British translation, it seems likely that the story was imported and translated by one of the many French refugees that came to Philadelphia in the 1790s and found entry in Matthew Carey's *The American Museum* before it was reprinted in 1798 by Samuel Bradford's *The Dessert to the True American* 1 (16): 3–4; 1 (17): 1–3; and lastly, in 1804 by *The Lancaster Hive; Devoted to Morality, Literature, Biography, History, Poetry, Agriculture* 2 (18): 72; 2 (19): 76; 1 (21): 84.

one of those benevolent characters that consider the wide world as their country, and the whole human race as their brethren. His negroes were distributed into little families. Among them were no dissensions, no jealousies, no thefts, no suicides, no conspiracies: the labours of the day gave place in the evening to the song and the dance; and they retired to rest, with hearts full of gratitude, satisfaction, and content.

About this time, a negro of Benin, known by the name of John, had instigated the slaves of two rich plantations to revolt, to massacre their masters, and to fly to the mountain. This mountain is in the middle of the island; it is almost inaccessible, and is surrounded with fruitful valleys, which are inhabited by negroes, called the wild negroes. These, having formerly deserted their services, settled in those valleys, from whence they often made cruel sallies upon their former masters; but now they seldom rise, except to revenge their brethren, who fly to them for refuge, from insupportable persecution. John had been chosen chief of those negroes, and had issued from the vallies with a considerable body of followers. The alarm was soon spread in the colony; troops were marched to the mountain, and soldiers distributed in those plantations that were defensible.

Wilmot assembled his slaves. "My friends," said he, "there are arms; if I have been a hard master to you, use them against me; but if I have behaved to you as an affectionate father, take them, and assist me in defending my wife and children." The negroes seized upon the arms, and swore they would die in his defence, and in the defence of those that were dear to him.

Amongst his slaves there was one, named Francisco, whom a friend of Wilmot's, called Filmer, had found abandoned on the shore of a Spanish colony; he had been barbarously maimed,[5] and one of his legs was newly cut off; a young negro woman was employed in stopping the blood, and in weeping the inefficacy of her cares. She had beside her a child but a few days old. They belonged to a Spaniard, who had taken this revenge on the negro, for abetting[6] Marianne, the woman, in her rejection of some dishonourable proposals which her master had made to her. Filmer purchased them of the Spaniard, who pretended that he had thus treated the negro, because he had surprised him performing the abominable ceremonies of the religion of Benin. Wilmot received them of his friend, who now also lived in his family. Marianne became the favourite of his wife; and Francisco, by his good sense and his knowledge of agriculture, acquired the confidence of Wilmot, and the esteem of every one.

This man came to his master at the beginning of the night. "The chief of the blacks," says he, "is a native of Benin; he adores the Great Orissa,[7] the Lord of life, and the Father of mankind; he must, therefore, be guided by justice and benevolence: he comes to punish the enemies of the children of Orissa; but you who have consoled them in their misery, he will respect. Let him know by one of our brethren of Benin, how you have treated your slaves, and you will see those warriors fire their muskets in the air, and throw their spears at your feet." His advice was followed, and a messenger dispatched to John.

When day appeared, it discovered a scene of desolation. Most of the houses within view, were on fire, and the plantations laid waste. In a few places, the cattle were seen feeding in security: but in most, the men and animals were discovered flying across the country, pursued by the exasperated negroes. John had given orders to spare neither man, woman, or child, in the places where his brethren had been harshly treated; in the others, he contented himself with giving liberty to the slaves, but he set fire to every house that was deserted. In his course he proceeded to the plantation of Wilmot, with a detachment of thirty men.

John, or rather Zimeo, (for the revolted negroes quit the names they have received on their arrival in the colonies,) was a young man, about two and twenty years of age; the statues of Apollo and Antinous do not shew more regular features, or more beautiful proportions. He had an air of grandeur, and seemed born for command. He was still warm from the fight; but, in accosting[8] Wilmot and Filmer, his eyes expressed affection and good will; the most opposite sentiments shewed themselves by turns in his countenance; he was almost, in the same moment, sorrowful and cheerful, furious and tender. "I have avenged my race," said he, "and myself; think not hardly, ye men of peace, of the unfortunate Zimeo; shrink not at the blood with which he is covered; it is that of the inhuman; it is to terrify the wicked that I set no bounds to my vengeance." Then, turning to the slaves, "choose," says he, "whether you will follow me to the mountain, or remain with your master." But the negroes falling at the feet of Wilmot, swore, with one voice, that they would rather die than leave him; that he had been a father to them, rather than a master; and that their servitude had been a blessing rather than a bondage.

At this scene Zimeo was affected and agitated with various emotions; lifting up to heaven his eyes, that were ready to overflow, "O Great Orissa!" cried he, "thou who hast formed the heart, look down on these grateful men, these true men, and punish the barbarians that despise us, and treat us as we do not treat the beasts that thou hast made for our use!"

After this exclamation, he gave the hand of friendship to Wilmot and Filmer; "thanks to Orissa!" says he, "I have found some whites that I can love! my destiny is in your power, and all the riches I have made myself master of, shall be yours, in return for the favour I have to ask of you."

Wilmot assured him that he would, without recompence, do him any service that was in his power: he invited him to repose himself, and ordered refreshments to be brought for his attendants.

"My friend," said he, "the great Orissa knows that Zimeo is not naturally cruel; but the whites have separated me from all I hold dear; from the wife Matomba, who was the friend and the guide of my youth; and from the young beauty, who was my heart's whole treasure. Think not hardly, ye men of peace, of the unfortunate Zimeo. You can procure him a ship, and you can conduct him to the place where those are detained, who are necessary to his existence."

At this moment, a young slave, a native of Benin, coming to speak with Wilmot, no sooner cast his eyes on Zimeo, than he gave a shriek, and retired with the utmost precipitation.[9] Zimeo was silent for a moment, when, turning to Wilmot and his friends, "listen, ye men of peace," said he, "to the story of my misfortunes; and acknowledge that I deserve your pity rather than your detestation.

"The great Damel, sovereign of Benin, whose heir I am, sent me, according to the ancient custom of the kingdom, to be educated by the husbandmen of Onebo. I was given in charge to Matomba, the wisest among them, the wisest of men. At the court of my father, his counsel had often prevented evil, and been productive of good. While he was yet young, he retired to that village, in which, for ages, the heirs of the empire have been educated. There Matomba enjoyed all the pleasures that a benign sky, a bountiful soil, and a good conscience can bestow. In the village of Onebo there were no animosities, no idleness, no deceit, no designing priests, no hardness of heart. The young princes had none but the most excellent examples before their eyes. The wife Matomba made me lose those sentiments of pride, and of indolence, that the court and my earlier instructors had inspired me with. I laboured the ground, like my master and his servants: I was instructed in the operations of agriculture, which makes all our riches: I was taught the necessity of being just, a duty incumbent on all men, that they may be able to educate their children, and cultivate their fields in peace; and I was shewn that princes, like the labourers of Onebo, must be just towards one another, that they and their subjects may live happy and contented.

"My master had a daughter, the young Ellaroe; I loved her, and soon found that my passion was returned. We had both of us preserved our innocence inviolate; I saw no other in the creation but her; she saw no other but me, and we were happy. Her parents turned this passion to our mutual advantage. I was obedient to every command of Matomba, in the hope of making myself worthy of Ellaroe; and the hope of preserving her place in my heart, made every duty delightful to her. My attainments were all due to her, and hers to me. Five years had we thus spent, with increasing attachment, when I demanded permission of my father to espouse Ellaroe. O how I cherished the thought, that she would be my companion on the throne, and my friend in every period of life!

"I was expecting the answer of my father, when two merchants of Portugal arrived at Onebo. They brought, for sale, some implements of husbandry, several articles of domestic use, and some trifles of dress, for women and children. We gave them ivory in exchange, and gold dust. They would have purchased slaves, but none, except criminals, are sold in Benin; and there were none of those in the village of Onebo. I questioned them with regard to the arts and the manners of Europe. I found in your arts many superfluities, and in your manners much contradiction. You know the passion which the blacks have for music and dancing. The Portuguese had many instruments unknown to us; and every evening they played on them the gayest and most enchanting airs. The young people of the village gathered together, and danced around them; and there I danced with Ellaroe. The strangers brought us from their ships the most exquisite wines, with liquors and fruits that were delicious to our taste. They sought our friendship, and we loved them truly. They informed us, one day, that they were now obliged to leave us, and to return to their country: the news affected the whole village, but no one more than Ellaroe. They told us, with tears, the day of their departure; they said they would leave us with less regret, if we would give them an opportunity to testify their regard, by entertaining us on board their ships: they pressed us to repair to them the next morning, with the young men, and the prettiest girls of the village. Accordingly, conducted by Matomba, and by some old people for the sake of decency, we set off for the ships.

"Onebo is but five miles from the sea, and we were upon the shore an hour after sunrise. We saw two vessels at a little distance from each other: they were covered with branches of trees, the sails and the cordage were loaded with flowers. As soon as our friends perceived us, they sounded their instruments, and welcomed us with songs. The concert and the decorations promised a delightful entertainment. The Portuguese came to receive us; they divided our company, and an equal number went on board each ship. Two guns were fired; the concert ceased; we were loaded with irons; and the vessels set sail.

(To be continued.)

MORAL TALES.

Zimeo.—Page 373.

HERE Zimeo stopt for a moment, then, resuming his story:—"yes, my friends," said he, "these men, to whom we had been prodigal of our wealth and of our confidence, carried us away, to sell us with the criminals they had purchased at Benin. I felt at once the misery of Ellaroe, of Matomba, and myself. I loaded the Portuguese with reproaches and threats: I bit my chains, and wished I could die: but a look from Ellaroe changed my purpose. The monsters had not separated me from her. Matomba was in the other vessel.

"Three of our young men, and a young girl, found means to put themselves to death. I exhorted Ellaroe to imitate their example; but the pleasure of loving and being beloved, attached her to life. The Portuguese made her believe that they intended for us a lot as happy as we had formerly enjoyed. She hoped, at least, that we would not be separated, and that she might again find her father.

"After having, for some days, wept the loss of our liberty, the pleasure of being always together stopped the tears of Ellaroe, and abated my despair.

"In those moments, when we were not interrupted by the presence of our inhuman masters, Ellaroe would fold me in her arms, and exclaim, O, my friend! let us endeavour to support and encourage one another, and we shall resist all they can do to us: assured of your love, what have I to complain of? and what happiness is it, that you would purchase at the expense of that which we now enjoy? These words infused into me extraordinary fortitude; and I had no fear but one—that of being separated from Ellaroe.

"We were more than a month at sea: there was little wind, and our course was slow; at last the winds failed as entirely, and it fell a dead calm. For some days, the Portuguese gave us no more food, than was barely sufficient to preserve us alive.

"Two negroes, determined on death, refused every species of nourishment, and secretly conveyed to us the bread and the dates that were designed for them. I hid them with care, that they might be employed in preserving the life of Ellaroe.

"The calm continued; the sea, without a wave, presented one vast immoveable surface, to which our vessel seemed attached. The air was as still as the sea. The sun and the stars, in their silent course, disturbed not the profound repose that reigned over the face of the deep. Our anxious eyes were continually directed to that uniform and unbounded expanse, terminated only by the heaven's arch, that seemed to enclose us as in a vast tomb. Sometimes we mistook the undulations of light for the motion of the waters; but that error was of short duration. Sometimes, as we walked on the deck, we took the resistance of the air for the agitation of a breeze; but no sooner had we suspended our steps, than the illusion vanished; and the image of famine recurring, presented itself to our minds with redoubled horror.

"Our tyrants soon reserved for themselves the provisions that remained, and gave orders, that a part of the blacks should be sacrificed as food for the rest. It is impossible to say, whether this order, so worthy of the men of your race, or the manner in which it was received, affected me most. I read, on every face, a greedy satisfaction, a dismal terror, a savage hope. I saw those unfortunate companions of my slavery observe one another with voracious attention, and the eyes of tigers.

"Two young girls of the village of Onebo, who had suffered most by the famine, were the first victims. The cries of these unhappy wretches still resound in my ears; and I see the tears streaming from the eyes of their famished companions, as they devoured the horrid repast.

"The little provisions, which I had concealed from the observation of our tyrants, supported Ellaroe and myself, so that we were sure of not being destined to the sacrifice. I still had dates, and we threw into the sea, without being observed, the horrid morsels that were offered to us.

"The calm continuing, despondency began to seize even our tyrants; they became remiss in their attention to us; they observed us slightly, and we were under little restraint. One evening, when they retired, they left me on the deck with Ellaroe. When she perceived we were alone, she threw her arms around me, and I pressed her with rapture in mine. Her eyes beamed with an unusual expression of sensibility and tenderness. I had never in her presence experienced such ardour, such emotion, such palpitation, as at that moment. Long we remained thus enfolded in one another's arms, unable to speak. "O thou," said I at last "whom I had chosen to be my companion on a throne, thou shalt at least be my companion in death!" "Ah, Zimeo!" said she, "perhaps the great Orissa will preserve our lives and I shall be thy wife." "Ellaroe," I replied, "had not these monsters by treachery prevailed, Damel would have chosen thee for my wife, as thy father had chosen me for thy husband. My beloved Ellaroe, do we still depend on the authority of Damel, and shall we now wait for orders that we can never receive? No, no, far from our parents, torn from our country, our obedience is now due only to our own hearts." "O, Zimeo!" cried she, bedewing my face with her tears. "Ellaroe," said I, "if you weep in a moment like this, you love not as I do." "Ah!" replied she, "observe, by the light of the moon, this unchangeable ocean; throw your eyes on these immoveable sails; behold, on the deck, the traces of the blood of my two friends; consider the little that remains of our dates, then—O Zimeo! Be but my husband, and I shall be contented!"

"So saying, she redoubled her caresses. We swore, in presence of the great Orissa, to be united, whatever should be our destiny: and we gave ourselves up to numberless pleasures, which we had never before experienced. In the enjoyment of these, we forgot our slavery; the thoughts of impending death, the loss of empire, the hope of vengeance, all were forgotten, and we were sensible to nothing but the blandishments of love. At last, however, the sweet delirium ceased; we found ourselves deserted by every flattering illusion, and left in our former state; truth appeared in proportion as our senses regained their tranquility; our souls began to suffer unusual oppression; weighed down on every side, the calm we experienced was awful and dead, like the stillness of nature around us.

"I was roused from this despondency by a cry from Ellaroe; her eyes sparkled with joy; she made me observe the sails and the cordage agitated by the wind; we felt the motion of the waves; a fresh breeze sprung up, that carried the two vessels in three days to Porto-Bello.[10]

"There we met Matomba; he bathed me with his tears; he embraced his daughter, and approved of our marriage. Would you believe it, my friends? The pleasure of rejoining Matomba, the pleasure of being the husband of Ellaroe, the charms of her love, the joy of seeing her safe from such cruel distress, suspended in me all feelings of our misfortunes: I was ready to fall in love with bondage; Ellaroe was happy, and her father seemed reconciled to his fate. Yes, perhaps, I might have pardoned the monsters that had betrayed us; but Ellaroe and her father were sold to an inhabitant of Porto-Bello, and I to a man of your nation, who carried slaves to the Antilles.

"It was then that I felt the extent of my misery; it was then that my natural disposition was changed; it was then I imbibed that passion for revenge, that thirst of blood, at which I myself shudder, when I think of Ellaroe, whose image alone is able to still my rage.

"When our fate was determined, my wife and her father threw themselves at the feet of the barbarians that separated us; even I prostrated myself before them: ineffectual abasement! they did not even deign to listen to us. As they were preparing to drag me away, my wife, with wildness in her eyes, with outstretched arms, and shrieks that still rend my heart, rushed impetuously to embrace me. I disengaged myself from those who held me; I received Ellaroe in my arms; she infolded me in hers, and instinctively, by a sort of mechanical impulse, we clasped our hands together, and formed a chain round each other. Many cruel hands were employed, with vain efforts, to tear us asunder. I felt that these efforts would, however, soon prove effectual: I was determined to rid myself of life; but how leave in this dreadful world my dear Ellaroe! I was about to lose her for ever; I had every thing to dread; I had nothing to hope; my imaginations were desperate; the tears ran in streams over my face; I uttered nothing but frantic exclamations, or groans of despair, like the roarings of a lion, exhausted in unequal combat. My hands gradually loosened from the body of Ellaroe, and began to approach her neck. Merciful Orissa! the whites extricated my wife from my furious embrace. She gave a loud shriek of despair, as we were separated; I saw her attempt to carry her hands towards her neck, to accomplish my fatal design; she was prevented; she took her last look of me. Her eyes, her whole countenance, her attitude, the inarticulate accents that escaped her, all bespoke the extremities of grief and of love.

"I was dragged on board the vessel of your nation; I was pinioned,[11] and placed in such a manner as to make any attempt upon my life impossible; but they could not force me to take any sustenance. My new tyrants at first employed threats, at last they made me suffer torments, which whites alone can invent; but I resisted all.

"A negro, born at Benin, who had been a slave for two years with my new master, had compassion on me. He told me we were going to Jamaica, where I might easily recover my liberty: he talked to me of the wild negroes, and of the commonwealth they had formed in the centre of the island; he told me that these negroes sometimes went on board English ships, to make depredations on the Spanish islands; he made me understand, that in one of those cruises, Ellaroe and her father might be rescued. He awakened in my heart the ideas of vengeance and the hopes of love. I consented to live: you now see for what. I am already revenged, but I am not satisfied till I regain the idols of my heart. If that cannot be, I renounce the light of the sun. My friends, take my riches, and provide me a vessel—"

Here Zimeo was interrupted by the arrival of Francisco, supported by the young negro who had so suddenly retired upon the sight of his prince. No sooner had Zimeo perceived them, than he flew to Francisco. "O, my father! O Matomba!" cried he, "is it you? do I indeed see you again? O Ellaroe!" "She lives," said Matomba; "she lives, she weeps your misfortunes, she belongs to this family." "Lead me, lead me,"—"See," interrupted Matomba, shewing him Wilmot's friend, "there is the man who saved us." Zimeo embraced by turns, now Matomba, now Wilmot, and now his friend; then with wild eagerness, "lead me," he cried, "to my love." Marianne, or rather Ellaroe, was approaching; the same negro, who had met Matomba, had gone in quest of her; she came trembling, lifting her hands and eyes to heaven; and with tears in her eyes, in a faint voice, she could hardly utter, "Zimeo, Zimeo." She had put her child into the arms of the negro, and after the first transports and embraces were over, she presented the infant to her husband. "Zimeo, behold thy son! for him alone have Matomba and I supported life." Zimeo took the child, and kissed him a thousand and a thousand times. "He shall not be a slave," cried he; "the son of my Ellaroe shall not be a slave to the whites." "But for him," said she, "but for him, I should have quitted this world, in which I could not find the man whom my soul loved." The most tender discourses at last gave place to the sweetest caresses, which were only suspended to bestow those caresses on their child. But soon their gratitude to Wilmot and his friend engrossed them wholly; and surely never did man, not even a negro, express his amiable sentiment so nobly and so well.

Zimeo, being informed that the English troops were on their march, made his retreat in good order. Ellaroe and Matomba melted into tears on quitting Wilmot. They would willingly have remained his slaves; they conjured him to follow them to the mountain. He promised to visit them there as soon as peace should be concluded between the wild negroes and the colony. He kept his word; and went thither often, to contemplate the virtues, the love, and the friendship of Zimeo, of Matomba, and of Ellaroe.

ENTREPRENEURS

ANTIPHILUS [PSEUDONYM]

*TO THE EDITOR OF THE WEEKLY MAGAZINE. MEMOIRS OF A SPY (1798)**

SIR,

IN the year 1793, I was summoned, in my character of physician, to the bed-side of a sick person, at a lodging-house, in Race Street. The incidents of this man's life were somewhat remarkable. I was able to collect from his own mouth, and from his papers, which, at his death, came into my possession, the following narrative, which I think not unworthy of publication.

The name of this man was Wimpfen. He was no more than ten years old when he eloped from his father's house, in the town of Lancaster in this state. His parents were absurdly indulgent, and had rendered him, by their mismanagement imperious and head-strong. He was seldom chidden, and still seldomer chastised by them. On one occasion, however, they thought proper to notice some offence of the lad, in a way which his pride could not brook. In a fit of resentment he resolved never more to enter his father's house. His character was remarkably adventurous and inquisitive. This, in conjunction with his passion, induced him to form his resolution.

His course he accidentally directed to Philadelphia. Any one would harbour and feed such a wanderer. A person at whose house he spent the night, having extracted from him the secret of his family, resolved to take him back the next day to his father. The lad received some intimation of this design before he went to bed, and in order to elude the execution of it, rose before day and departed without warning or taking leave. In this way he arrived, at length, at Philadelphia. He roamed about the streets, asked and obtained food when he was hungry; and slept at night under a pent-house. The hazard he had run of being carried home, against his will, taught him caution and duplicity. He answered evasively or falsely to the questions that chanced to be put to him. His

* SOURCE: Antiphilus [pseud.]. 1798. "Memoirs of a Spy." *The Weekly Magazine of Original Essays, Fugitive Pieces, and Interesting Intelligence* 2 (15): 41–45.
PUBLICATION HISTORY: The story of an American spy evolves from the ambitious but ill-fated magazine project that James Watters launched in Philadelphia in April of 1798, which folded in August of the same year when Watters died in the yellow fever epidemic. Among his contributors was Charles Brockden Brown, as well as a number of unknown American writers hiding behind such pseudonyms as Antiphilus, the name of an ancient Greek artist.

petition being limited to a breakfast or dinner, and his air being thoughtless and gay, those to whom he applied for the first two or three days, were satisfied with merely giving him what he asked.

On the fourth day he was wandering as usual, without any fixed object, along Second street. He began to feel his situation to be desolate and irksome: He reflected on the affection which his parents had always manifested for him, and the sorrow, to which his sudden disappearance had probably given birth. He began to think seriously of returning home, and was employing his untutored understanding in devising the best means for this end, when he met a boy much younger than himself, weeping bitterly. In his rambles, on the day before, he had seen this child sitting at the door of an house on Market street. On enquiry the boy informed him that he was lost. Wimpfen bade him be of good courage, and immediately conducted him home. The mother of the lost child had already missed her darling; had been seized with the utmost consternation; and had dispatched messengers to all quarters in search of him, when Wimpfen made his appearance at the door, leading the wanderer by the hand.

The joy and gratitude of the mother may be easily conceived. Notice was taken of Wimpfen, and the obvious enquiries made as to his name and condition. Wimpfen was dexterous[12] and deceitful; and he pretended to have come from Jersey. His parents he said were dead, and his elder brother had turned him out of doors. Mrs. Bilden and her husband were good folks; their fortune was considerable; and little Frank was their only child. They consulted a moment with each other, and resolved to afford the stranger an asylum.

The boy soon became a troublesome guest. He was mischievous, turbulent, and incontrollable. He was put to school together with Frank, but was always beating and tormenting his companion, though he never failed to defend him from the violence and insults of any other. When about fourteen years of age he happened to play the truant. He spent the greater part of the day in the fields, flying his kite. In the evening he returned into the city, but lingered in the streets, fearful of the enquiries and chastisement which were preparing for him at home. In this state of suspense, he met a school-fellow, whom he persuaded to accompany him to the riverside. His companion, in complying with his request, disobeyed the positive injunctions of his parents, and did not yield without great reluctance to the solicitations of Wimpfen. They strolled from one spot to another, gazing at the ships and talking on school-boy topics. A ship, of a larger size than ordinary, attracting Wimpfen's attention, he proposed to his companion to go on board and view her more closely. After great importunity the boy consented, but in stepping from the wharf to the vessel, unfortunately stumbled, fell into the water, and was drowned.

Terrified at this disaster, and conscious in what degree it was imputable to him, he retired in confusion from the spot. He stopped near a vessel that lay within gun-shot of the former, and employed himself in mournfully reflecting on his situation. The captain of this vessel, happening to be standing near, and noticing his apparent distress, entered into conversation with him. He hearkened to the solicitations of this man, and consented to embark with him as a sort of domestic in the cabin. The vessel was preparing to leave the port, that very evening, and, in a few days, Wimpfen found himself on the ocean.

The behavior of the captain had, at first, been studiously kind; but as soon as they had got to sea, it underwent a total alteration. He was capricious and cruel; and beat the unhappy boy, in the most inhuman manner, and for the most trivial faults. The youth was of a most daring and impetuous spirit. This treatment, so unexpected, and so little according with the captain's promises, by which he was induced to embark with him, could not fail to inspire him with resentment and vengeance.

One day after dinner, having left a plate upon the deck, which a pig, thrusting his nose against it, chanced to break into pieces, the captain, in transport of fury, began to beat him. He bore the most cruel chastisement without a tear or a murmur, though this firmness, which the captain called obstinacy, tended only to prolong his punishment. As soon as it was finished, the captain retired to his berth and fell asleep. Wimpfen waited in sullen silence till he observed that the eyes of the tyrant were closed. He then deliberately took down a loaded pistol that hung in the cabin, and, bringing it close to the captain's head, discharged it. Luckily his aim was not infallible, and the ball only grazed his temple. The sleeper awoke in the utmost terror, and the crew hurried to the spot. Wimpfen calmly related what he had done, and professed his resolution to execute, on the first opportunity, his imperfect vengeance. The captain's cowardice was equal to his cruelty: He began to find that his own safety required a change of measures: Henceforth, Wimpfen was treated with more lenity.[13]

The first hour, after his arrival at Bristol, whither the ship was bound, he made his escape, and once more, pennyless and friendless, committed himself to the wide world.

He was wandering in the precincts of this city, uncertain as to his future projects, when three persons rushing upon him, seized, and carried him before a magistrate. Having as they thought, identified his person, he was conducted, free of all charges, to London. A robbery to a great amount, had been committed a few weeks before, in the neighbourhood of London. Wimpfen's stature and person, remarkably coincided with those of the highwayman, but, on his arrival in London, being confronted with the person robbed, the mistake was instantly detected. The witness was a gentleman by name Ayscue. The countenance and accents of the robber, who was one of his discarded domestics, were perfectly known to him, and were found to be very different from those of Wimpfen. The robber, like Wimpfen, was a mere youth.

He was immediately discharged, but Ayscue was desirous of making him some compensation for the danger and inconvenience to which he had been subjected. His youthful appearance prepossessed him likewise, in his favour. He was remarkably tall and manlike for his age. Wimpfen gave a candid account of his condition and adventures, and consented to enter into Ayscue's service.

This man was a lawyer, and though young, had already attained considerable eminence. He was newly married, and lived in an opulent style. Wimpfen's station was easy, and his master, finding him of an inquisitive and ardent spirit, treated him with few of the reserves to which a servant is supposed to be entitled. He enjoyed considerable leisure, and had free access to his master's books and instruments. He passed three years in a very tranquil manner, and in the hourly improvement of his understanding. At the end of this period, a young lady, the sister of his mistress, became a member of the family.

Wimpfen's integrity did not keep pace with the improvements of his understanding. His heart was impressed with the charms of this young lady, who joined the corrupt habits of a boarding-school with talents, of no mean order, and an intemperate vivacity. Permit me to draw a veil over this part of his life: Perhaps his assertion is true that his own virtue was the object of seduction, and that the lady had fallen from purity previously to his acquaintance with her. Be that as it may, his master threatened him with vengeance, which he could appease only by marriage with the young lady, who was farther recommended by a small fortune. The evidences of depravity which his wife's subsequent conduct displayed, occasioned so much disgust, that he put himself in possession of her ready money and retired to France.

His purse was soon exhausted by the dissipations of Paris. By his dexterity and address he made himself useful to the American Negociators, who had lately arrived in that capital. By this, and other means, he gleaned a temporary subsistence. His subtlety and knowledge of the world had received considerable accessions during a two years' abode at Paris; but the same cannot be said of the firmness and integrity of his principles.

The war commenced between France and England.[14] The British Ambassador had opportunities of knowing the capacity of Wimpfen, and confided in him an important, but secret commission, to be executed at Paris. No consideration had more weight with Wimpfen than his own interest; yet such was the force of the patriotic principle in this man, that the indirect injury done to his native country by benefiting her great enemy, rendered his new employment insupportably irksome. He seized the first opportunity of changing sides. He made a bargain with the French government, and withdrew into England. He pretended, to his old employers that his commission at Paris had been suspected, and that, in order to avoid the punishment that impended over him, he had been compelled to a precipitate flight. This conduct answered two purposes: He attained by it, new gratuities from the English government, and drew closer the veil which concealed his present purposes.

He was a colleague of *Francis de la Motte*,[15] and occupied the same house in Bond street. The fate of that gentleman is well known. He was indicted in 1781, for treasonable practices, condemned, and executed at Tyburn. Wimpfen, though the coadjutor of *De la Motte*, and no less culpable, by his wonderful dexterity extricated himself from the ruin in which his companion was involved, and continued to carry on his trade of *Spy* till the conclusion of the war.

While he remained in England he dropped all intercourse with his wife and his quondam master. After the peace of 1783, there being no longer any demand for his services, his revenue was dried up. He had, however, by frugality, left himself not destitute. With what he had saved, he retired into Languedoc; but his restless and enterprising disposition would not allow him to remain longer than a year in his present situation. He returned to Paris, and solicited the Office of Foreign Affairs for some commission.

At this period several persons were secretly dispatched to India, to counterwork by money and intrigue, the progress of the British arms in that quarter. Wimpfen offered to accompany them; but falling sick at Brest, they were forced to embark without him.

On his recovery he returned to Paris. Some accident introduced him to the Compte de Mirabeau,[16] whose discernment justly estimated the capacity of Wimpfen. From this period, till the death of that celebrated intriguer, he attached himself to his person with unshaken fidelity. He was his secretary, his emissary, his confidant, and his negociator. Wimpfen's talents qualified him for inferior parts; parts, indeed, which demanded equanimity and skill, perhaps, in a degree equal to those occupied by his friend; but they were less brilliant, and operated on the fortune of his patron, rather than on those of the nation.

The active genius of Mirabeau found constant employment for Wimpfen. The opportunities of near inspection better qualified him for the biographer of his patron than any other person living: His pictures would have been accurate and forcible, but perhaps deficient in wisdom.

After the death of this man France became a scene of too much danger and calamity for Wimpfen to remain in it. He had no thoughts, however, of returning to his native country: His attention was bent towards England, when, by chance, in a Paris Coffee-house, he met with a countryman, by name Lesley. They recognized each other, with some difficulty, and after the mention of various incidents which had occurred in their early youth. Lesley, like himself, was a native of Lancaster, and one of the companions of his childhood: He had passed a life of sobriety and sameness: He was early apprenticed in Philadelphia; and had now come to France on a mercantile adventure.

This interview wrought a most singular revolution in the feelings of Wimpfen. The ideas of home and of childhood; the image of his parents, whose distress, on account of his elopement, was painted in pathetic colours by his companion, and who were still alive and in straitened circumstances, recurred to him with so much force as to melt him into tears. He was seized with an ardent longing to return and spend the remainder of his life, near his natal spot and in the bosom of tranquility. The longer he contemplated this scheme, the more fondly he cherished it; and Lesley being shortly to set out for Bourdeaux, and there to embark for America, he resolved to accompany him. Suitable arrangements were easily made, and he arrived in this city, in June, 1793.

Shortly after he was seized with a lingering disease. I was called upon as a physician, and attended him till his recovery. During this period our frequent intercourse produced a considerable intimacy, and he made me acquainted with all the important incidents in his life.

His health was scarcely restored when he was seized by the reigning disease,[17] which had already made considerable progress. The house was immediately deserted by its other inhabitants, and I was obliged to perform the office of his nurse. His death speedily put an end to my danger. His papers he bequeathed to me, and his parents have been placed, by the acquisition of the money which he brought with him, in a comfortable situation. He died in the thirty seventh year of his age.

PHILIP FRENEAU

THE INEXORABLE CAPTAIN: A SHORT STORY (from Mr. SLENDER's Journals.) (1788)*

THE island of Barbadoes was formerly very fertile, and employed prodigious fleets in exporting its productions. The case, however, has been long otherwise. The lands are exhausted, the seasons are not so moist as formerly, and want and poverty are, of consequence, every hour and minute to be met with in this once so delightful a spot. I formerly visited it in a very distressed time, when war had wasted both continents, and the seas were covered with public and private ships of war. No provision vessels had arrived in a long time, and the public shores on the island were nearly consumed. At length there came in a small barque from a distant part of the continent, and no sooner was she brought to her moorings than we saw crowds of people besieging her on every side. Every complexion that Nature had shaded between the remotest extremes of white and black, was observable in this variegated host, and every countenance was strongly marked with anxiety and solicitous concern. Every one wished to become a purchaser. An engrosser[18] came down, and offered to take the whole, if an English shilling per bushel was abated in the price. His proposal was not agreed to, and, to complete his chagrin, the company dismissed him with a universal hiss.

A POOR woman had, with much ado, procured a conveyance on board, and was telling the master of the barque a lamentable story indeed. Her husband had, the other day, lost both his legs and an arm in an engagement with a French privateer. She now had him to provide for, as well as seven helpless children. The privateer to which he belonged had taken no prizes of any considerable value, so that there was nothing to expect from that quarter; and she now brought the last two *pieces of eight*[19] she had in the world, for which, in regard to her peculiar ill fortune, she hoped the master of the barque would not insist upon his full price; but that he would order two bushels to be measured out into her basket.

* SOURCE: Freneau, Philip. 1788. "The Inexorable Captain: A Short Story. (From Mr. Slender's Journals.)." *The Miscellaneous Works of Mr. Philip Freneau, Containing his Essays, and Additional Poems*, 128–33. Philadelphia.

PUBLICATION HISTORY: Freneau was a talented writer of social essays and stories. Francis Bailey, Freneau's publisher and printer, advertised the volume in his publication *The Freeman's Journal* as "Performances in Prose and Verse." Freneau's other prose writings frequently appeared under the pseudonyms Robert Slender and Hezekiah Salem.

IT is impossible for me to relieve all the *stricken deer*, replied he, but should I even grant your request, the quantity you mention would be but a small and trivial supply to you and yours; and when it is gone, what will you or they be better of it?

IT would prolong our existence a few days, answered the woman, very rationally; and HE who permitted you to reach our port with this small supply, will, perhaps, by the time it is expended, send us a greater abundance.

I HOPE they will not drop in till I have disposed of my cargo, said the master of the barque; and I would advise you, my honest girl, to borrow some money from your friends, as it is my determination not to recede a single stiver[20] from the price I have fixed.

I HAVE no friend, answered the woman, that will lend me the tenth part of a groat.[21]

THE commander of the barque, upon hearing this, retired to his cabin, and did not appear again till the woman returned homewards as she came—with an empty basket!—

"HE must be a very hard-hearted man," said one of the islanders present.

THAT may be possibly the case, replied I; but only observe the hypocrisy and insincerity of mankind: the woman had a sufficiency of money to purchase one third of a bushel at the specified price; but she would not rely upon the benevolent Being, vulgarly called *Providence*, for any thing under the present and precise supply of *two bushels*.

"SHE had a right to make the best bargain she could," said the islander.

And so has the master of the barque, answered I; for, you may rely upon it, the officer of the customs will not abate him a farthing of his fees.

"BUT where is that pity and compassion," cried the islander, "and those other emotions of sympathy, which ought to sway the breast of every MAN on these trying occasions?"

HE would give but a sad account of his voyage to his owners, returned I, if he was not, even upon such occasions, proof to all the scenery of misery, as well as deaf to the voice of pity.

THE vessel was by this time drawn toward the wharf, and a stage laid to the shore.

A THIN man of a pale complexion now attracted my notice; who led a couple of mules with several empty bags on their backs;—the poor animals were almost as thin and meager as himself.

A TRANSIENT sparkle of joy kindled up in the eyes of all three at the sight of a large heap of corn that had been just measured out to a rich planter; but as it moved off in the plantation cart, the momentary flash was at an end, and the heavy gloom of sadness succeeded in its place.

CRUEL illusion, said I—how bitterly are they oftentimes deceived who place their hearts and affections on things below, even when their desires are justifiable in themselves.

THE thin man then stepped up to the master of the barque, and began to tell him that he possessed two acres of land among the mountains, upon which he had found means to support a female companion and a considerable number of children for several years; but that the dry weather had been of such long continuance the present season, that the seed of all his hopes had perished in the ground; and that a small quantity of cotton, and a little coffee (neither of which were yet ripe) were in their whole dependence.

AND what is all this to me, my good friend, said the commander of the little barque.

I WAS thinking, replied the other, that if your honour would let me have five or six measures out of your cargo, I would give you the coffee and cotton, as they now stand in the field, in pledge of payment; and by the time your honour returns to this island a second time, I would have both articles in prime order, ready to deliver into your hands.

AND who will be responsible to me, replied the tar,[22] that you will not in the mean time have ran away, or removed to some other place, or will not, upon my return, swear point blank that you never saw or heard of me before in your life; at best, you will be concealed in your mountains, and I might as well seek for the bones of the *Cyclops* in Sicily, as expect any success in ferreting you from your den.

MY principles would not suffer me to act in that manner, said the thin man.

And my principle is never to trust to the honour of mankind, retorted the other; so that if you cannot produce the *one thing needful*, you and your cattle had better be packing, without more ado.

THE man turned about with tears in his eyes, and looked pitifully at his mules, and his mules looked at him, and the looks of both were full of regret and disappointment.

THE master of the barque then stepped to the quarter deck and took a large dram of brandy.—But, if you would reflect a moment, continued he (returning and addressing the thin man) you would be at once sensible of the impropriety of your request. The hard hand of necessity has also driven me hither to make the most of a trifle, and that without loss or delay of time. You and I are two beings that have this day met by accident, and could reciprocally spend a month in relating the story of our mutual wants and difficulties. Believe me, we have not sailed from the gardens of paradise, nor cleared out from the bosom of affluence. I have, at this terrible season of the year, come a long way, no less than six hundred leagues, over a stormy ocean, in a feeble barque, which will, perhaps, never accomplish my return. Absent from those I love, and the scenes natural to men, I have risqued the cruelty of enemies, the horrors of shipwreck; have patiently endured the beating shower, long, dreary nights, and cold, pinching winds!—And a thousand difficulties and mischances may yet attend me on my way to my native land—and all for what?—You would have me return home with a parcel of fine promises, a hundred millions of which would not ballast my vessel, so as to enable her to carry sail on her return.

I DO not perfectly comprehend the meaning of these arguments, said the thin man; but if my wife was here, I think she could answer them: She has a devil of a tongue, and an understanding as keen as a razor.

KEEP her at home, then, in God's name, answered the tar; for I have one of exactly the same stamp to hold arguments with on my own coasts.

THE man and his mules then returned sullenly to the mountains.

BUT, you will say, to what purpose is all this idle story?—I will candidly confess that there is very little instruction to be gathered from it, more than this, *That necessity alone renders one half of the world insensible to the miseries and wants of the other.*

Notes

1. Set free by the Spanish when the English conquered the island in 1655, they formed independent Maroon communities (Lockley 2009, ix–xxiii). These runaway slaves settled in the inaccessible inland mountains much like the rebellious slaves led by Zimeo.
2. Mate: dejected, downcast, discouraged.
3. Imprecations: curses.
4. Persecuted in England, many members of this religious group settled in the Americas, especially in liberal Pennsylvania. The pacifistic Quakers were early leaders in the effort to abolish slavery, both in Britain and in the United States, for example, through the activities of Anthony Benezet, founder of the first anti-slavery organization.
5. Maimed: disabled, wounded.
6. Abetting: encouraging, assisting.
7. Orissa: name for minor gods and spirits worshipped by the Yoruba people in

modern-day Nigeria. Slaves exported their religion to Cuba, the West Indies, and from there to the rest of the Americas.

8. Accost: to meet.

9. Precipitation: confusion, sudden and hurried action.

10. Porto Bello, the harbor town founded by the Spanish at the isthmus of Panama, in 1597.

11. Pinioned: having the arms bound or shackled.

12. Dexterous: clever, crafty, cunning.

13. Lenity: mildness, gentleness.

14. The American war of independence was a world conflict involving the major European powers. The Paris Treaty of 1783 ended the war.

15. Francis Henry de la Motte was a former French lieutenant executed for high treason in front of a huge crowd in 1781; his life and death inspired various literary works.

16. Honoré Gabriel Riqueti, comte de Mirabeau, French writer and politician, was involved in the French Revolution as speaker of the Third Estate.

17. He suffered from a venereal disease, probably syphilis.

18. Engrosser: someone who wants to acquire the whole of the commodity to monopolize the market.

19. Two pieces of eight: Spanish dollar, a silver coin.

20. Stiver: a currency denomination, a nickel.

21. Groat: one of several coins used in the British West Indies.

22. Tar: informal word for seaman, sailor.

Suggestions for Further Reading

Slavery

Frederic [pseud.]. 1789. "The Desperate Negro." *The American Museum, or, Universal Magazine* 6 (6): 433–36.

Hammon, Briton. 1760. *A Narrative of the Most Uncommon Sufferings and Surprizing Deliverance of Briton Hammon, A Negro Man*. Boston.

Marrant, John. 1785. *A Narrative of the Lord's Wonderful Dealings with John Marrant, a Black, with the Assistance of Reverend William Aldridge*. London.

Rush, Benjamin. 1787. "The Paradise of Negro Slaves: A Dream." *The Columbian Magazine* 1 (5): 135–38.

"The Wretched Taillah: An African Story." 1792. *The Massachusetts Magazine: or, Monthly Museum* 4 (4): 250–51.

Entrepreneurs

Bradford, William. 1856. "[Thomas Allerton]." In *History of Plymouth Plantation*, edited by Charles Deane, 291–93. Boston.

Brown, Charles Brockden. 1798. "Arthur Mervyn, or Memoirs of the Year 1793." *The*

Weekly Magazine of Original Essays, Fugitive Pieces, and Interesting Intelligence 2 (20): 193–230; 2 (22): 257–62; 2 (23): 290–96; 2 (24): 322–27.

Brown, Charles Brockden. 1798. "Man at Home." Essay-serial in *The Weekly Magazine of Original Essays, Fugitive Pieces, and Interesting Intelligence*, published from February 1798 to April 1798 in thirteen installments.

"The History of Tom Varien." 1759. *New-England Magazine of Knowledge and Pleasure* 3: 3–13.

Mather, Cotton. 1702. "Pietas in Patriam: The Life of His Excellency Sir William Phips." In *Magnalia Christi Americana*, 1:164–230. London.

PART IV

CULTURES OF PRINT

THIS SECTION FOCUSES ON processes of textual travel that characterize short narratives in the Americas as a result of complex cultural translations and traffic. The selection of texts considers the ways in which stories that migrated from Europe to the Americas have been reclassified by editors for changing audiences, times, and circumstances. In some cases, such as in the popular stories on premature death ("Valeria: An Italian Tale," 1799, for example) or the widely read oriental tales (such as "Firnaz and Mirvan: An Eastern Tale," 1792), it becomes clear that the early "American" story is less a creation of a single author than a product of multiple authorships and editorial interventions (Haberman 2008). Its success, or its "becoming American," depends less on its being "original"—that is, penned by an American writer (although most stories were published anonymously)—than on its brevity and variety. These features were essential to the medium in which most narratives were published: the magazine, whose miscellaneous sections on art, poetry, literature, and science are frequently compared by editors to a "Bee Hive, enriched by the aromaticks of every field" ("General Preface" 1790, ii) and whose use of short pieces derives from an effort to reduce printing costs and accommodate contemporary reading habits.

Eighteenth-century short narratives often acquire multiple "lives" as they cross generic and linguistic boundaries. For example, collections or individual foreign tales are translated into English and published separately as extracts in newspapers or magazines, as can be seen in "Azakia" (1783) and "The Child of Snow" (1792). Some have an "afterlife" as reprints or serve as templates for nineteenth-century short stories. Along the way they were renamed, stripped of their origins, and sometimes rewritten. The early story in the Americas was often the result of acts of literary piracy and verbatim copying, as well as the editors' relentless hunt for short tales to satisfy the desultory reading habits of their audience. More recent studies demonstrate that readers and publishers "routinely forced fiction to migrate into other forms of writing—a kind of transtextual operation that turned fiction into other genres such as aphorism, moral essay, magazine article, character sketch, political disquisition, and so on" (Flint 2011, 46).

The stories in this section highlight the workings of a transatlantic print culture in which figures from Orientalism, sensationalism, and Native American history were especially popular. After *The Arabian Nights*—a collection of Persian, Arabian, and Indian folktales—had been translated into English in 1706, Oriental tales became popular in English literature throughout the eighteenth and the nineteenth centuries. Editors of leading literary journals of the period issued stories from *The Arabian Nights* to meet the demand and interests of their readers. In 1764 James Ridley published *The Tales of the Genii: Or, the Delightful Lessons of Horam, the Son of Asmar*, under the pseudonym Sir Charles Morell, based on *The Arabian Nights*. The genii are supernatural creatures who do one's bidding when summoned, as in the "History of Prince Zeyn Alasnam and the King of the Genii," for instance. "Firnaz and Mirvan" contains similar magic themes, as the anonymous author combines characters and narrative elements borrowed from German, French, and English Oriental tales. The story's idyllic Persian setting, with nymphs and the spirit Firnaz, creates a magical atmosphere in which Mirvan—an evil despot—dreams of his rise and fall, conquering "new worlds" and "invading the liberties of others" before being ousted by a "European hero," a possible reference to Alexander the Great. Disguised as an Oriental dream tale, "Firnaz and Mirvan" could be read as an allegory on human vanity and a lust for power that stands in the way of pursuing a life of contentment, vividly contrasting the effects of civilization with the simplicity of nature. Its appearance in an American magazine in 1792 reveals how the decentralized transatlantic culture of reprinting provides various and generically divergent reading and writing practices for a civic culture in which the distribution of power—in both domestic and public spheres—plays an increasingly important role.

Sabina, the unknown author of "Louisa: A Novel" (1790), likewise embeds the story of the misfortunes and final rise of the protagonist within the context of the Barbary captivity, combining the Oriental setting with elements of other popular genres. Published in Isaiah Thomas's *The Massachusetts Magazine* in Boston (1789–96), it is one of the first Algerine captivity stories, written in the form of a fictitious memoir. Moreover, *The Massachusetts Magazine* was on the verge of becoming the most attractive and popular periodical in Boston. Thomas, who had already published *The Massachusetts Spy* (1770–1820) and earlier *The Royal American Magazine* (1774–75), eked out a particular niche for his periodical by satisfying the popular demand for sentimental stories. He avoided elite erudition and offered short "amusing but instructive" pieces for a readership that, "not having many leisure moments, will be more likely to read a short essay on any subject, than to set down and peruse in course a lengthy dissertation" ("The General Observer No. 1" 1789, 9). Compared to the many other short-lived periodicals of the early national period, Thomas was fairly successful at building the magazine around a network of correspondents and collaborators. *The Massachusetts Magazine* was not only a self-proclaimed "asylum for native Genius" ("General Preface" 1790, i), i.e., encouraging submissions from local authors, but it also established a discursive community based on notions of friendship and mutuality. The magazine created the impression that readers and contributors (the "friends" as they were called) had an equal share in patching together a general miscellany for an enlightened public. Thus, Thomas's magazine spelled out a communitarian space for private and collective readings, built a collaborative authorship via a network of corresponding agents, and organized representational solidarity.

Sabina was one of the main contributors to Thomas's magazines and much acclaimed by the magazine's readers. The use of the pseudonym Sabina did not reveal the author's gender, since men frequently used female pen names (see, for instance, the note signed by "Anna" preceding Margaretta Faugeres's story, "An Account of a Murder," in this section). "Louisa: A Novel" portrays the adventures of a female protagonist traveling through North America, the Caribbean, Europe, and Africa. Its numerous intertextual references contain a universal message on the equality of the sexes as well as on the abolition of slavery. The story unfolds a romance with female heroines and emphasizes their importance in creating a community capable of overcoming national and ethnic differences, as indicated by the cross-cultural marriages at the end of the story. Similar to "Amelia, or the Faithless Briton," which had been published earlier in *The Massachusetts Magazine*, the story is highly innovative in using embedded tales, transatlantic settings, alterations between showing and telling, shifts of perspective, and the amalgamation of various themes and developments that culminate in the turning point in the story. Its deistic tone and ambiguous racial message prevented the story from being further circulated in the pages of North American magazines, especially in light of Thomas Paine's *The Age of Reason* (1794) and its controversy over Deism. Nevertheless, its transatlantic themes had an afterlife in both Susanna Rowson's play *Slaves in Algiers* (1794) and Royall Tyler's *The Algerine Captive* (1797).

While earlier studies stress either particular national themes or original authorship as central criteria for incorporating stories into a canon of early American short fiction, the short narratives assembled in this section evolve from migrant stories that circulated in magazines and show how foreign literature is repackaged and redeployed so that an "American" story results. Michel Certeau (2008, 174) speaks in this respect of a readerly "appropriation" of texts, an activity through which readers construct a text's meaning for themselves, refashioning what they consume. "Azakia: A Canadian Story" and "The Child of Snow" are transnational stories, having appeared in France, Germany, and England before migrating to North America. Both stories document a pattern of reclassification based on the pluralities of texts, overlapping genres, and motifs assembled in magazines. "Azakia: A Canadian Story," one of the most widely circulated transatlantic Indian tales, remained in print until 1816. The prose tale of the love triangle involving the French officer St. Castins, the Huron beauty Azakia, and the chieftain Ouabi was reprinted in Matthew Carey's *The American Museum, or Universal Magazine* in 1789. The story is a translation of French author Nicolas Bricaire de la Dixmerie's "Azâkia: Anecdote Huronne," which he had published in *Contes philosophiques et moraux* in 1765. Dixmerie's collection expanded into three volumes in 1769, becoming a transatlantic steady seller. "Azakia: A Canadian Story" was translated and reprinted in England and North America. This story also resonates with a transnational tradition of European–Native American romances, as indicated by translations into Swedish, German, and Portuguese (Johnson 2009). As the numerous reprints in American magazines show, the postrevolutionary United States was just one country among many in which the story became popular. Drawing upon Carey's reprint, Sarah Wentworth Morton reworked the history of the Baron de St. Castins and his marriage to the daughter of an Abenaki chief in a verse tale titled *Ouâbi: or The Virtues of Nature. An Indian Tale. In Four Cantos* (1790). Given the workings of transatlantic print culture circulating the figure of the American Indian as an international icon, Morton invests in this network without gaining the wider popularity the story attained on an international level.

Similarly, the short tale "The Child of Snow" marks the transition of fictitious stories from the newspaper into the literary medley of the miscellanies. It transports literary elements and sentiments that matched the overall design of Thomas's *The Massachusetts Magazine*, which also intended to create an audience by its appeal to a popular rather than elite taste. "The Child of Snow" circulated in American newspapers and magazines from July 4, 1787, beginning with the *Charleston Morning Post and Daily Advertiser*, and having its final appearance in *The Boston Weekly Magazine and Ladies' Miscellany* of 1818. The story is about a woman who becomes pregnant in the absence of her husband, a traveling merchant, and his revenge for her infidelity. Upon the husband's return, she attributes her son's birth to a miraculous conception induced by a falling snowflake, inadvertently swallowed while she was leaning outside her window. This motif is taken up by the husband, who takes his son with him on a long journey and, after selling him to a Saracen slave trader, returns home to tell his wife that the boy melted away on an especially hot day. "The wife knew perfectly well the merchant's meaning," the narrator concludes, and adds the maxim that establishes again the continuity between her infraction and punishment: "She durst not, however, break out, but was obliged to swallow the liquor she had brewed."

Critics identify this rather short, flat piece of prose as an American story but are ignorant of its roots in German and French medieval literature (Werlock 2010, x). They recognize in it a successful combination of folkloristic material with a domestic background, namely, the American merchant traveling for his business. It also matches the literary tradition of instructive and moral tales about sexual misconduct and marital infidelity, and thus fulfills an eighteenth-century narrative purpose: the fusion of realism and didacticism. In *The American Short Story before 1850*, Eugene Current-García (1985, 13) highlights, in addition to the story's themes, the particular narrative elements that make this tale a forerunner of the nineteenth-century short story. Its combined use of "irony, novel detail, both realistic and fantastic, and its matter-of-fact tone" makes it an authentic American tale. Yet the story was borrowed from "Mr. Le Grand's Tales of the Twelfth and Thirteenth Centuries." Pierre Jean-Baptiste Legrand d'Aussy's collection of thirteenth-century French tales appeared in Paris under the title *Fabliaux ou Contes des douzième et treizième siècles, traduits ou extraits d'après les manuscrits* (1779). A first English translation was published in London in 1786, titled *Tales of the Twelfth and Thirteenth Centuries. From the French of Mr. Le Grand*. John Williams, the translator, reissued the collection as *Norman Tales* in 1789. The French medieval tale

"De l'enfant qui fu remis au soleil" mutated into the English story "The Child Melted by the Sun," and American newspaper reprints ascribe their borrowings to the English translations.

The story itself is a fabliau, a genre of medieval comic tales frequently depicting sexual or obscene topics in an unabashedly humorous way. The fabliau was never limited to any one social class, and writers borrowed freely from it, as did, for instance, Geoffrey Chaucer in his fourteenth-century *Canterbury Tales*. Eighteenth-century editors frequently used such "little fables" to compensate for the lack of original stories at hand, but they were also reprinted because of their simple, unsophisticated, and practical style. The fabliau favors a materialistic view of everyday life as it depicts people from the lower and middle classes. It is altogether more expansive and less didactic than the fable, since it avoids a summary of the moral and puts a greater emphasis on telling a story. Its expansive meaning refers to a process of readerly appropriation made possible by textual cues that function, according to Frow, as "metacommunications" (2006, 115). The meaning may stand out in very obvious ways, such as the husband's "project of revenge" in "The Child of Snow," or it may come to the fore in statements of condensed information: "It is needless to give the particulars of the journey, or an account of the countries through which he passed." The fabliau usually contains a twist at the end of the story, typically in the form of an outwitted character. Apart from its brevity, these general attributes certainly account for the fabliau's circulation in the amusement section of American newspapers before such short pieces found their entrance into the miscellanies.

This section also highlights the wide distribution of sensationalistic short narratives in the Atlantic world of the eighteenth and early nineteenth centuries. Magazine editors quickly learned to exploit their readers' appetite for transgressive short narratives; they obtained factual and fictional stories from all available sources to cater to a growing taste for sensationalistic topics about outsiders, shape-shifters, and marginal characters, often accompanied by morally instructive remarks. Readers could, however, easily grasp the story's imaginary happening because it fell into what has been called "light reading" or "small tales" that appealed to an unspecialized audience fascinated by short fictions. While periodical studies discuss early literary magazines as "virtual coffeehouses" (Gardner 2012), which aim to foster a republican order among readers and writers alike, sensationalist stories such as Margaretta Faugeres's "An Account of a Murder" (1781) and the reprint of a French ghost story show how magazines also served as a space that embellished the abnormal, eccentric, weird, and incredible in order to build a periodical business upon liminal fantasies that could be freely tapped by the readers. In the "rational age" of the late eighteenth century, abnormality was inherently interesting. Human nature was imagined to go berserk in foreign settings. There were, however, numerous exceptions, and as magazine fiction shows (even before Washington Irving and Edgar Allan Poe), the domestic and the foreign overlap in stories about liminal figures. Literary magazines teem with stories about mobility that come from liminality and from fellow human beings in liminal states—those places in between the accepted social structure. Not unlike later nineteenth-century short stories (Nathaniel Hawthorne's tales, for instance), these early liminal texts reveal the complex nature of human reality often at odds with social reality.

In 1796 *The New York Weekly Magazine* printed a short, anonymously published narrative titled "An Account of the Murder of Mr. J—Y—, upon his family, in December, A.D. 1781." Although the magazine paid homage to republican virtues, the editors equally satisfied their readers' growing appetite for sensational accounts of crime and murder. Execution sermons and confessions were the leading literary forms to portray perpetrators and to control domestic fantasies about crime (see the confessions of Owen Syllavan and Thomas Powers in Part I). "An Account of the Murder of Mr. J—Y—," written by Margaretta Faugeres, marks the movement toward a more profane but graphic short narrative on crime. Faugeres retells the story of an actual familicide that occurred in 1781 in upstate New York. Misguided by religious delusions, the farmer, James Yates, killed his wife, Elizabeth, and their four children: two daughters and two sons. Despite the strong religious subtext (since Yates had obviously converted to the Shaker religion), the murder is set within Gothic conventions and highlights a monstrous lunacy in the face of an inscrutable evil as one of the key features of the new carnal literature of crime (see Charles Brockden Brown's "Somnambulism"). Faugeres's account of the family's slaughter also imitates the language of captivity narratives, which is in tone similar to the well-known *History of Maria Kittle*, authored by her mother, Ann Eliza Bleecker, and published posthumously by her daughter in 1793.

Similarly, "Valeria: An Italian Tale"—a story about premature death—has a long pre-history in the context of the transatlantic culture of print and marks the transition from apparition narratives to the supernatural tale in the nineteenth century. Drawing upon an earlier collection of French criminal reports and court decisions, Jean-Pierre Claris de Florian fleshed out a ghost story in his *Nouvelles nouvelles* (Paris, 1792). Florian titled his story "Valeria: An Italian Tale." In the same year, an English translation appeared as *New Tales from the French of M. Florian* in London. American editors pirated the increasingly popular anthologies of short tales emerging in the 1790s in England, freely borrowing from them without acknowledging their sources. The London version appeared serialized with dramatic cliff-hangers in the American *Literary Museum, or Monthly Magazine* in 1797. While Florian's version controls the transgressive experience of the lovers by quoting authorities from classical antiquity in the story's introduction, the abridged reprints migrate from the dogmatic to the literary use of the supernatural by leaving out the introduction and creating a situation of oral storytelling. The narrator relates how, at a Christmas house party in the Languedoc, as the youthful company were telling each other stories of "the marvelous, ghosts and apparitions," a young Italian lady called Valeria introduced her story by calling herself a ghost. She explained that after having been refused permission to marry her lover Octavian, she was deceived into marrying a cousin. Discovering the deceit immediately after the wedding, she fainted and became delirious; "the disease rapidly increased, and after a paroxysm of sixty hours" she expired. Valeria was placed in the family vault, but Octavian—having obtained access to the vault and kissing her—felt her breathe. He warmed her in his embrace and took her to his house, where a physician "answered her to life." Appearing to her parents and husband as a ghost, she caused the former to repent their actions and the latter to relinquish his claim.

This version appeared in the first, 1806 volume of the British magazine *La Belle Assemblée, or Bell's Court and Fashionable Magazine Addressed Particularly to the Ladies* (1806–37; founded by John Bell). The story was reprinted in Baltimore a year later by Eliza Anderson, retitled "Valeria, or the Ghost Alive." Anderson was the first woman to edit a general-interest magazine in the United States, and in 1806 she founded *The Observer* and adopted the pen name Beatrice Ironside for her satirical and witty editorials. Within the pages of her magazine, Anderson fought journalistic vendettas against critics who were outraged over her translation of a scandalous French novel (Sophie Cottin's *Claire d'Albe*, 1798). Like earlier editors, Anderson was continually in search of material that would attract and retain subscribers, and she recognized the story's sensational potential. In the print context of *The Observer*, the story is not simply one with a happy resolution for the lovers, but one in which the threshold-crossing and reintegration of the protagonist evokes ambiguity. Valeria's final reprimanding of her parents' and former husband's behavior contests prevailing notions of domestic authority and paternal power as questionable standards of communal life.

This section shows that in the pages of the magazine, the world of the text encounters the world of the reader. In contrast to specific modes of organizing textual materials that impose their intentions and meanings on the reader (i.e., dogmatic discourses such as religion or politics), the magazine's function lies in the actualization of texts—since magazines were sometimes read aloud. Rearranging, decontextualizing, or extracting texts from other sources, magazines invest texts with new meaning and status and thus increase the range of textual appropriations on the readers' side. In doing so, magazines move beyond specific reader groups and appeal to various communities of new readers and their changing reading habits, aptitude, and predilections.

ORIENTALISM

ANONYMOUS

*FIRNAZ and MIRVAN: An Eastern Tale ([1752] 1792)**

IN the earlier ages of the world, mankind knew no other ties but those of nature. No throne was then erected upon the ruins of liberty, and no men were taught like the savage of the forest to bow the neck, to force, and usurpation.

* SOURCE: Anonymous. (1752) 1792. "Firnaz and Mirvan: An Eastern Tale." *The New York Magazine, or Literary Repository* 3 (10): 628–30.

PUBLICATION HISTORY: The characters of Firnaz and Zohar appear in Christoph Martin Wieland's verse tales "Zemin und Gulhindy" and "Der Unzufriedene," published in *Erzählungen* (1752). They were adapted into the French story "Firnaz and Zohar," published in the Genevan magazine *Choix Littéraire* (1755–60; vol. 8), and in *Contes Moraux*, published by Madame d'Uncy (1763, vol. 1). A further augmentation titled "Firnaz and Mirvan" appeared in English in *The Orientalist: A Volume of Tales after the Eastern-Taste. By the Author of Roderick Random, Sir Launcelot Greaves, &c. and others* (1764). This pen name was used by Tobias George Smollett, but the volume is almost certainly not by him. Subsequently, the story was widely published in English magazines: 1774. *St. James's Magazine or Memoirs of our Own Times* 1 (August): 317–19, and English and German collections of tales, like *Novelettes Moral and Sentimental*, published in London (1785), or *Palmblätter: Erlesene morgenländische Erzählungen* (1800). *The New York Magazine* reprint was probably borrowed from the English collection *Elegant Tales, Histories, and Epistles of a Moral Tendency*, published in London (1791) and edited by the Reverend John Adams. Before that, the story was been published as "The Discontented Man: An Eastern Tale" in 1784. *The Gentleman's and Lady's Town and Country Magazine; or, Repository of Instruction and Entertainment* 6 (October): 253–56; 7 (November): 281–84. In England, the story was also published, under the title "Zohar: An Eastern Tale," in 1788. *The European Magazine & London Review* (August): 122–24, and (September): 206–8. This version migrated to America: 1791. *The Massachusetts Magazine; or, Monthly Museum. Containing the Literature, History, Politics, Arts, Manners & Amusements of the Age* 3 (4): 235–37; 3(5): 273–75 and both publications were ascribed to "Wieland," indicating the German Enlightenment writer as their source. "Firnaz and Mirvan: An Eastern Tale" was also published in 1792. *The New York Magazine, or Literary Repository* 3 (10): 628–30.

The earth covered with riches supplied a healthful and harmless repast, and at once gave her inhabitants security and content.

In those happy times it was, that fortune had showered down its gifts upon Mirvan, who took up his residence by the borders of the Caspian Sea.[1] Here, in a country replete with every convenience that could supply necessity, and every charm that could invite the eye, he enjoyed, or might have enjoyed uninterrupted tranquility. He was rich—but he was not happy; wisdom requires no abundance to make man content. Tho' the education of this youth was cultivated with all imaginable assiduity,[2] yet his natural impatience taught him to spurn the blessings with which he was surrounded, and carried his wishes even beyond the capacity of nature to satisfy. His soul soon saw only a disgusting uniformity in the good which he enjoyed. What remedy for a pain that seemed incurable? though nature be never so indulgent, she is poor to the desiring son of folly.

One day, fatigued with winding through all the mazes of his anxious desires, he insensibly fell asleep. Firnaz, the king of the Genii,[3] had compassion upon his wretched situation, and undertook to cure him of his allusions, by convincing his imaginations in a dream of truths he had seemed to despise when waking.

Mirvan fancied himself placed on the summit of a mountain, where, leaning against the trunk of a spreading cedar, he enjoyed at one view, all the possessions of his ancestors, which covered the valley beneath. But far from regarding this wealth with joy, he burst into complaint and invective. Assaulted by a thousand different desires, he walked forward with an uncertain pace, when suddenly his eyes were struck with a light that seemed more than terrestrial. His surprise was still encreased by the appearance as a cloud with all the beautiful variations of the rainbow, which ambrosial perfume, Firnaz, king of the Genii, conducted to the place where the discontented youth was standing; and thus addressed him: "Son of mortality, speak thy griefs, in order to find redress."[4] Encouraged by the voice, the youth returned, "The dull uniformity of my condition is insupportable; the morning differs not from the night, and to-day resembles yesterday; all my life appears but a moment lengthened by disgusting repetition. The valley and the forest are stripped of their beauty, in my eye.—Even the charms of the beauteous Thyrza herself, are no longer pleasing since she has blest me with enjoyment."

Favourable genius, continued he, for thy looks bespeak thy compassion, change the country which we now behold, into a region resembling that possessed by those beings who reside above the stars. Let it contain an abstract of all those beauties which are dispersed round the creation, that all may flatter my senses, and that my soul may have entire fruition in all that imagination can conceive of pleasure.

He wish'd, and the indulgent genius soon complied with his importunate request. The face of nature grew ten thousand times more beautiful than ever rapturous poet had fancied. The violet and the amaranthus[5] sprung up beneath their steps. The zephyr,[6] enchanted with this delightful landscape, wasted its odoriferous breath on every side. All that could gratify sense, or excite satiety; were there in profusion. Mirvan now began to revive; he perceived himself placed upon a bed of roses, over-shaded by a bower of never-fading green. In the enthusiasm of his rapture he arose, traversed the charming plain with an hasty step. Here distracted in a variety of beauty, he seemed at a loss what to prefer. The juicy anana, the delicate lotos, by turns, attract his hand and his eye; his ears are flattered by the consort of the grove.—Like a weary traveller, our youthful complainant seemed now at ease, having come to the seat of destination. He had not wandered long in this ideal scene of beauty, when he discovered seven nymphs[7] who fixed their regards upon him.—They moved with unspeakable grace, and all their looks served to inspire pleasure. Mirvan saw and was enchanted with their beauty; the other charms of the country now seemed lost in the comparison. The nymphs seemed to be conscious of his passion, and assuming an air of modesty, fled to the thickest shades, sure of being pursued.

Thus blest and blessing, he at first thought his raptures would never end. But scarce were eight days passed in this abode, when the minutes began to lengthen, and new wishes to interrupt his happiness. His ears were fatigued with continued harmony, his eyes with the repetition of beauty. The reasoning principle seemed sunk on the bed of sloth, and the soul had no opportunity of vigorous exertion.—I detest, cried he, a life where nothing is found but softness and ease, no variety to amuse, no danger to excite resolution. Ah! would Firnaz but once more hear my prayer, it is not to spend my days in the arms of pleasure, I could wish to embark in greater raptures, I could wish for power, as I see the plain without limits lying around me, I would desire also to govern a people with unbounded authority.

He had scarce spoken when an invisible arm seizing him instantly, transported him through the air. He beheld a country without limits, diversified with forests of cedars whose tops seemed to reach the clouds, large rivers divided it, at once supplying an easy conveyance, and giving fertility. Beautiful cities were scattered up and down without number. All that you see, cried his conductor, is thine. Mirvan, with a joyful heart bowed to the ground, and thanked the indulgent genius. He scarce concluded this instance of gratitude, when he found himself in the midst of a circle of heroes and ancient sages, who chose him their king, even before he had time to return from his astonishment. His brows were bound with a diadem, and the silver sounding-trumpet proclaimed his accession among the people. The populace thronged around to kiss the steps of his throne, while numberless camels came loaded with all the riches of the East, and the spices of the neighbouring Isles.

The ears of Mirvan were charmed with the martial notes of the trumpet, and the neighing of the horses equipped for war: his heart began to beat for conquest, and as they who wish for enemies easily create them, he soon went to war; attacked the foe and was victorious. One conquest seemed only to induce him to wish for more: he went from victory to victory, till all his neighbours became tributary, or all their countries laid in ruin. He first then began to form the wish of a once famous European hero,[8] namely, that of new worlds to conquer; but the time approached that his vanity was to be humbled. A distant country that had, with jealous eyes, seen his progress in invading the liberties of others, began to fear for their own; a love of freedom supplied them with both conduct and courage. They attacked the enemy of mankind with a force, which it was impossible to resist; the army of slaves fell by myriads: the hero now began to consider that he was but man: he fled for safety to the forest, alone, deserted by the crowd of flatterers, and now given up a prey to famine, fatigue and his own reflections still more mortifying than either. After a long journey he found himself in the midst of a plain, encircled by a mountain. He reposed himself on a bank by a glassy rivulet that poured from a neighbouring hill. The soul of Mirvan seemed all discord and confusion: wretch that I am, cried he, why was I born to this variety of distress? why brought into the world to survive every felicity? the poor peasant who feeds upon roots and water; the wandering savage that hunts for a precarious meal is happier far than I; I will not, cannot survive it! He had scarce finished, when throwing himself headlong into the water, he there expected to terminate a wretched existence; when the fancied coldness of the waves gave an instant shock, which awaked him from his dream. Beside him lay the lovely Thyrza, his favourite wife, more beautiful than the morning; his attendants came with submissive assiduity, to know his pleasure: in short, he found all his possessions real, all his wants imaginary, and ever after retained a proper share of gratitude, for the benefits he enjoyed from heaven, without once murmuring at its having been more indulgent to others.

SABINA [PSEUDONYM]

*L O U I S A.—A NOVEL (1790)**

Resignation to the will of Providence is most certainly a duty, and few even pretend but that a calm compliance with our fate, however severe, renders that fate less irksome.[9] To be cheerful in adversity, is thought a proof of great mind; to be humble in prosperity, is a proof of a good one. A person who practices the *one*, may certainly the other. Goodness and greatness are terms almost synonymous with me; why then should we sink beneath our species, by repining at the decrees of a being infinitely wise, merciful and just; who is acquainted with our wants, who knows what is best suited to our situations, and is sensible of our erroneous wills. I have met with many proofs, that condescension, resignation and benevolence, are frequently rewarded in this state. The following tale is perhaps an example.

Louisa was not a regular beauty, bur her softness, her sprightliness and delicacy, that sensibility that diffused itself over her features, gave such a charm to every thing she said or did, that beauties were often overlooked in her company, and she never had the mortification to be neglected. A person that had seen her would have said she was a pretty girl; and when they had conversed with her, they would find she had an art of interesting the feelings.

Her father had been attentive to her education; it was polite[10] and useful; it was such as taught her not to fret at little evils, and to bear great misfortunes without murmuring. He was constantly inculcating lessons of patience, cheerfulness and resignation; he frequently repeated Pope's universal prayer,[11] as the best human production; he made her acquainted with history, and early inspired a love of poetry. She read many speculations and philosophical essays, and was soon an habitual moralist. As for religion, the Bible was put into her hands, and she was taught, rather to make that the guide of her life, than a subject of her conversation.

Her mother was a most excellent woman, and knowing it was necessary

* SOURCE: Sabina [pseud.]. 1790. "Louisa: A Novel." *Massachusetts Magazine, or, Monthly Museum of Knowledge & Rational Entertainment* 2 (2): 78–82; 2 (3): 147–51.

PUBLICATION HISTORY: Sabina is a female author's pseudonym for a regular contributor to Isaiah Thomas's *Massachusetts Magazine*. Her career exemplifies an early stage of a writer's stardom. The name is probably borrowed from an early appearance of the pseudonym in the *Spectator* (1712). Sabina's readers dedicated poems to her and celebrated the writer as the "mistress of the moral tale." She contributed under numerous pseudonyms to magazines in Boston and New York. Besides "Louisa: A Novel," other important narratives for which she was held in high esteem by her readership are the story "Almira and Alonzo" (1789) and her contribution to the essay series "The Dreamer" (1789–90) in the *Massachusetts Magazine*.

that a female should be a good housewife, as well as an agreeable companion, rendered Louisa a useful member of society by instructing her in every domestick accomplishment. There was no employment in the family way, however servile, but what she was well acquainted with: She must know how to obey before she learnt to command; and in order to have business well performed by servants, a mistress must understand it herself.

The first time Louisa had occasion to practice that fortitude she had learned, was at the death of her mother. When Louisa was eighteen years old, she lost this excellent parent, and none ever felt a loss more severely. The gentle girl for a time gave a loose to sorrow, and shed a torrent of tears; but when she saw a father sinking under his own misfortunes, lamenting his separation from the loved companion of his life, she bade her heart to cease its throbbing, and bowed submission to the stroke; and by her constant attention, her unwearied endeavours to sooth her father's grief, and calm the anguish of his heart, she taught him almost to forget the wife he had lost, in the contemplation of her daughter's virtues.

Louisa managed the family in her mother's room; and her conduct was so just, so highly commendable, that she became the object of universal esteem: But scarcely had she begun to smile with serenity and innocence, when her remaining parent was taken off by an apoplexy.[12] Judge, ye daughters of sensibility—judge what must be her emotions, and lend a tear to Louisa's woes! At first she sunk beneath them—she felt herself alone—she looked with horrour and anguish upon every object around her; but she saw not a father to protect her through the maze of life, nor an indulgent mother to guide her in the paths of rectitude.

The reverend Evander[13] and his amiable companion contributed not a little to raise the dejected fair one; they had long lived in the neighbourhood, and been the sincere friends of her departed parents; this endeared them, this rendered them revered and respected by Louisa; she attended to their advice, and Evander settled her affairs, and kept every thing that might perplex her from her knowledge. She was mistress of the mansion she lived in, and had about four thousand pounds in money, besides a large farm that was around the house. Louisa settled a little plan for her conduct; she regained her cheerfulness, and became satisfied with the decrees of Providence; and her poor neighbors had every day reason to bless her generosity and humanity.

She became acquainted, by accident, with Pallador;[14] he was a worthy young man, possessed of an affluent fortune that was at his own disposal; had received a good education, and was pleasing in his person. Their sentiments were similar, and it was not long before their hearts formed the tenderest and most interesting emotions in favour of each other. Pallador persuaded and pressed with all the energy of a youthful lover to be made happy; and Louisa, convinced his passion was sincere, and certain of his merit, could not deny his entreaties. As far removed from a prude as from a coquette, she had not a sensation that virtue blushed to own, and by the advice of Evander, gave him her hand about a year after the death of her father. They removed to town as soon as the marriage knot was tied, and soon became the happiest pair in the circle of their acquaintance. Their felicity received an addition the second year of their marriage by the birth of a little daughter. Their infant Elvira soon became the delight of Pallador, and the darling of Louisa. Every day was ushered in by a succession of rational amusements; their affability pleased all their acquaintance, while their liberality taught the hearts of the poor to sing for joy. But alas! how transient is human felicity—how variable is the lot of mortals!—of this, Louisa is a striking proof.

Pallador's affairs became distressed by the villainy of a man who pretended that Pallador's father had defrauded him of large sums of money. The man commenced a lawsuit against him, and by the chicanery and subterfuges of law, involved him in difficulty. By corrupting of evidences, he gained his case, and deprived Pallador of every acre he possessed. The expenses he had been at had drained his purse, and his wife's ready money was spent in the vain pursuit of what was already gone. Pallador possessed a feeling heart, and he looked with horror upon the state to which he was reduced. He caught Louisa to his breast with agony, and looked with distress upon his little Elvira; he exclaimed that he had ruined the best of women, and complained of his hard lot in terms forcible and tender. The behaviour of his wife bespoke the soul of Louisa; she viewed him with sympathy, and endeavoured to render his situation more agreeable, and to sooth the anguish of his heart. She represented with all the oratory of female eloquence, with all pathos of expressive tenderness, that happiness did not consist in affluence; that she could not be poor while her Pallador lived, and while the blessing of health bloomed on the cheek of Elvira; that contentment, love, and a farm, was sufficient; and as they were possessed of these, she did not doubt they should experience more real felicity in retirement than they ever could in the noise and bustle of a town. Thus persuaded, thus caressed, Pallador again became calm, and blessed the day that gave him Louisa; he prepared to follow her advice, and every thing was made ready for the country. They were universally beloved; even adversity had not cooled the friendship of many, and not a few offered to provide some post for Pallador. But a state of dependance was what he could not bear; he preferred freedom to gaiety, and left the metropolis with less uneasiness than he expected. Any one, to have seen Louisa, would have supposed her removal a matter of choice. Far from being depressed by the necessity, she kept up her spirits, and though calculated to shine in a publick life, though qualified to make a figure in the highest station, though in the bloom of youth, she left those scenes of vivacity with smiles of affability. When they arrived at Louisa's paternal seat, the neighbours all assembled to see and welcome them, to express their joy at their return, and sorrow for misfortunes that could not be avoided. There is something truly teaching in expressions of rustick sympathy; it touched the hearts of Louisa and Pallador, and they strove to deserve the good will of those worthy but uncultivated souls. Evander was not the last to pay his respects and testify his affections; a social intercourse was soon established between the families. This state would have been quite agreeable to Louisa, if it could have pleased her husband; but an ambition to shine in courts, and to appear in scenes of gaiety and festivity, had taken possession of his mind; retirement became disgusting; solitude was irksome; even Louisa, though not less beloved, became less pleasing. A languor[15] seized his spirits, and a decline soon followed, and in a few months the physicians pronounced his disorder incurable. It was now that Louisa felt the full force of all her troubles; she watched his bed with unceasing assiduity; she hung over him with inconceivable distress; her soul grew sick with anguish, and was harrowed up with trembling expectations; but even hope deserted her; yet she kept her distressing forebodings concealed when in his presence, lest it should affect him; but it was vain, and vain was every aid that was administered; he languished four months, and fell a prey to his misfortunes. "Be comforted, my Louisa, (said the dying husband) be resigned to the decree that takes me from you; be attentive to your life and health, for our daughter's sake." "Speak not of comfort, (replied she) I am deaf to every ray of hope—I do not wish to be happy—I dismiss the phantom expectation. Oh my husband!—Oh my Pallador! Must I outlive you—must I lose you? I survived the best of parents—I murmured not at the will of Heaven—I was deprived of fortune, and I smiled at the occurrence; but must I be deprived of what is dearer than all?" Here her sorrows grew unutterable—she wept not—she spake not—a dead calm, a distressing silence—all the agony of misery burst upon her, when she beheld her husband a corps[e] before her. The soul of Pallador had fled and left the worn out form; the spirit had ceased to animate the clay, and Louisa was a widow; a word that in my opinion, connects every idea of wretchedness, and conveys the very energy of sorrow, the very emphasis of woe. Ye daughters of misfortune, who have wept the lover and the friend; who have seen the husband of your youth, the dear object of your fondest wishes, pale and cold before you; who have one dismal moment beheld yourselves and infant offspring deprived of your protectors; it is to you this page is dedicated; it is you that can feel her woes; and, ye souls of sensibility, it is not necessary to describe the scene; your fancies have already formed the interesting, distressing group, and you have "lent the sigh to sorrows not your own."

Louisa was seized with a violent fever, that had well nigh proved fatal, and recovered by slow degrees. The good Evander was constantly with her, and strove by lessons of piety and patience to support her under her afflictions; and though it was some time before she recovered her health, it was longer before she had any spirits. The attention of Evander and his amiable wife, the noble fortitude of her disposition, her affability, the playful innocence of her daughter, all helped to dissipate her melancholy; the lenient hand of time poured balm and oil into her wounded heart, and her duty taught her to be resigned.

Eighteen months had now passed since the death of Pallador, and not a day had fled, but she had bedewed with a tear for his virtues, and a sigh to his memory. Her circumstances were not straitened, but they were limited; she was frugal from inclination and habit; she was liberal from principle; in being so she gratified the darling purity and delicate feelings of her soul; and when she relieved the distressed, she felt herself happier and richer. It is true she could not give according to her inclination, but she gave to the extent of her ability; and she gave freely and without ostentation; she taught her wants to be limited by her fortune; she loved to see others happy, and encouraged an innocent mirth.

A part of Louisa's little estate was bounded by the sea; a number of stately oaks and lofty pines concealed it from view; but the gentry[16] around used to walk or ride upon the beach, which was several miles in length at low water; it was entirely smooth and even, and the eye could here behold vessels of almost every nation passing and repassing, laden with the riches of the East, or the more necessary produce of America. At one end a small monument had been erected to the memory of two young men who were surprised here by a Moorish vessel, and died in slavery. But there was no reason for fears of this kind at present; peace had long been established between the lawless freebooters and the British nation.[17] Evander had been on a visit for a few days to a sister, who was confined by a languishing disorder, and supposed to be near her end. His wife sent, and desired Louisa and her little Elvira would spend the day with her; it was the first of September; the weather was remarkably fine; the day was spent very agreeably; we are loth[18] to part from scenes of pleasure. Louisa determined to tarry the evening; a servant had been sent home with the little girl at sun set, and the amiable Porsena and Louisa passed the evening in sociable and sensible chat. It was very pleasant, and at nine o'clock Louisa bid good night to her friend, and prepared to walk homeward unattended. The servant had not returned that carried Elvira home, and Louisa would not permit the maid to go home with her, as she was not fearful. Conscious of the goodness of her own heart, she suspected no evil from others. Vice is suspicious because it is vicious. Virtuous minds are not apt to be startled without they are really in danger; and even then virtue seldom shrinks. It was thus with Louisa; she walked alone, fearless, and surveying the beauties of the evening, she reflected how often she had walked there, leaning on the arm of her father or her husband; she felt the sigh rising in her bosom, and the tear stealing down her cheek; she did not suppress the one, or wipe off the other; but she took a kind of mournful pleasure in indulging the sensations that occasioned them. It was but the fourth part of a mile from Evander's to her house, to cross the field; but three times that distance round the beach to the avenue that led to her mansion; the grass was wet with the dew, and she chose the latter way as the most agreeable. She had got almost fronting her own dwelling, when she observed a vessel at anchor in the ocean, and a boat, rowed by four men, approaching the shore; an impulse of fear taught her to quicken her pace, and this was increased by seeing the men leap from the boat and pursue her. She ran up the avenue; they followed her; her fright deprived her of strength; she called aloud for help, and sunk panting to the ground. Her cries were in vain, her breath was lost, and the villains seized her, and conveyed her on board the boat that rowed towards the vessel. Louisa fainted when they first seized her, but their endeavours to lift her into the vessel awaked her from her swoon; she looked up and saw a parcel of men in strange habits[19] around her; this suggested to her the idea of her situation, and she relapsed into a second swoon.[20] It is now necessary to inform the reader, that this was an Algerine privateer, that was returning from an unsuccessful cruise, and had anchored to supply herself with water. The captain was sordid, and he was attached to women. When they saw Louisa, a supposition that she would be an acceptable present to him, induced them to seize her as abovementioned. Whatever sentiments the captain conceived of Louisa when he first saw her, his interest overcame them all, and that taught him to consider Louisa as a very valuable prize. The privateer had been fitted out by a noble Turk, whose name was Osmen. The natural abilities of his mind were good, and he had cultivated them with great care; he had learnt the different languages, and was polite and affable; not addicted to any vice, but promoting every virtue that he had any knowledge of; he indulged in sensuality, because it was customary; he was affluent; had hundreds of slaves employed about his gardens; his haram[21] was filled with the beauties of the east; almost every one thought it an honour to be noticed by him, and strove every thing to render themselves agreeable, and to give him pleasure. All but the fair Fatima;[22] she alone was disconsolate and unhappy; a Greek by birth, and a Christian by education; she had been a slave four months; her uncommon beauty had raised Osmen's admiration when first he beheld her; but Fatima's heart soon experienced the tender passion; she loved Osmen, and that love rendered her situation more dangerous than it would otherwise have been; she could not submit to his wishes, and her love was such she could give him no reason; it was with difficulty she denied him, but it was impossible for her to talk before him; she had sense, she had wit, and knew how to express it to others; to Osmen she was silent, and as a silent pensive beauty, Osmen admired her, and he ceased to solicit, till she should see fit to grant.

(*To be concluded in our next.)*

L O U I S A.—A NOVEL.

[Concluded from page 82.]

LET us now return to Louisa; she was left with the pirates in a swoon; as soon as she recovered, and saw the full extent of her misfortunes, she fell on her knees, and besought the Captain to return her to the shore: she offered him all she possessed; she intreated, she prayed, but it was vain. Hally,[23] for that was his name, was wedded to interest, and determined to pursue the path that led to it. How strange it is that any heart should be so calloused[24] to distressed virtue; he absolutely refused her. The first days of her captivity were almost a state of distraction; but it was silent; she was neither loud nor fretful in complaints. The Captain and the crew treated her with civility and respect; neither insult nor impropriety were offered to her, and every convenience that the vessel could afford, she was indulged with. She had now time to indulge the disagreeable feelings of her heart; and when she reflected that Providence ordered every thing; that it was wrong to repine, she endeavoured to resign herself to her fate, and to do nothing contrary to her conscience or honor, and leave the event to Heaven. Her bitterest moments were on account of Elvira; for her she shed many tears, and many to the memory of Pallador, who was always in her mind. By degrees she became calm; the Captain appeared to be a man of some capacity, and Louisa conversed with him upon a variety of subjects, and endeavoured to sooth her inquietude by informing herself of the customs and manners of the nations he had been among. The vessel's crew at first treated Louisa with respect, because that Hally commanded it; but a wish to render Louisa less unhappy arose in every breast, before she had been on board a week; they laid aside the natural ferocity of Turks, and became complaisant and obliging; so great is the influence of a virtuous and well educated female. They were four and twenty days performing their voyage, and at the end of that time arrived at Algiers. Hally immediately informed Osmen that he had brought an ornament to his Haram; and gave such a description of Louisa as raised his curiosity to see her; before her arrival, he was sunk in a state of tasteless apathy; every thing was unpleasing, or indifferent to him; he demanded Hally's price for his captive, and paid without reluctance. Louisa now became the slave of Osmen, and in that state we must now behold her; but her mind was neither depressed nor daunted; she rose above captivity, and triumphed over misfortunes; she absolutely refused to adorn herself in the magnificent apparel that was brought her; but put on a light mourning robe; in this dress she was conveyed to the Haram of Osmen, who waited with impatience to see her. A certain dignified grief sat upon her countenance; a calmness was diffused over her features, which were softened by misfortunes; she paid that respect to Osmen that she thought his due, as a person to whom heaven had given the power of directing her life. At present, Osmen, far from assuming the haughty master, thought he could not please his fair slave more, than to appear the gallant admirer, and immediately professed himself her lover, expecting compliance to every wish. But instead of this, he was astonished at the mortifying refusal that he received—at the fire and virtuous indignation that sparkled from her eyes; he retired, chagrined and affronted. But the next morning he renewed his visit, and renewed the proposal that had so offended her the evening before. "I am your slave, (said Louisa) but my mind is free; I will never be a slave to vice; guilt shall never stain my cheek with crimson, nor remorse torture my conscience. Command me to the most menial[25] employment, or the most laborious toil, and you shall see me fulfill my duty by my obedience. But my honor I will preserve; for know, Osmen, that I will not outlive it, and I trust the God I worship will not forsake it." Osmen saw she was fixed; he was surprised at the steady purpose of her soul, and admired her reliance on Providence; and a sentiment more respectful than love took possession of his soul; he began to revere her as a superiour being,[26] and promised solemnly to give her delicacy no further pain from his passion. From this time Louisa was calm, and waited in firm reliance, that the Being she served would one day deliver her from captivity, and restore her to her daughter, for whom she felt every pang of maternal affection.

The happiness of a state of felicity receives an increase by the participation of friendship; and the same divine flame is capable of lessening the severest troubles. Louisa found a solace for her afflictions in the company of Fatima; of all the ladies in the Haram, she alone possessed those virtues that are requisite to constitute a sincere and lasting friendship; the rest were light, vain, trifling and frivolous, incapable of thought or reflection; they sang, danced, laughed, and partook of every amusement that a state of confinement could afford. Fatima and Louisa mingled sorrows, and by a reciprocal confidence softened the afflictions of each other's hearts. Louisa strengthened Fatima's principles, and inspired her with a fortitude that she wanted; while Fatima's hapless love was a beautiful lesson to Louisa, and taught her that there was a possibility of her being more wretched than she was; she had not a fatal passion to combat with, and the evils of captivity were not embittered by any emotions that were inconsistent with reason or virtue. Not a day passed, in which Osmen did not visit the Haram, not from the motives that formerly drew him there, but to refine his understanding, and improve his mind with Louisa's conversation. Fatima was always of the party, and by degrees she gained courage to say some things that shewed Osmen her mind was as amiable as her person was lovely. One day as they were seated in a terrace that overlooked a vast extent of country, Osmen gave his fair hearers an account of the laws and customs of his nation; and Louisa in return informed him of the manners of the British. One subject brought on another, and at length the revolution and independence of America became the theme. I am no politician said Louisa; it is I think quite out of the female line to be of any party; I revere virtue wherever I see it, and love the good and the noble soul as well in the uncultivated African, as in the polished European. I know little of the revolution; but I love, revere, and esteem their illustrious chief.[27] He is, continued she, brave, gentle and generous; he is prudent, valiant, and discreet; he is a faithful friend, the best of husbands, and the parent of all around him; he unites the polite courtier with the learned politician, and the famous warriour with the gentle characteristicks of peace. While she made this eulogium on a character so revered, Osmen listened with attention; reflected, and he admired what he wished to imitate. I am brave, said he—my country acknowledge it; I am kind to my servants; but does it become a man to keep his fellow creatures in bondage? I endeavor to make their bonds easy; but still it is slavery; the godlike man, Louisa has mentioned, has, it is said, been fighting for liberty, while I detain as captives, hundreds that have as good a right to liberty as I; he is a tender husband, and experiences every pleasure that the caresses of an amiable woman who loves him from principle and inclination can give. But I can never know such soft endearments; can the caresses of captives give pleasure to a soul? can the false blandishments of women who are confined, and who perhaps would prefer the meanest of my slaves to me, give any satisfaction to the mind? In these and other reflections he passed the night; and in the morning, renewed his visit to the Haram. As he entered the apartment, the ladies were seated together opposite the door; he thought he never saw them look so lovely; the conversation turned upon the tender passion and Louisa gave so sweet a description of the happiness of a married life, when two tender hearts are inspired by the same flame, that Osmen was touched to the soul; and Fatima bursting into tears, hid her blushing face in Louisa's bosom. There is something in beauty in distress, that affects the most obdurate heart; and while Fatima discovered new beauties by her sensibility, he expressed his sorrow for her troubles, and begged in the strongest terms to be made acquainted with her griefs, that he might endeavour to remove them. A consciousness of her affection put it out of her power to speak—and to hide her sentiments she left the room. As soon as she was gone, Louisa availed herself of Osmen's present sentiments, and informed him of Fatima's many struggles, and tenderness towards him. Pleased and astonished to find himself an object of real love, he left Louisa—but not till she had discovered his sentiments were favourable to her friend.

He left Louisa to advise with the noble spirited Alphonso, who was a slave, though he felt not bondage. Osmen was his generous master, and all he required of him was to be his friend. Alphonso was an Englishman, with an accomplished person, an affluent fortune, and a thousand virtues. He felt a load of affliction without repining,[28] he had lost an amiable wife and an infant daughter, about a year before the period of which I am speaking. Grief for their death rendered every place irksome—and a hope to dissipate his melancholy, suggested the idea of travelling. After visiting France, he embarked for Spain, and in going from thence to Leghorn[29] in an American vessel, he was taken prisoner, and carried to Algiers. Generous hearts, and noble souls, are congenial,[30] and claim acquaintance at first meeting, though the most different corners of the globe, had given them birth, Osmen became the purchaser of Alphonso, and found no price too great to purchase such a friend, and it was to him he repaired; told all that had passed between Louisa, Fatima and himself; and mentioned every doubt that arose in his mind. It is easy to imagine what advice Alphonso gave him; fired with a curiosity to see his amiable countrywoman, and behold the female whose virtues had wrought such a change in Osmen's bosom, Alphonso requested leave to converse with Louisa; this was granted the next day, and Osmen introduced him to the Haram. In that visit Alphonso was pleased with Louisa, and felt the melancholy of his heart dissipate in her presence. But how great was the surprise of Louisa, or the joy of Fatima, when Osmen told them, that it was his intention to alter his manner of living, and emancipate his slaves; to such as chose to stay in Algiers, he would give sufficient to support them, with liberty to marry the ladies of his Haram, if it was pleasing to them; to those that wished to visit their native land, he would give sufficient to carry them home, and would provide them a safe passage. "But," said he, "will not Fatima set the example? shall Osmen alone be wretched? or will she give him her hand, and in the sight of heaven, become his wife?" It is not easy to express Fatima's feelings. It is sufficient to say, that every thing was executed as had been planned. The ladies of the Haram were delighted with the thoughts of freedom; the men who had been unhappy in bondage, were rejoiced at liberty; many of these had connections at home; to these, Osmen provided the means of a quick return, with something to carry with them; those who had no families, preferred a connection with the smiling beauties of the east, were settled in some of Osmen's country seats, with every convenience of life. In a few weeks, the generous Osmen gave his hand to Fatima. This unexpected happiness had dissipated her melancholy, smiles of satisfaction were displayed upon her countenance, the roses of health revisited her cheek; she conversed with sprightliness, and Osmen was charmed with her good sense and affability. Alphonso and Louisa were present at the ceremony; at a recollection of former happiness, they shed tears, and were equally surprised at each others emotions. In a walk in one of Osmen's delightful gardens, Alphonso told Louisa the sorrows of his heart, and learnt the labyrinth through which she had passed with emotions of surprise and admiration; he was charmed with her virtues, with her unaffected goodness; and resolved to devote the remainder of his life to her. He informed Osmen of this resolution, who highly applauded it, and notwithstanding his reluctance to part with his European friends, he prepared them a passage to the Havannah, and sent two caskets of valuable jewels on board the ship; and with many tears, took leave of them, promising to visit them in England, with his Fatima, in the course of a year. After an agreeable passage, Alphonso and Louisa

arrived at Bacelona, and finding a ship ready to sail for Portsmouth, in England, went directly on board, and soon got safe to the place. That very day they arrived, Alphonso procured a post chaise, and set out for the place of Louisa's residence; it was several hundred miles, and they were six days performing the journey. In the course of that time, and the preceding voyage, they became fully acquainted with each other; similiar merit produced the strongest friendship, and ripened into the tenderest affection. Louisa promised if her daughter was still alive, to connect herself with Alphonso. She had been absent a year; and the last day's journey was filled with anxiety as well as hope; they stopped at the worthy parson's, who was astonished to see her, having been fully convinced that Louisa was drowned, and carried off by the tide, the night she was missing. Elvira had been with this worthy couple ever since, and had enjoyed uninterrupted health; she instantly knew her mamma. It is unnecessary to add more, except that Alphonso and Louisa were married, after Alphonso had settled a handsome fortune on Elvira, to whose education he pays every attention. He likewise settled a handsome annuity[31] upon Evander; and after rendering every neighbour around them happy, they set out for Alphonso's seat, where they still live patterns of virtue and fidelity; and blessings to all around them.
SABINA.

MIGRANT FICTIONS

[NICHOLAS BRICAIRE DE LA DIXMERIE]

*AZAKIA: A CANADIAN STORY (1783)**

THE ancient inhabitants of Canada were, strictly speaking, all savages. Nothing proves this better than the destiny of some Frenchmen, who first arrived in this part of the world. They were eaten by the people, whom they pretended to humanize and polish.

* SOURCE: [Nicholas Bricaire de la Dixmerie]. 1783. "Azakia: A Canadian Story." *Universal Magazine of Knowledge & Pleasure* 72 (500): 59–63.
PUBLICATION HISTORY: "Azakia: Anecdotes Huronnes" first appeared in volume 2 of Nicholas Bricaire de la Dixmerie's *Contes philosophique et moraux* (Paris 1765, 187–209). An English translation appeared under the title "Azakia: A Canadian Story" in the London-based *Universal Magazine of Knowledge & Pleasure* (1783), which was reprinted by Matthew Carey in his *The American Museum* in 1789. In 1784 a first German translation was printed in *Hannoverisches Magazin* 21 (March 12): 322–36, acknowledging the *Universal Magazine* as its source. This trans-

New attempts were more successful. The savages were driven into the inner parts of the continent; treaties of peace, always ill observed, were concluded with them; but the French found means to create in them wants which made their yoke necessary to them. Their brandy and tobacco easily effected what their arms might have operated with greater difficulty. Confidence soon became mutual, and the forests of Canada were frequented with as much freedom by the new inmates as by the natives.

These forests were often also resorted to by the married and unmarried savage women, whom the meeting of a Frenchman put into no terrors. All these women for the most part are handsome, and certainly their beauty owes nothing to the embellishments of art; much less has it any influence on their conduct. Their character is naturally mild and flexible, their humour gay; they laugh in the most agreeable and winning manner. They have a strong propensity to love; a propensity which a maiden in this country may yield to, and always indulges without scruple, and without fearing the least reproach. It is not so with a married woman: she must be intirely devoted to him she has married; and what is not less worthy of notice, she punctually fulfils this duty.

An heroine of this class, and who was born among the Hurons,[32] one day happened to wander in a forest that lay contiguous to the grounds they inhabited. She was surprised by a French soldier, who did not trouble himself to enquire whether she was a wife or a maiden. Besides, he found himself little disposed to respect the right of a Huron husband. The shrieks of the young savage in defending herself brought to the same place the Baron of St. Castins, an Officer in the troops of Canada. He had no difficulty to oblige the soldier to depart, but the person he had so opportunely saved had so many engaging charms, that the soldier appeared excusable to him. Being himself tempted to sue for the reward of the good office he had just rendered, he pleaded his cause

lation was reprinted in *Der Neuschottländische Kalender auf das Jahr 1788*, an almanac printed in Halifax, Canada, without page numbers. The story circulated widely in American and English magazines: 1783. *Hibernian Magazine, or, Compendium of Entertaining Knowledge* (March): 128–32; 1789. *The American Museum, or Repository of Ancient and Modern Fugitive Pieces* 6 (September): 193–98; 1792. *The Bee: or Literary Weekly Intelligencer* 7 (February 1): 180–87; (February 8): 220–23; 1794. *The Monthly Magazine; or, Vermont Magazine* 1 (May): 62–65; 1 (June): 132–35; 1797. *The New-York Magazine, or Literary Repository* 2 (1): 31–37; 1798. *The Dessert to the True American* 1 (3): n.p.; 1 (3): n.p.; 1803. *Village Magazine* 1 (19): 73–76; 1804. *Philadelphia Repository and Weekly Register* 4 (January 14): 9; 4 (January 21): 17. The story had a late print in 1816 in John Bell's *La Belle Assembleé; Being Bell's Court and Fashionable Magazine* in January and *New-York Weekly Museum* 25 (October): n.p. Adaptations of the story can be found in Sarah Wentworth Morton's *Quâbi: or, The Virtues of Nature. An Indian Tale. In Four Cantos. By Philenia, a Lady from Boston* (1790) and Jacques Grasset de Saint-Sauveur *Hortense, ou la jolie courtisane* (1796).

in a more gentle and insinuating manner than the soldier, but did not succeed better. "The friend that is before my eyes hinders my seeing thee," said the Huron woman to him. This is the savage phrase for expressing that a woman has a husband, and that she cannot be wanting in fidelity to him. This phrase is not a vain form; it contains a peremptory refusal; it is common to all the women of those barbarous nations; and its force the neighbourhood of the Europeans and their example were never able to diminish.

St. Castins, to whom the language and customs of the Hurons were familiar, saw immediately that he must drop all pretensions; and this persuasion recalled all his generosity. He therefore made no other advances than to accompany the beautiful savage, whom chance alone had directed into the wood, and who was afraid of new rencounters. As they passed on, he received all possible marks of gratitude, except that which he at first requested.

Some time after St. Castins, being insulted by a brother Officer, killed him in a duel. This Officer was nephew to the General-governor of the colony, and the Governor was as absolute as vindictive. St. Castins had no other resource than to betake himself to flight. It was presumed that he had retired among the English of New-York; which, indeed, was very probable; but, persuaded that he should find an equally safe asylum among the Hurons, he gave them the preference.

The desire of seeing again Azakia, which was the name of the savage he had relieved, contributed greatly to determine him in that choice. She knew immediately her deliverer. Nothing could equal her joy at this unexpected visit, and she declared it as ingenuously as before she had resisted his attacks. The savage, whose wife she was, and whose name was Ouabi, gave St. Castins the same reception, who acquainted him of the motive of his flight. "May the great Spirit be praised, for having brought thee among us, replied the Huron! This body," added he, laying his hand on his bosom, "will serve thee as a shelter for defence, and this head-breaking hatchet will put to flight, or strike dead thy enemies. My hut shall be thine: thou shalt always see the bright star of the day appear and leave us, without any thing being wanting to thee, or any thing being able to hurt thee."

St. Castins declared to him that he absolutely desired to live as they did, that is, to bear a part in their labours and their wars; to abide by their customs; in short, to become a Huron; a resolution which redoubled Ouabi's joy. This savage held the first rank among his people; he was their grand Chief, a dignity which his courage and services had merited for him. There were other Chiefs under him, and he offered one of the places to St. Castins, who accepted of the rank only of a private warrior.

The Hurons were then at war with the Iroquois,[33] and were intent on forming some enterprise against them. St. Castins would fain make one in the expedition, and he fought as a true Huron; but was dangerously wounded. He was brought back with great difficulty to Ouabi's house on a kind of litter. At this sight Azakia appeared overwhelmed with grief, but, instead of vain lamentation, she exerted all possible care and assiduity[34] to be of service to him. Though she had several slaves[35] at command, she depended only on herself for what might contribute to the solace of her guest. Her activity equalled her solicitude. One would have said that it was a lover watching over the precious life of her beloved. Few could help drawing the most flattering consequences on such an occasion; and this was what St. Castins did. His desires and his hopes revived with his strength. One only point disconcerted his views, which was the services and attentions of Ouabi. Could he deceive him, without adding ingratitude to perfidy? But, said St. Castins, arguing the case with himself, the good-natured Ouabi is but a savage, and he cannot be so scrupulous herein as many of our good folks in Europe. This reason, which was no reason in fact, appeared very solid to the amorous Frenchman. He renewed his tender advances, and was surprised to meet with new refusals. "Stop! Celario (which was the savage name that was given to St. Castins;) stop," said Azakia to him; "the shivers of the rod which I have broke with Ouabi have not yet been reduced to ashes. A part remains still in his power, and another in mine. As long as they last, I am his, and cannot be thine." These words, spoke in a peremptory manner, quite disconcerted St. Castins. He dared not insist upon the matter farther, and fell into a melancholy reverie. Azakia was deeply affected by it. "What can I do?" said she to him; "I cannot become thy companion but by ceasing to become the companion of Ouabi; and I cannot quit Ouabi without causing in him the same sorrow thou feelest in thyself. Answer me, has he deserved it?"—"No!" cried out Celario, "no! he deserves to be intirely preferred before me; but I must abandon his dwelling. It is only by ceasing to see Azakia that I can cease to be ungrateful to Ouabi."

These words chilled with paleness the young savage's face: her tears flowed almost the same instant, and she did not endeavour to conceal them. "Ah! ungrateful Celario!" cried she, with sobs, and pressing his hands between her own; "is it true, ungrateful Celario! that thou hast a mind to quit those to whom thou art more than the light of the bright star of the day? What have we done to thee that thou shouldst leave us? Is any thing wanting to thee? Dost thou not see me continually by thy side as the slave that wants but the beck[36] to obey? Why wilt thou have Azakia die of grief? Thou canst not leave her without taking with thee her soul: she is thine, as her body is Ouabi's . . . . . . The entrance of Ouabi stopped the answer of St. Castins. Azakia still continued weeping, without restraining herself, without even hiding for a moment the cause. "Friend," said she to the Huron, "thou still seest Celario, thou seest him, and thou mayest speak to and hear him; but he will soon disappear from before thine eyes: he is going to seek after other friends." . . . "Other friends," cried the savage, almost as much alarmed as Azakia herself; "and what, dear Celario, what induces thee to tear thyself from our arms? Hast thou received here any injury, any damage? Answer me; thou knowest my authority in these parts. I swear to thee by the great Spirit, that thou shalt be satisfied and revenged."

This question greatly embarrassed St. Castins. He had no reasonable subject for complaint, and the true motive of his resolution ought to be absolutely unknown to Ouabi. There was a necessity of pretending some trivial and common reasons, which the good Ouabi found very ridiculous. "Let us speak of other things," added he; "to-morrow I set out on an expedition against the Iroquois, and this evening I give to our warriors the customary feast. Partake of this amusement, dear Celario." . . . "I am equally willing to partake of your dangers and labours," said St. Castins, interrupting him; "I shall accompany you in this new expedition."—"Thy strength would betray thy courage," replied the Huron Chief; "it is no great matter to know how to face death; thou shouldst be able to deal death among the enemy; thou shouldst be able to pursue the enemy, if they are put to flight, and thou shouldst be able to fly thyself, if they be an over match. Such were at all times our warlike maxims. Think now therefore only on getting thyself cured, and taking care of this habitation during my absence, which I confide to thee." It was in vain for St. Castins to make a reply. The warriors soon assemble, and the feast begins. It was scarce over when the troops marched off, and St. Castins remained more than ever exposed to the charms of Azakia.

It is certain that this young savage loved her guest, and loved him with a love purely ideal, without doubting that it was such a love. She even took a resolution which others who loved as she did certainly would not have taken, which was to procure for St. Castins the opportunity of obtaining from another what herself had obstinately refused him. The charms of the rival she gave herself were well calculated to attract his regards. She was but eighteen years old, was very handsome, and, which was not less necessary, was still a virgin. It has been before observed, that a maiden enjoys full liberty among the North American Indians. St. Castins, encouraged by Azakia, had divers conferences with Zisma, which was the name of this young Huron lady, and in a few days he could read in her eyes that she would be less severe than his friend. It is not known whether he profited of the discovery: at least it did not make him forget Azakia, who, on her side, seemed to have no inclination to be forgotten. St. Castins felt himself, notwithstanding all his interior struggles, more attracted towards her. An incident, which everywhere else might have contributed to unite them, had like to have separated them for ever.

They were informed by some runaways, who had made more speed than others, that Ouabi had fallen into an ambuscade of the Iroquois, that he had lost some of his party, and that he himself was left on the field of battle. This news filled St. Castins with true sorrow. His generosity made him set aside all views of interest. He forgot, that in losing a friend he found himself rid of a rival. Besides, the death of this rival might also occasion that of Azakia. Her life, from that moment, depended on the caprice of a dream. Such was the force of a superstitious custom, sacred from time immemorial among these people. If, in the space of forty days, a widow, who had lost her husband, sees and speaks to him twice successively in a dream, she infers from thence that he wants her in the region of souls, and nothing can dispense with her from putting herself to death.

Azakia had resolved to obey this custom, if the double dream took place.[37] She sincerely regretted Ouabi; and though St. Castins gave her cause for other sorrows if she was to die, the prevalency of the custom had the ascendant over inclination. It is not easy to express the inquietudes, the terrors that tormented the lover of this beautiful and credulous Huron. Every night he fancied her a prey to those sinister visions; and every morning he accosted[38] her with fear and trembling. At length he found her preparing a mortal draught: it was the juice of a root of the citron-tree; a poison which in that country never fails of success. "Thou seest, dear Celario," said Azakia to him, "thou seest the preparation for the long journey which Ouabi has ordered me to make" . . . "Oh Heavens!" said St. Castins, interrupting her, "how can you believe in a foolish dream, a frivolous and deceitful delusion?" "Stop, Celario," replied the Huron, "thou deceivest thyself Ouabi appeared to me last night; he took me by the hand, and ordered me to follow him. The weight of my body opposed his order. Ouabi withdrew with a mournful countenance. I called him back, and the only answer he gave me, was to stretch out his arms to me, and he afterwards disappeared. He will return without doubt, dear Celario; I must obey him, and after bewailing thy hard lot I will swallow this draught, which will lull my body into the sleep of death; and then I will go and rejoin Ouabi in the abode of Souls."

This discourse quite dismayed St. Castins. He spoke against it every thing that reason, grief, and love could suggest to him most convincing; nothing seemed to be so to the young savage. She wept, but persevered in her design. All that the disconsolate Celario could obtain from her was by supposing, that, though Ouabi should appear to her a second time in a dream, she would wait, before she put herself to death, to be assured of his; of which St. Castins was resolved to know the truth as soon as possible.

The savages neither exchange nor ransom their prisoners! contenting themselves to rescue them out of the enemy's hands whenever they can. Sometimes the conqueror destines his captives to slavery; and he oftener puts them to death. Such are particularly the maxims of the Iroquois. There was therefore reason to presume, that Ouabi had died of his wounds, or was burnt by that barbarous nation. Azakia believed it to be so more than any other; but St. Castins would have her at least doubt of it. On his side, he re-animates the courage of the Hurons, and proposes a new enterprise against the enemy. It is approved of. They deliberate upon electing a Chief, and all voices unite in favour of St. Castins, who had already given proofs of his valour and conduct. He departs with his troop, but not till after he had again Azakia's word that, notwithstanding all the dreams she might yet have, she would defer, at least till his return, the doleful journey she had designed to take.

This expedition of the Huron warriors was attended with all imaginable success. The Iroquois believed them to be too much weakened, or too discouraged to think of undertaking any thing, and themselves were on their march to come and attack them; but they were no way cautious how they proceeded. It was not so with St. Castins's band of warriors. He had dispatched some of his people to reconnoitre. They discovered the enemy without being seen by them, and returned to give advice thereof to their Chief. The ground was found very fit for lying in ambuscade; and the Hurons availed themselves so well of it, that the Iroquois saw themselves hemmed in, when they believed they had no risque to run. They were charged with a fury that left them no time to know where they were. Most of them were killed on the spot; and the remainder maimed or grievously wounded. The Hurons march off directly to the next village, and surprise the Iroquois assembled there. They were going to enjoy the spectacle of seeing a Huron burnt; and already the Huron was beginning to sing his death song. This no savage, whom the enemy is ready to put to death, ever fails to do. Loud cries, and a shower of musket balls, soon dispersed this curious multitude. Both the fugitives, and those that faced about to resist, were killed. All the savage ferocity was fully displayed. In vain St. Castins endeavoured to stop the carnage. With difficulty he saved a small number of women and children. He was apprehensive particularly, that in the midst of this horrid tumult Ouabi himself was massacred, supposing he was still living, and was in that habitation. Full of this notion, he ran incessantly from one place to another. He perceived on a spot where the battle still continued a prisoner tied to a stake, and having all about him the apparatus of death; that is, combustibles for burning him by a slow fire. The Chief of the Hurons flies to this wretched captive, break his bonds, knows him, and embraces him with transports of joy. It was Ouabi.

This brave savage had preferred the loss of his life to that of his liberty. He was scarce cured of his wounds, when life was offered him on the condition of remaining a slave; but he had chosen death, determined to procure it, if refused to him. The Iroquois were a people that would spare him that trouble; and, one moment later, his companions could not have saved him.

After having dispersed or made slaves of the remains of the Iroquois in that quarter, the Huron army marched home. St. Castins wanted to give up the command of it to Ouabi, which he refused. On the way, he informed him of Azakia's purpose to die, persuaded that he was not alive, and that he required her to follow him; he acquainted him also of the poison she had prepared on that account, and of the delay he had obtained from her with great difficulty. He spoke with a tenderness and emotion that deeply affected the good Ouabi, who called to mind some things he did not much attend to at the time, but he then let him know nothing of what he intended. They arrive. Azakia, who had another dream, fancied this return as the signal of her fate. But how great was her surprise to see in the number of the living the husband she was going to meet in the abode of Spirits! At first she remained motionless and mute; but her joy soon expressed itself by lively caresses and long discourses. Ouabi received the one, and interrupted the others. Afterwards addressing himself to St. Castins: "Celario," said he, "thou hast saved my life, and what is still dearer to me, thou hast twice preserved to me Azakia. She therefore belongs more to thee than to me. I belong to thee myself. See whether she be enough to acquit us both. I yield her to thee through gratitude, but would not have yielded her to deliver myself from the fire kindled by the Iroquois."

What this discourse made St. Castins feel is hard to be expressed, not that it seemed so ridiculous and strange to him as it might to many Europeans: he knew that divorces were very frequent among the savages. They separate as easily as they come together. But, persuaded that Azakia could not be yielded up to him without a supernatural effort, he believed himself obliged to evince equal generosity. He refused what he desired most, and refused in vain; Ouabi's perseverance in his resolution was not to be conquered. As to the faithful Azakia, who had been seen to resist all St. Castins's attacks, and to refuse surviving the husband whom she believed dead, it might perhaps be expected that she would long hold out against the separation her husband had proposed to her. This she made not the least objection against. She had hitherto complied only with her duty; and thought she was free to listen to her inclination, since Ouabi required it of her. The pieces of the rod of Union were brought forth, put together, and burnt. Ouabi and Azakia embraced each other for the last time, and from that moment the young and beautiful Huron was reinstated in all the rights of a maiden. It is also said, that by the help of some missionaries, St. Castins put her in a condition of becoming his wife according to the rules prescribed to Christians. Ouabi, on his side, broke the rod with the young Zisma; and these two marriages, so different in the form, were equally happy. Each husband, well assured that there were no competitors, forgot that there had been any predecessors.

ANONYMOUS

*The CHILD of SNOW (1792)**

AN active and industrious merchant, had occasion often to be abroad for a considerable time together, in the pursuit of his traffick. During one of his voyages, which lasted for more than two years, it happened that his wife became enamoured of a young neighbour. Love, which is restrained with difficulty, soon brought them together; but they managed their affairs in so bungling[39] a manner, that at the expiration of about nine months, the merchant's wife found

* SOURCE: Anonymous. 1792. "The Child of Snow." *Massachusetts Magazine, or, Monthly Museum of Knowledge and Rational Entertainment* 4 (12): 718–19.
PUBLICATION HISTORY: The subject matter of the story and the first Latin version can be found in an eleventh-century Cambridge collection of songs, *The Carmina Cantabrigensia*. One of the songs, the "Modus Liebinc," has become known as the snow child sequence. The story of a merchant's unfaithful wife emerged out of South German folk traditions. A French version of the story appeared in Pierre Jean-Baptiste Legrand d'Aussy's collection of thirteenth-century French tales under the title *Fabliaux ou contes des douzième et treizième siècles, traduits ou extraits d'après les manuscrits* (Paris, 1779). A first English translation was published in London in 1786, titled *Tales of the Twelfth and Thirteenth Century. From the French of Mr. Le Grand*. A first American appearance was in the *Charleston Morning Post and Daily Advertiser* in 1787 under the title "The Child Melted by the Sun." The story appeared in twelve newspapers in 1787 (South Carolina, Massachusetts, Connecticut, New Jersey, Pennsylvania, New York); there are three appearances for 1790 (Rhode Island, New York, South Carolina) and two for 1800 (Massachusetts, Vermont). The final publication was in 1818: *Boston Weekly Magazine and Ladies' Miscellany* 2 (31): 122–23.

herself for the first time a mother. The husband, on his return, was greatly surprised to find this acquisition to his family, and asked his wife to what accident they were indebted for it.—"Sir," said she, "I happened one day to be reclined above stairs at the window, giving vent to my grief for your absence. It was in the winter season, and there was at the time a heavy fall of snow. As I cast up my streaming eyes to heaven, and heaved a sigh on thinking of you, a flake of snow accidently made its way into my mouth, and I immediately found that I had conceived this child whom you now see."

The merchant on hearing this story, did not betray the least symptoms of discontent or ill humour. "Thanks be to God," said he; "I have wished for an heir, and he has sent me one: I am satisfied and thankful for his bounty." He, indeed thenceforward, affected the most entire satisfaction, never offered the least reproach to his wife, but lived in the same good understanding with her as before. Nevertheless this was all dissimulation—he had formed inwardly a resolution to be one day or another amply revenged.

The child, however, grew up, and had attained the age of fifteen, when the merchant, who was still occupied with his project of revenge, thought seriously of putting it into execution. –"Wife," said he one day, "you must not be afflicted, if I once more take my leave of you for a time. I am going upon a long journey to morrow; and I desire you will get ready my baggage, and that of my son: For I mean to take him with me, that he may acquire some knowledge of trading while he is young." "Alas!" replied the mother, "I am much grieved to hear that you are going to take him abroad so soon; but since it is for your satisfaction and his advantage, I submit. God be with you both, and bring you back in safety." Matters being thus arranged, the merchant set off early next morning; and took the Child of Snow along with him.

It is needless to give the particulars of the journey, or an account of the countries through which he passed. It is enough to mention, that on his arrival in Genoa, he found a Saracen[40] merchant bound for Alexandria, to whom he sold the boy as a slave. Afterwards having settled his own affairs at leisure, he returned home.

The imagination of a hundred poets combined would not give you an adequate description of the distraction of the mother, when she saw the merchant return without her son. She tore her hair, and fell into a fit of phrenzy.[41] At length having recovered herself, she conjured her husband to tell her without reserve what had happened to the youth. The husband expected all this uproar; and therefore was not puzzled for an answer. "Wife," said he "one cannot arrive to my age, without having had experience enough in the world, to know the necessity of reconciling one's self to whatever may happen. For what do we gain by giving way to our affliction? Listen with fortitude to the misfortune that happened to us in the country whence I come. Your son and myself were, on a sultry day, climbing up a steep and lofty mountain. It was about noon, the sun was vertical over our heads and burned like fire. When, behold, on a sudden, your son began to dissolve, and melted before my eyes! I would have offered him assistance, but knew that it would be vain; for I recollected that you told me he sprang out of a flake of snow."

The wife knew perfectly well the merchant's meaning. She durst not, however, break out, but was obliged to swallow the liquor which she had brewed.

SENSATIONALISM

ANNA [PSEUDONYM]

*An Account of a Murder Committed by Mr. J.—Y—, Upon His Family, in December, A.D. 1781 (1796)**

To the EDITOR of the NEW-YORK WEEKLY MAGAZINE.

SIR,

the inclosed Account I transmit to you for publication, at the particular request of a friend, who is well acquainted with the circumstances that gave rise to it.—It is drawn up by a female hand, and she here relates respecting Mr. Y— what she knew of him herself, and what she had heard of him in her father's family,

* SOURCE: Anna [pseud.]. 1796. "An Account of a Murder Committed by Mr. J.—Y—, Upon His Family, in December, A.D. 1781." *The New-York Weekly Magazine; or, Miscellaneous Repository* 2 (55): 20; 2 (56): 28.

PUBLICATION HISTORY: The story was probably written by the writer and political activist Margaretta Faugeres (1771–1801), the daughter of Ann Eliza Bleecker (1752–1783). Faugeres amalgamates two stories of lurid family murder. In 1781, James Yates, an upstate New York farmer, murdered his family; Faugeres knew about his case through her family's history, since Yates was under arrest in Bleecker's house before he was sent off to prison in Albany. Another source is Judge Stephen Mix Mitchell's *A Narrative of the Life of William Beadle, of Weathersfield. . . . The Particulars of the "Horrrid Massacre" of Himself and Family* (Hartford 1783). The magazine version heavily borrows from Beadle's narrative. Given the fact that Charles Brockden Brown was on close terms with some members of the Bleecker family, he knew about the story, which became a source of inspiration for his novel *Wieland; or, The Transformation. An American Tale.* New York, 1798. The story was twice reprinted: 1796. *The Philadelphia Minerva* 2 (81): n.p.; 2 (82): n.p.; 1797. *South-Carolina Weekly Museum and Complete Magazine of Entertainment and Intelligence* 1 (July): 813–16.

where he had been an occasional visitant; as I have no reason to believe that this transaction has ever appeared in print, you will be pleased to give it a place among your original compositions.

ANNA.

NEW-YORK, *May 17, 1796.*

AN ACCOUNT
OF A MURDER COMMITTED BY MR. J.—Y—, UPON HIS FAMILY,
IN DECEMBER, A.D. 1781

THE unfortunate subject of my present essay, belonged to one of the most respectable families in this state; he resided a few miles from Tomhanick,[42] and though he was not in the most affluent circumstances, he maintained his family (which consisted of a wife and four children,) very comfortably.—From the natural gentleness of his disposition, his industry, sobriety, probity and kindness, his neighbours universally esteemed him, and until the fatal night when he perpetrated the cruel act, none saw cause of blame in him.

In the afternoon preceding that night, as it was Sunday and there was no church near, several of his neighbours with their wives came to his house for the purpose of reading the scripture and singing psalms; he received them cordially, and when they were going to return home in the evening, he pressed his sister and her husband, who came with the others, to stay longer; at his very earnest solicitation they remained until near nine o'clock, during which time his conversation was grave as usual, but interesting and affectionate: to his wife, of whom he was very fond, he made use of more than commonly endearing expressions, and caressed his little ones alternately:—he spoke much of his domestic felicity, and informed his sister, that to render his wife more happy, he intended to take her to New-Hampshire the next day; "I have just been refitting my sleigh," said he, "and we will set off by day-break."—After singing another hymn, Mr. and Mrs. J—s—n departed.

"They had no sooner left us (said he upon his examination) than taking my wife upon my lap, I opened the Bible to read to her—my two boys were in bed—one five years old, the other seven;—my daughter Rebecca,[43] about eleven, was sitting by the fire, and my infant aged about six months, was slumbering at her mother's bosom.—Instantly a new light shone into the room, and upon looking up I beheld two Spirits, one at my right hand and the other at my left;—he at the left bade me destroy all my *idols*,[44] and begin by casting the Bible into the fire;—the other Spirit dissuaded me, but I obeyed the first, and threw the book into the flames. My wife immediately snatched it out, and was going to expostulate,[45] when I threw it in again and held her fast until it was entirely consumed:—then filled with the determination to persevere, I flew out of the house, and seizing an axe which lay by the door, with a few strokes demolished my sleigh, and running to the stable killed one of my horses—the other I struck, but with one spring he got clear of the stable.—My spirits now were high, and I hasted to the house to inform my wife of what I had done. She appeared terrified, and begged me to sit down; but the good angel whom I had obeyed stood by me and bade me go on, "You have more idols, (said he) look at your wife and children." I hesitated not a moment, but rushed to the bed where my boys lay, and catching the eldest in my arms, I threw him with such violence against the wall, that he expired without a groan!—his brother was still asleep—I took him by the feet, and dashed his skull in pieces against the fire-place!—Then looking round, and perceiving that my wife and daughters were fled, I left the dead where they lay, and went in pursuit of the living, taking up the axe again.—A slight snow had fallen that evening, and by its light I descried my wife running towards her father's (who lived about half a mile off) encumbered with her babe; I ran after her, calling upon her to return, but she shrieked and fled faster, I therefore doubled my pace, and when I was within thirty yards of her, threw the axe at her, which hit her upon the hip!—the moment that she felt the blow she dropped the child, which I directly caught up, and threw against the log-fence—I did not hear it cry—I only heard the lamentations of my wife, of whom I had now lost sight; but the blood gushed so copiously from her wound that it formed a distinct path along the snow. We were now within sight of her father's house, but from what cause I cannot tell, she took an opposite course, and after running across an open field several times, she again stopped at her own door; I now came up with her—my heart bled to see her distress, and all my *natural feelings* began to revive; I forgot my duty, so powerfully did her moanings and pleadings affect me, "Come then, my love (said I) we have one child left, let us be thankful for that—what is done is right—we must not repine, come let me embrace you—let me know that you do indeed love me." She encircled me in her trembling arms, and pressed her quivering lips to my cheek.—A voice behind me, said, "This is also an idol!"—I broke from her instantly, and wrenching a stake from the garden fence, with one stroke levelled her to the earth! and lest she should only be stunned, and might, perhaps, recover again, I repeated my blows, till I could not distinguish one feature of her face!!! I now went to look after my last sublunary treasure, but after calling several times without receiving any answer, I returned to the house again; and in the way back picked up the babe and laid it on my wife's bosom.—I then stood musing a minute—during which interval I thought I heard the suppressed sobbings of some one near the barn, I approached it in silence, and beheld my daughter Rebecca endeavouring to conceal herself among the hay-stacks.—

(To be concluded in our next.)

AN ACCOUNT OF A MURDER COMMITTED BY MR. J——Y——, UPON HIS FAMILY, IN DECEMBER, A.D. 1781.

(Concluded from page 20.)

AT the noise of my feet upon the dry corn stalks—she turned hastily round and seeing me exclaimed, "O father, my dear father, spare me, let me live—let me live,—I will be a comfort to you and my mother—spare me to take care of my little sister Diana[46]—do—do let me live."—She was my darling child, and her fearful cries pierced me to the soul—the tears of *natural pity* fell as plentifully down my cheeks, as those of terror did down her's, and methought that to destroy *all* my idols, was a hard task—I again relapsed at the voice of complaining; and taking her by the hand, led her to where her mother lay; then thinking that if I intended to retain her, I must make some other severe sacrifice, I bade her sing and dance—She complied, terribly situated as she was,—but I was not acting in the line of my duty—I was convinced of my error, and catching up a hatchet that stuck in a log, with one well aimed stroke cleft her forehead in twain—she fell—and no sign of retaining life appeared.

I then sat down on the threshold, to consider what I had best do—"I shall be called a murderer (said I) I shall be seized—imprisoned—executed, and for what?—for destroying my idols—for obeying the mandate of my father—no, I will put all the dead in the house together, and after setting fire to it, run to my sister's and say that Indians have done it—"I was preparing to drag my wife in, when the idea struck me that I was going to tell a *horrible lie*;" and how will that accord with my profession? (asked I.) No, let me speak the truth, and declare the good motive for my actions, be the consequences what they may."

His sister, who was the principal evidence against him, stated—that she had scarce got home, when a message came to Mr. J——n, her husband, informing him that his mother was ill and wished to see him; he accordingly set off immediately, and she not expecting him home again till the next day, went to bed—there being no other person in the house. About four in the morning she heard her brother Y——call her, she started up and bade him come in. "I will not (returned he) for I have committed the unpardonable sin I have burnt the

Bible." She knew not what to think, but rising hastily opened the door which was only latched, and caught hold of his hand: let me go, Nelly (said he) my hands are wet with blood—the blood of my Elizabeth[47] and her children.—She saw the blood dripping from his fingers, and her's chilled in the veins, yet with a fortitude unparalleled she begged him to enter, which—as he did, he attempted to seize a case knife, that by the light of a bright pine-knot fire, he perceived lying on the dresser—she prevented him, however, and tearing a trammel from the chimney, bound him with it to the bed post—fastening his hands behind him—She then quitted the house in order to go to his, which as she approached she heard the voice of loud lamentation, the hope that it was some one of the family who had escaped the effects of her brother's frenzy, subdued the fears natural to such a situation and time, she quickened her steps, and when she came to the place where Mrs. Y——lay, she perceived that the moans came from Mrs. Y——'s aged father, who expecting that his daughter would set out upon her journey by day break, had come at that early hour to bid her farewel.

They alarmed their nearest neighbours immediately, who proceeded to Mrs. J——n's, and there found Mr. Y——in the situation she had left him; they took him from hence to Tomhanick, where he remained near two days—during which time Mr. W—tz—l (a pious old Lutheran, who occasionally acted as preacher) attended upon him, exhorting him to pray and repent; but he received the admonitions with contempt, and several times with ridicule, refusing to confess his error or *join* in prayer—I say *join* in prayer, for he would not kneel when the rest did, but when they arose he would prostrate himself and address his "father," frequently saying "my father, thou knowest that it was in obedience to thy commands, and for thy glory that I have done this deed." Mrs. Bl——r, at whose house he then was, bade some one ask him who his father was?—he made no reply—but pushing away the person who stood between her and himself, darted at her a look of such indignation as thrilled horror to her heart—his speech was connected, and he told his tale without variation; he expressed much sorrow for the loss of his dear family, but consoled himself with the idea of having performed his duty—he was taken to ALBANY and there confined as a lunatic in the goal, from which he escaped twice, once by the assistance of Aqua Fortis,[48] with which he opened the front door.

I went in 1782 with a little girl, by whom Mr. Bl——r had sent him some fruit; he was then confined in dungeon, and had several chains on—he appeared to be much affected at her remembrance of him, and put up a pious ejaculation[49] for her and her family—since then I have received no accounts respecting him.

The cause for his wonderfully cruel proceedings is beyond the conception of human beings—the deed so unpremeditated, so unprovoked, that we do not hesitate to pronounce it the effect of insanity—yet upon the other hand, when we reflect on the equinimity[50] of his temper, and the comfortable situation in which he was, and no visible circumstance operating to render him frantic, we are apt to conclude, that he was under a strong delusion of Satan. But what avail our conjectures, perhaps it is best that some things are concealed from us, and the only use we can now make of our knowledge of this affair, is to be humble under a scene of human frailty to renew our petition, "Lead us not into temptation."[51]

May, 27, 1796.

ANONYMOUS [JEAN-PIERRE CLARIS DE FLORIAN]

*VALERIA: AN ITALIAN TALE (1799)**

THERE seems to be a prejudice in the world against the belief of spirits; and yet we forget that the best writers both of Greece and Rome, and historians the most famous for their veracity and philosophy, have attested their existence. Plutarch relates, how Brutus, being in his tent at midnight, a short time before the battle of Phillippi, saw a terrible vision—"a man of enormous size, and hideous countenance, of whom at first, he was afraid, but seeing that the phantom neither did nor said any thing to him, but merely kept moving round his couch; he at length asked him who he was? The phantom replied—I am thy evil

* SOURCE: [Jean-Pierre Claris de Florian]. 1799. "Valeria: An Italian Tale," *The Dessert to the True American* 1 (38): 1–2; 1 (39): 1–2; 1 (40): 1–2.

PUBLICATION HISTORY: The story of a premature burial has a long history as *mythes flottans* in European literature. The story of the lovers as living dead became known through Giovanni Boccaccio's novel *Filocolo*, written in the fourteenth century. It recurs in a slightly altered version in François Gayot de Pitaval's many-volumed compilation of judicial cases and court decisions published in Paris in the 1730s. The French writer Jean-Pierre Claris de Florian drew upon Gayot's story and fleshed it out into a ghost story in his collection *Nouvelles nouvelles* (Paris, 1792). Florian titled his story "Valeria: An Italian Tale." In the same year, an English translation appeared as *New Tales from the French of M. Florian* in London. The London version came out under the title "The Apparition: A Tale" in the *American Literary Museum, or Monthly Magazine* in 1797. Three years later, a much shorter version of this now "horrid tale" appeared in John Harrisson's *The New York Weekly Museum* (1788–1811). An altered and more dramatized version of Florian's narrative appeared in the first 1806 volume of the British magazine *La Belle Assemblée, or Bell's Court and Fashionable Magazine Addressed Particularly to the Ladies* (1806–37). The story was reprinted in Baltimore a year later by Eliza Anderson, who edited the short-lived magazine *The Observer* (1807). Anderson borrowed the story and published it as "Valeria, or the Ghost Alive!"

FIG. 4: Engraving from Winslow, Jacques-Bénigne. 1746. *The Uncertainty of the Signs of Death, and the Danger of Precipitate Interments and Dissections, Demonstrated, I. From the Known Laws of the Animal Oeconomy. II. From the Structure of the Parts of the Human Body. and, III. From a Great Variety of Amusing and Well-Attested Instances of Persons Who Have Return'd to Life in their Coffins, in their Graves, Under the Hands of the Surgeons, and After They Had Remain'd Apparently Dead for a Considerable Time in the Water. With Proper Directions, both for Preventing such Accidents, and Repairing the Misfortunes Brought upon the Constitution by them. To the Whole is Added, a Curious and Entertaining Account of the Funeral Solemnities of Many Ancient and Modern Nations, Exhibiting the Precautions they Made Use of to Ascertain the Certainty of Death. Illustrated with Copper Plates*, opposite page 43. London. © The British Library Board. G.19084.

genius, and you shall see me near Phillippi. Brutus replied—it is well, I shall see you there; and immediately the vision disappeared. Afterwards, making ready for battle near the city of Phillippi, the night before the engagement, the same phantom appeared to him again, without saying a word; by which Brutus understood that his hour was come!"

Pliny the younger, in his letters, affirms, as a certain fact, the story of the philosopher, Athenodorus, who, having made purchase at Athens of an old mansion, which every one refused, because every night a spectre there made its appearance, boldly waited to see it. It came at length, dragging a massy chain, and made signs to the philosopher to follow it. Athenodorus, who was at that moment busy, made signs to it, in his turn, to wait a little. The spirit increasing the rattling of its chains, and the philosopher, taking his lamp, rose and followed it, who, conducting him to the court in which the house stood, disappeared suddenly. Athenodorus marked the spot, to know it again. The day following, he assembled the magistrates, who ordered the ground to be dug up, and found some human bones confined by chains. They were collected, and publicly interred; from which period the house was no more disturbed.

If examples more recent be required, we may consult the memoirs of the famous Aggrippa d'Aubigny, grandfather of Madame Maintenon, so notorious for his zeal for Calvinism, his rigid frankness, and inflexible integrity. He had lost his mother. "I was," says he, "in my bed, and entirely awake, when I heard some one enter my apartment, and I perceived at my bed side, a woman, remarkably pale, whose cloaths made a noise against my curtains: these she withdrew, stooped towards me, and, giving me a kiss as cold as ice, she, in a moment vanished!"

Shall we then call in question what Plutarch, Pliny and d'Aubigny have affirmed? or shall we say, to justify our incredulity, that these men were weaker than we are?

Without pursuing this discussion, I am about to relate a fact, which I had from the person to whom it happened. This person is still alive, at the city of Florence, and will confirm the testimony. This is the manner in which I was told this wonderful anecdote.

I was, during an interval of absence from the service, at a small place in Languedoc,[52] where I was born, when several friends invited me to spend the Christmas in an old castle built in some rocks in the midst of the mountains of Cevennes. The mistress of this mansion had assembled some young damsels, officers and agreeable neighbours. Good humour and frankness prevailed amongst us all—each had a pleasure in finding himself one of the society; none wished to shine exclusively of the rest, or disputed whose turn it was to hold forth. Each was satisfied with the rest, and the rest with him. We laughed all the day. In the evening, seated in a circle round a large fire, we told tales, sung ballads, and finished our evenings delightfully. The young ladies of Languedoc, not wanting in imagination (a thing common enough in this country) were particularly delighted with stories of spirits. Each had his tale to tell.—The season, the place, the occasion. All added to the effect which these fearful recitals produced. The nights were long and dark, the country was buried in snow, and the owls, the old inhabitants of the tower in which was the saloon, answered each other through the cracks, by their slow and monotonous cries: add to this, it was the time of advent, when every body knows that apparitions are most frequent.[53] Thus, when the tale began, the circle insensibly contracted; as it proceeded, it still became less, and they who pretended to laugh, were often ready to expire from terror; and it often happened that the reciter was seized with a sudden fit of tremour, his voice changed, he became speechless; and ventured not to look either to the bottom of the great hall, whence the noise of chains was fancied to proceed; nor yet towards the chimney, from which something was expected to descend.

We had in our party a young Italian, named Valeria Orsini, whose indifferent health had brought her to Montpellier, to consult our physicians. She had, at that place, formed an intimacy with the lady of our castle, who had invited her to the country, during the absence of count Orsini, her husband, whom unexpected business had obliged to return to Florence. This younger stranger was very amiable: to great vivacity she united an enchanting sweetness, an evenness of temper, which nothing interrupted. Her conversation was lively and impressive, though her person and features announced nothing but mental desert.[54] Her large black eyes were very languishing, her look inspired tenderness, her beauty and conciliating grace seemed to obtain fresh power from the paleness which ever marked her countenance. Her lips also partook of this paleness; for, when Valeria spoke, a statue of alabaster seemed to be animated! when she did not speak, she did not the less attract attention; and indeed she personally gave a striking idea of the story of Pygmalion![55]

Amongst all our females, Valeria gave proofs of the greatest resolution, in hearing those fearful recitals. She was never agitated, and often smiled; and, without appearing to doubt the truth of the tales she heard, she had merely the air of supposing them easy of explanation. The story of a councellor of

Thoulouse, to whom a man who had been assassinated, and buried for six months, appeared one evening, to reveal his murderers: That also of a married man of Lyons, who, having in a transport of jealousy killed his wife, saw her every night appear at eleven o'clock, and lie down by his side! A multitude of other anecdotes of a similar kind, very well authenticated, but nevertheless very wonderful, seemed, to Valeria, as mere common events. We were almost angry with her, and we one day expressed to her our astonishment at her not being at all affected by what she heard. Hear her answer:

"My friends, it seems very reasonable that any story of apparitions should astonish you, since the greater part of you, perhaps, have never seen one?" "You have, then, madam," said I—She smiled, with seeming contempt. "I have done more," she replied, "I have been, and am still one myself! It is a spirit who now addresses you!" At these words all the party uttered a loud shriek, and fled from her precipitately; and were, indeed, pressing towards the door, when Valeria, with that sweet and tender voice, the tones of which were irresistible, called us back, and entreated us to be seated; and, whilst taking each alternately by the hand, at the same time, that we looked upon her with terror, and discovered each some new appearance in her person, which we had never seen before, and which favoured of the other world, she spoke to us as follows:

"It is no fault of mine, my friends, if I have been dead these ten years!—There is no one to whom this might not have happened; but what does not happen quite so often is, that since that period, I have found myself infinitely happier; I have enjoyed a felicity I never knew before, and which, thanks to heaven, yet continues. It is true, that the troubles I endured during my life, well paid for the happiness I enjoyed since my death. It is necessary that I tell you every thing which happened to me till that fortunate moment, and you will see that my death alone could insure my tranquility in the world!

"I was born at Florence, and my parents were noble and affluent. My father and mother had no child but myself. I was brought up beneath their roof, where my good and tender mother compensated by her care, her love, and her caresses for the uneasiness I suffered from the severity of my father. That old man, estimable in many respects, was proud of his high birth, the honours he had obtained in the service of the emperor, and every day made himself miserable, because he had no son to inherit his titles. My poor mother suffered his ill humours with a sweetness, which sometimes disarmed my father; but vanity soon resumed her empire.—He believed himself without a child, because he was without a son!

"The palace we inhabited at Florence, was next to a house where dwelt a venerable gentleman, not very rich, but highly esteemed. He was called the Marquis Orsini. A long time a widower, he dedicated his life to the education of Octavius, his only son, whose age was nearly the same as my own.

"My father and the old Orsini had formerly served together; they esteemed and frequently saw each other; and young Orsini was, from his childhood, accustomed to come often and familiarly to our house; and my mother always took affectionate notice of him.

"I was hardly ten years old, when Octavius became the friend of my heart. He was so mild so handsome, and so amiable, that I loved him more than ever sister loved a brother. I told him all my pleasures and my troubles, and was the confidant of his secrets; and, as if we had foreseen the sorrows it was to cause us, we took care to conceal our mutual passion. Before my father and mother, we appeared to be indifferent: our amusements seemed to occupy us entirely; sometimes we even disputed, but as soon as we got into the garden, or a little grove at the end of it, we had no longer any restraint.

"Octavius spoke of nothing but his tenderness. He pressed and would kiss my hands; often he ventured to embrace me vowing never to have any wife but Valeria. I, on my part, made a similar vow, and I received his innocent caresses without a blush. 'Till the age of fourteen, no remorse, no fears interrupted our tender passion. Octavius was then sixteen. I perceived that I loved him more than I had ever done any thing before; but a secret whispering told me, that I ought no longer to walk alone in the grove with Octavius. From this moment I avoided such walks; and I took away from him, in our sports that unreserve which had constituted their delight. Octavius made heavy complaints. I wished to tell him my motives, and, with this view, for the last time, I consented to meet him in the solitary grove. But whether my father had any suspicions, or whether chance there directed him he approached us, in a green walk very much shaded, where I was sitting on a bank of turf. There was room only for myself; accordingly, Octavius was kneeling before me, holding my hands and addressing me with much vivacity; and as he spoke in a low tone, from the fear of our being overhead, our faces in a manner met. In this position my father surprized us; his anger was equal to our terror: he ordered me, in a terrible voice, to go to my mother; I instantly obeyed. I heard him at a great distance reprimanding Octavius—forbidding him ever to enter our doors; and I saw the poor youth retire weeping from our mansion.

(To be continued.)

VALERIA: AN ITALIAN TALE.
(Continued from our last.)

"I suffered as much as he, for I loved as tenderly as I was beloved.—This love, formed in my infancy, could only terminate with my life. The outrageous reproaches which my father heaped upon me;—his menaces, and the violence in his deportment,[56] did but increase my tenderness. I did not deserve the cruelty with which he treated me. Obstacles irritated me the more; and whilst with eyes declined, and in a melancholy silence, I heard my father in a rage swearing to sacrifice me if ever I again saw Octavius—I pronounced in a low tone, a vow to be his, and his only.

"The day succeeding this dreadful adventure, as I was with my mother, who, without endeavouring to excuse me, tried to appease my father's wrath who should enter but the father of Octavius, the Old Marquis Orsini; his air and venerable aspect inspired confidence and esteem. My father, on seeing him, ordered me to leave the room—I obeyed; but the interest I had in knowing what should pass compelled me to stay at the door and listen. I heard this conversation: 'My lord,' said the father of Octavius, 'I came here to solicit pardon and grace. My son has told me every thing. I have blamed his temerity;[57] but excuse me, if a father's tenderness compassionates his love. My son adores your daughter, and he presumes to think that he is beloved. In opposing their mutual partiality, you will make two beings wretched—you will be so yourself; for at our age, my old friend, nature can only compensate us for all we have suffered, by making us spectators of our children's happiness. You know the family of Octavius; it is without stain, and may aspire to an union with yours. Nothing but your opulence can make this an unequal match, but keep this if you think proper. You may still hope one day to have an heir—I wish heaven might grant it you; if it does, my joy will equal your own. Give Valeria no more than Octavius will receive from me: this will be enough to make them happy. Retain the rest in your own hands for your son, if you shall happen to have one, or to give it to mine in proportion as he shall merit your esteem and tenderness.'

'I am astonished,' replied my father, with a cold and disdainful air, 'how a man, discreet as you are, could indulge such ideas. Grant that ever your son, by his supposed accomplishments, shall arrive at the highest situation in the state, you would doubtless suppose it the highest honour for him to obtain the hand of my daughter. Since at present he has nothing but an idle youth to plead, a mysterious presumption, and the advantage of having offended me, do you think that I can possibly give my consent to this union?'

'I presume,' interrupted the old gentleman, 'that you are sensible and upright—that you love your daughter—that in the bosom of a father, pride cannot obliterate the sweetest and most sacred of duties. I think, moreover, that the son of your friend does you no dishonour by loving Valeria; and if in the warmth of your anger you forget that he is the son of your friend, I shall be obliged to remind you that his father at least is your equal.'

"At this expression my mother was eager to stop the conversation; she spoke in so high a tone that old Orsini could not hear my father's reply. He instantly took his leave; and from this moment the most determined hatred succeeded to thirty years of friendship.

"Judge of my sorrow: no more hope of seeing Octavius again—no opportunity of conveying to him any news of my own condition, or to hear of his. My father surrounded me with spies—forbade me to go out, even to mass.—He never spoke to me—I never saw him, but at the hours of meals, when he never turned his eyes towards me. I was in his house as a stranger, whom pains are taken to instruct that she excites no emotion. My health soon declined, and I should have sunk under it, but for the tender care, the kindness, and the pity of my mother, she never left me a moment; she supported my almost exhausted courage, giving me hopes that my father might yet one day be appeased. She ventured not to speak to me of Octavius; but all that she said, in some respect related to him, and all her consolations brought my lover to my remembrance; and without ever mentioning his name, she talked to me incessantly.

"Time rolled away without any diminution of what I suffered, when one evening I availed myself of the absence of my father, to go and afflict myself alone in the green walk, where my misfortunes commenced. I wished to sit on the same turf, where I had once been seated near Octavius. I watered it with my tears: I remembered all that he had said to me; I repented my former vows—when suddenly a man appeared, and fell prostrate before me. In terror I attempted to fly, but the voice of Octavius detained me.

'Hear me,' said he, 'I have but a moment and it is the last—for this night I leave Florence; my father has procured for me a company of horse in the service of the emperor. War is declared against Prussia.[58] I go to join the army—to perish or deserve you. I hope—I am determined to distinguish myself so much in my first campaign, that the emperor finds desire to know me—which, if ever he does, I will declare to him my love. Joseph[59] is young, and doubtless susceptible—he will pity my misfortunes; and may, perhaps, interest himself in my behalf with the Great Duke, his brother.[60] Your father cannot resist the Grand

Duke; and your hand may become the reward of my constancy[61] and valour. I ask of you but one year, Valeria;—promise me to resist but for one year, the commands of your father; after this period, I shall either be no more, or deserve to be your husband.'

"I heard him with extreme agitation: I could hardly breathe; my heart palpitated[62] with love, hope, and terror. I vowed to be faithful to him whilst I lived, and to die a thousand times sooner than except of any other husband. We agreed to write to each other, by means of one of our domestics already gained, by Octavius and who had now given him admission. A slight noise which we heard, compelled us to separate. I tore my hand from that of Octavius; and returning precipitately to my chamber, passed the remainder of the night in tears.

"For the first six months which followed the departure of Octavius, I experienced no alteration at home. My father always treated me with the same harshness—my mother with the same affection. The domestic in the interest of my lover, regularly brought me his letters; every day they informed me of some new success. General Laudohn[63] had conceived a great friendship for Octavius; had made him his aid-de-camp, and promised to promote him to the highest rank. But the war was long and tedious, and offered few opportunities of showing personal valor. The great talents of Frederick and his brother Prince Henry,[64] disconcerted the projects of the sagacious Laudohn. No battles—no surprizes—the two Prussian heroes foresaw every thing—their genius predominated over accident, and commanded fortune; and probably, for the first time, personal bravery and chance were banished from war. At the end of ten months I abruptly ceased to hear from Octavius. Fearful for his life, but not of his constancy, I wrote letter after letter, counting every moment of the post. The domestic our confidant, went incessantly to inquire, and always returned to tell me, that there was nothing for me. Afflicted by this continued silence, I sent to old Orsini's to make particular inquiry whether he had heard from Octavius. The answer calmed my anxiety in one respect, but not in another: Octavius, they said, had written the preceeding evening; he has very well—was made a colonel, and was going to pass the winter at Vienna with General Laudohn.

"I was unjust enough to reproach my lover, and dared to think that he had forgotten me. I instantly ceased to write, and made some vain attempts to banish him from my heart. Alas!—I only encreased my sorrow; his image every where followed me: I saw him every instant, as I had seen him on the night we parted. I might well determine and vow to banish from my mind those sweet recollections; they recurred to me perpetually, and I was ever thinking that I would think no more of Octavius.

"At this point there arrived from Germany a cousin of my father, who took up his residence at our house. He was a tall thin man, from forty-five to fifty years old, of a cold and austere character. He talked of nothing but his nobility. He had employed his whole life, and the little understanding he had, to study and to know by heart all the genealogies of Europe. He was perfectly acquainted with the year, the month, and the day of all contracts of marriages that had been made in Germany since the decline of the Roman Empire. He knew all the families, and all their branches, of the Electors, the Palatines of Poland and Hungary; and for some years, to fill up his tedious hours of leasure, he busied himself in arranging the titles of the Ottoman family, and the different branches they had produced, to the sixty-fourth generation; which did not fail, as he said, to give him a vast deal of trouble, on account of the prodigious number of sultans which had entered into that family, not always the most delicate in the subject of alliances.

"This cousin, who was named Count Heraldi, on the very first evening of his arrival, after having, during supper-time, asked my father a multitude of questions concerning the gentlemen of Tuscany, inquired, with an air of indifference, whether a certain Marquis Orsini lived in Florence? My father, in a sour manner, replied, 'That he knew nothing about him,'—'But I must know,' replied Heraldi, 'for in passing through Vienna, about three weeks since, I dined with General Laudohn, on the very day of the marriage of his niece to a son of this Marquis Orsini. This young man, whom I found to be very amiable, learning that I was coming here, gave me a letter for his father, made me promise that I would see him, and give him a particular account of the marriage festival, and of the happiness which I saw that he enjoyed with his bride.' I heard this speech, more dead than alive. My father knit his brows, without making any reply. My mother looked at me, trembling all over, and the cruel Heraldi proceeded to relate—'that the young lady had fallen in love with Orsini; that the emperor had interested himself in the marriage, and that a regiment had been the portion of the general's niece!' Every thing was consistent with what he had before said. I no longer doubted the perfidy of Octavius, and certain of my misery, in spite of all my efforts to dissemble my afflictions, my strength failed me, and I fell lifeless, in the arms of my mother. They carried me away. Returning to myself, I found that I was in bed, surrounded by my maids, and supported by my mother, who embraced me, with many tears.

"The horrid condition of my mind, soon brought on a burning fever. It was long and painful: my mother never left me, even my father, during the six weeks of my illness, distinguished me by much tenderness, watched over me, called me his daughter, and seemed to have restored me to his affection. His severity, indeed, had never estranged my love, and I was so sensible of the return of that of my father, that in an interval, when taking my hand, and fixing his eyes upon me, which were full of tears, he enquired how his dear Valeria found herself? I could not restrain my transport, and throwing my arms around his neck, I pressed my face to his, and, weeping at the time, said—'Yes, my father, I am your own Valeria. I am your dutiful child, and, from this moment, the only wish of my heart shall be to obey you.'

"This word determined my fortune. I had perceived that my father had always intended me for my cousin Heraldi. This relation had our family name, and this name was decisive with my father. To him it was an essential happiness to see his family revive, and to leave all his wealth to a descendant from his ancestors. He spoke to me on this subject, without asking—without exacting any thing; but he told me, 'he should expire with grief if I did not take pity on his weakness.' Octavius was married, Octavius was faithless! I was incensed against Octavius. To me it seemed delightful to be able to love another. I consented, and gave him my promise. How could I not give? how could I disobey my father, who did not command, he only intreated.

"The preparations for my marriage were made with a celerity of which I did not dare to complain, but which filled me with terror. My mother said nothing—she sighed, and concealed her tears. My father redoubled his tenderness to me. Heraldi loaded me with presents, and spared me any professions of a love to which I could not listen—The dispensarion arrived from Rome, and the contract was signed. They dressed me, covered me with diamonds, and led me to the altar.

"I pronounced the formidable vow, without any extravagant emotion: almost indifferent to my situation; troubling myself but little about a fate that could not possibly be happy, which, indeed, I knew was to be supported with more or less of suffering. After mass I left the choir, surrounded by my family, held by the hand of Heraldi, who seemed to feel no great deal of joy, when, at the gate of the church, as I advanced to use some holy water, lifting my eyes, I saw, resting against a pillar, a young man; pale, trembling, his hair and dress in great disorder, his eyes wild and staring, who, regarding me with a fixed countenance, approached and said, in a hollow broken tone, 'I wished, Valeria, to see you consummate your enormous crime—I have seen it—am content, and am about to die!'

"Saying thus, he vanished. I fainted, without any recollection. Indeed, from that moment I remembered nothing: relapsing into my former illness, I experienced still greater and more seeming danger. I was never free from delirium. My disease made a rapid progress; and all that I have since learned from my mother is, that after a paroxysm, which continued many hours, I sunk into an extreme weakness, and apparently expired in her arms.

(To be concluded in our next.)

VALERIA: AN ITALIAN TALE.

(Concluded from our last.)

"My mother was likely to follow me! My father was in despair. Heraldi wept, but the calamity seemed without remedy. I was interred. They carried me, with much funeral pomp, to the sepulchre of my family, which was in a chapel of our cathedral. There my coffin was placed, along some bars of iron: the stone of the tomb was replaced, and I was left in this scene of death.

"What passed afterwards had better be related by Octavius than by me. He has often told it me, 'that having formed a fixed purpose of going to conceal himself in some of the Apennine Dessarts, to finish his miserable life, the condition in which he had seen me, the news of my illness, repeated every where, detained him in Florence.'—You may very easily imagine his distraction[65] when informed of my death: almost wild with despair, and considering himself my murderer, he formed the mad project of entering my tomb, and killing himself on my coffin. The very evening of my interment, he bribed the sexton, and both of them, at midnight, with a dark lanthorn, entered the church, and, removing the stone of the vault, descended the steps. Soon as Octavius beheld my bier, he darted forwards, tore away the linen which concealed my countenance, and pressing his mouth to my pale lips, did not think he should want the aid of his sword to put a period to his life.

"Miracle of love! Miracle, which they who have never loved cannot possibly believe, the soul of my lover revived mine! From my lips, pressed with such vivacity and tenderness by his, a sigh escaped, Octavius perceived this: Octavius, transported, uttered a loud cry, snatched me from my coffin, and pressed me to his bosom; mine, from that moment, beat again! I made a slight motion. Octavius, transported with joy, took me in his arms, ascended the steps, gained the gate of the church, and, without stopping a moment, flew to the house of his father, where placing me on a bed, every assistance was afforded me.

"I at length opened my eyes; my first looks met those of Octavius and his father, with a physician, who already answered for my life. I cannot describe my feelings. I seemed to wake from a long dream! I did not think myself alive, but I recognized Octavius. I could not speak to him, but I had the delight of seeing him. I found myself tolerably well, and yet was not certain that I was alive. Three days and three nights hardly restored me to myself. At the end of this time, the sleep I enjoyed, without being sensible of it, and the nourishment I took without knowing it, gradually restored me to my senses. My memory revived. I recollected my mother, my marriage, and the spot where I had seen my lover. There my ideas were suspended. But I understood what he said. I comprehended that I was in the house of Octavius—I was sensible that it was he who pressed my hand; and my love, the warmth of which had never left me, every moment brought to me again something I had forgotten.

"I soon found myself in a state to hear and listen to Octavius, and to learn from his lips all that had happened to me. The idea of his marriage, his perfidy, then presented itself to my disordered mind. As soon as I could at all converse rationally, I spoke to him of his marriage with the niece of general Laudohn. Octavius believed me still in a delirium.—General Laudohn had no niece.

"Octavius was returned from the army, but he was not a colonel. He had never been at Vienna; but availing himself of a leave of absence, he had obtained with difficulty—unhappy that for the space of two months I had never written to him, he had travelled night and day, bringing with him a letter from Laudohn, recommending him to the Grand Duke. He alighted from his horse, just as I entered the church: he had followed me to the altar, and in his anxiety and grief, was determined, at least, to reproach me for my perjury.

"I then learned that Heraldi, probably in concert with my father, had invented this detestible falshood; and that betrayed by the domestic in whom I had placed confidence, they had intercepted the letter of my lover. This discovery excited in me an aversion for the perfidious Heraldi, with the extremest contempt, and indeed, horror, that was invincible. No crime in my eyes was equal to the horrible means he had employed, and yet I was the wife of this monster. I was condemned to live his wife, and to consecrate my days to him. This afflicting idea again reduced me to despair; I lamented my tomb, and once more wished to visit it.

'My dear child compose yourself.' said the elder Orsini. 'I am now come from the Great Duke: I have myself carried him the letter from the brave Laudohn; and was determined to inform him myself of all that had happened. This generous prince heard me patiently; he takes you under his protection. He has written to the holy father to dissolve your unnatural marriage. I doubt not but he will say you have died for Heraldi—live now for Octavius. Thus religion as well as justice will defend you against your tyrants. I have only one favour to ask of you—it is, that no person may see you, nor be informed of our secret, till our courier shall return from Rome. Your peace and happiness depends on this precaution.'

"These words restored me to hope. I promised the good old man, whom I now called my father—I even swore to obey his advice, and never depart from his house. Where, alas! could I be better. Octavius was with me—Octavius spoke to me incessantly of his love and our union. My health was restored—I was happy already—and was about to be more so. I soon had lost every trace of my disease. I found myself what I had been in my earlier youth, and I retained of my sufferings only that paleness which you have observed in me:—fearful vestige[66] of the grave, which nothing can remove!

"The time soon approached, when the courier was to return from Rome, when a wonderful accident seemed to threaten a disappointment of all our hopes.

"It was the holy week. My pious mother had educated me in those religious principles, which, thanks to heaven, I have never forgotten. I mourned in secret that I could not go to the church on those sacred days, when penitence appeases the justice of a merciful Deity. I would not mention to Octavius the necessity which my heart felt, of returning thanks in his temple to the God who had preserved me, but I determined at all events, to fulfill so sacred a duty. I availed myself of the only moment, when I accidentally found myself alone. I wrapped myself in a black veil, through which I could not possibly be discovered. On holy Thursday I left the house at nine in the evening, and hastened towards the cathedral to worship our Saviour. The church was full of people, who in profound silence, with hands clasped together, their eyes fixed upon the ground, offered their prayers to the altar on which the Host was placed. This altar alone was illuminated by an immense number of flambeaus[67]—all the rest of the building was in profound darkness. I remained concealed behind a pillar; I addressed my prayers to the Saviour of the world, and entreated him to watch over her, who had no hopes but from his pity and almighty power.

"In rising to go away, I felt a violent desire to look at the chapel where I had been interred. It was very near, and I accordingly approached it. What did I not see!—In the alley which led to the vault, I saw and knew my father, and mother on their knees at my tomb, and my husband, Heraldi, in mourning, weeping near my father, who seemed absorbed in the profoundest thought. My mother, near the railing which confined the vault, was praying with many tears. I could hardly refrain crying out. I darted involuntarily towards her, and was stopped only by the grate. My mother did not hear me; she was too absorbed. I contemplated her a long time in tears, when suddenly I saw her stoop forwards, take hold of the iron railing to support herself, and with great tenderness, bend herself almost to the ground, pronouncing the name of Valeria—at the same time she kissed the marble of my tomb. I was no longer mistress of myself!—I pressed her hand to my lips, and mourned aloud!

"By this movement, the veil which covered me was thrown aside without my perceiving it. My mother, in astonishment, raised her head, saw, and recognized her daughter. She pronounced my name aloud, and reached her arms towards me. My father and husband also saw and remembered me. My father remained motionless. Heraldi advancing, opened the iron door. I would have fled, but the crowd prevented me. Heraldi approached me; he had extended his hand to take hold on me; and I had been lost, if in this moment, love had not inspired me. 'Forbear! said I to him in a tone which I made as terrible as I could:—'at least respect after her death, her whom you deluded in her life!—You, alone, caused my death—leave me—lament your crime—and avert the anger of heaven!

"Having said this, Heraldi, frozen with terror, heard me without daring to stir from this place. I concealed myself beneath my veil, and, with a composed step, advanced to the door of the church. The people made way for me—I got cut—fled with celerity, and gained the house of Octavius, without any person's presuming to follow me. The next day, in Florence, nothing was talked of but the apparition which had appeared in the cathedral. Nobody could doubt it—a thousand witnesses had remembered me. Many added, that having pushed away the hand of my husband, who pursued me, my five fingers had left in his clothes—five marks of fire. Others asserted, that Heraldi had destroyed me, and I came to demand justice.—All accused him with a loud voice, of being the murderer of his wife. The people murmered against Heraldi, followed him with reproaches, and even threw stones at him; his life indeed, was no longer secure.

"Happily the courier returned, bringing from the holy father a brief which annulled my marriage, as being fraudulently contracted. As soon as the Grand Duke received it, he sent for Orsini, and concerted with him what measures to pursue, and the very next morning I went to the palace with Octavius and his father. The prince was exceedingly kind to us, condescended to converse with us, on our dearest interests; and when he was told that my father and mother, with Heraldi, were come in obedience to his orders, he made us enter a closet, where I thus heard him address my father:—

'It seems, sir, that strange means were taken to make your daughter marry a person whom she could not love.—Your repentance is revenge enough; and the tears which I see in your eyes take from me the power of reproaching you. Death has broken this ill-fated bond: and if by a miracle, which the people believe, your daughter should be restored to life, this marriage will be null and void.—This is the brief of his holiness, declaring it to be so, and I am about to make it public. Choose then, Count Heraldi, whether to resist me in a matter so disgraceful to you, or to sign a renunciation of your pretented rights, and to depart instantly for Vienna. My kindness will then follow you, and you will restore tranquility to my capital, which your presence interrupts.'

"Heraldi was not long in replying: he made his renunciation in the term dictated by the Grand Duke; when taking leave of his Imperial highness, he that moment left Florence, promising never to return."

'But this is not all,' said the Grand Duke, addressing himself to my father, 'your daughter is yet alive!'—A shriek from my mother here interrupted him.—'You will see her again,' he continued, 'but your daughter can never be happy but as the wife of young Orsini. He it was who delivered her from the tomb.—She resides in his house.—Gratitude, paternal love, and the fame of Valeria, all enjoin you to assent to their union. If my entreaty does not weaken claims so strong, I entreat of you Valeria for Octavius: he deserves her, for he has won the esteem and friendship of Laudohn. Give your consent to this marriage, I promise you a regiment for your son-in-law; and for yourself, will secure a 'riband of the order of Maria Theresa.'—"My father replied only with a bow. He consented to the request of the prince; and my mother, bathed in tears, entreated to see her daughter. I could wait no longer: I hastily opened the door, threw myself into the arms of my mother, who, I thought, would have died of joy. That of my father, was equally lively. He pressed me to his bosom, entreated me to pardon his faults, and heaped caresses both on Octavius and the elder Orsini. We all fell at the feet of the Grand Duke, unable to find words to express our gratitude. My marriage was not long delayed; it was solemnized[68] in the Grand Duke's palace. From this moment, entirely occupied with pleasing the husband I adore—the venerable Orsini who loves me as his daughter—my excellent mother—who never leaves me—I spend my days tranquilly in the sweets of friendship, gratitude, and love; and I thank heaven, that I was dead for a short time, to live ever afterwards in felicity."

Notes

1. The Caspian Sea is the largest enclosed body of water on earth, situated between modern-day Russia, Azerbaijan, Iran, and Kazakhstan.

2. Assiduity: attention.

3. The genie is an invisible spirit mentioned in the Koran and part of Arabian demonology. It is believed by Muslims to inhabit the earth and influence mankind by appearing in the form of humans or animals. The term was adapted into English from the French translators of *Arabian Nights*.

4. Redress: relief, improvement.

5. Amaranthus: a family of plants.

6. In Greek mythology, Zephyr is the god of the west wind, generally a gentle breeze.

7. An allusion to the seven daughters of Atlas and Pleione, in star tales otherwise known as Pleiads.

8. European hero: reference to Alexander the Great (356–323 BC), who conquered Asia, or Christopher Columbus (c. 1451–1506), who opened up the conquest of the western hemisphere.

9. Irksome: disgusting, tedious; dissipate: to scatter, pass away.

10. Polite: emphasizing sociability and refined conversation.

11. Alexander Pope (1688–1744) published his poem "The Universal Prayer" in 1738 and attached it to *An Essay on Man*. Modeled after the Lord's Prayer, the poem rejects fatalism and blind determination. It holds that Jehovah, Jove, and the Lord are adored in "every clime . . . by saint, by savage, and by sage."

12. Apoplexy: bleeding within internal organs, nowadays called a stroke.

13. A name of Greek origin, meaning "good man" or "strong man." Evander of Pallene was a deific hero from Arcadia who brought Greek knowledge to Italy. Evander is also a character in the pastoral play *Evander and Alcimna* (1770), by the Swiss Samuel Gessner (1730–87). His idyllic pastorals and edifying moral reflections were reprinted in North American magazines in the 1770s and 1780s.

14. The name appeared in a number of plays circulating in eighteenth-century America, such as Shakespeare's *Cymbaline* (1609) and John Ford's *The Lovers' Melancholy* (1628) and also refers to a Spanish folksinger.

15. Languor: mental suffering or distress, longing or grief.

16. Derived from old French, it originally referred to high-born people. In England it frequently meant the untitled nobility, and in colonial America it denominated the well-bred gentleman farmers and their land-owning families.

17. The reference here is to the Barbary pirates and privateers who launched their raids into the Atlantic Ocean and the Mediterranean Sea from their ports in North Africa. The cities of Tunis, Tripoli, and Algiers were also known as the Barbary Coast. Until 1776 and the signing of the Declaration of Independence, American ships and colonists were protected by British treaties with the Barbary States. When in 1784, Barbary pirates began to capture American vessels and peoples, the government was forced to pay ransom and tribute to the Barbary States. Tensions between the United

States and the Barbary States grew throughout the 1790s and finally war was declared in 1800. Accounts about Barbary corsairs and reports about the captivity in North Africa found entry into European literature and captivity stories abounded since the sixteenth century.

18. Loth: reluctant, unwilling.

19. Habit: clothing.

20. Swoon: fainting fit.

21. Haram: mid-seventeenth-century Arabic word literally meaning "prohibited place," hence sanctuary or women's quarters.

22. Fatima: popular female character in Oriental tales, such as Anne Claude Philippe Comte de Caylus's *Oriental Tales Collected From Arabian Manuscripts in the Library of the King of France* (1745), but also in moral tales about Fatima in literary magazines such as the *Universal Magazine* (March 1772) and *The Gentleman and Ladies' Town and Country Magazine* (May 1784). The character became popular in tales anonymously reprinted in American magazines throughout the 1790s and the opening decade of the nineteenth century.

23. Corsairs and captains were frequently English or European renegades and outcasts who brought naval expertise to the piracy business and enabled the Barbary pirates to make long-distance slave-catching raids as far away as the North Atlantic.

24. Callousness: a hardened state of mind, want of feeling.

25. Menial: lacking reward, prestige, undignified.

26. The allusions to providence and God in the text refer to the American version of deism. In general, deists believed in reason and rejected revelation, since they held that the observation of the natural world helps man determine the existence of God. Nevertheless, Benjamin Franklin and Thomas Jefferson maintained that besides the free agency of man and the rational course of nature exists a "particular Providence," showing that God intervenes in human affairs.

27. George Washington (1732–99), elected first president of the United States in 1788, was revered as the "father of the nation."

28. Repining: discontent, complaint.

29. Leghorn: a province in Italy, nowadays called Livorno.

30. Congenial: partaking in the same disposition, temperament.

31. Annuity: a yearly grant or income.

32. Hurons: indigenous people of North America belonging to the Wyandot language group (Great Lakes regions and Georgian Bay); they were Native allies to the French during the Seven Years' War (1756–63) and known to the French through the encounters with Samuel de Champlain (1574–1634).

33. Known as the "People of the Longhouse" or Haudenosaunee, the Iroquois were a league of numerous indigenous nations and tribes in North America. Given the Hurons' involvement in the fur trade and their alliance with the French, the Haudenosaunee and Huron were traditional enemies.

34. Assiduity: attention.

35. Since pre-Columbian times, slavery among indigenous tribes took many forms

in the Americas. Unlike chattel slavery, indigenous enslavement was part of trade, war, or status, but often also necessary to maintain tribal demography.

36. The slightest indication of will or command.

37. The Iroquois, Huron, and Seneca American Indians developed a dream cult to act out their dreams socially. They regarded dreams as the hidden or unconscious area of the psyche. An understanding of dreams makes hidden desires known, because they were considered the basis of individual and social problems.

38. Accost: to approach and to speak to.

39. Bungling: clumsy, unskillful.

40. Saracen: Roman and Greek name for the nomadic peoples of the Arabian desert, by extension a Muslim.

41. Phrenzy: mental derangement, temporary insanity.

42. In 1769, James and Ann Eliza Bleecker moved to Tomhanick, a rural estate, twenty miles from Albany, upstate New York.

43. The story's female characters, Yates's wife, Elizabeth; his sister, Nelly; as well as the daughters, Rebecca and Diana; all embody female icons of chastity and motherhood. Rebecca typifies the powerful mother in the Bible. In Genesis, Rebecca marries Abraham's son Isaac and replaces Isaac's mother, Sarah. She determines the fate of the Jewish. After the father's death, Rebecca hands over Isaac's estate to her favorite son, Jacob.

44. Idol: an image or material object that represents a deity, frequently worshipped with blind devotion.

45. Expostulate: to demand why, to complain.

46. The name of the Roman goddess symbolizes an independent, virtuous, and compassionate woman. In Roman mythology, she protects children.

47. Elizabeth is a biblical figure, in both the Old and the New Testament. In Hebrew her name means "My God is abundance." Many saints and queens also carry this name.

48. Invented in alchemy, it is a highly corrosive solution, also called "strong water," which consists of nitric acid and water.

49. Pious ejaculation: ejaculatory prayer was at a devotional practice that involved praying immediately in reaction to what one witnesses, also as a means to include prayer in daily routines.

50. Equ[a]nimity: evenness of mind or temper.

51. Matthew 6:9–13 renders the story of Jesus teaching his disciples to pray by giving them an example that is called the Lord's Prayer: "Our Father which art in heaven, Hallowed be thy name. Thy kingdom come, Thy will be done in earth, as it is in heaven. Give us this day our daily bread. And forgive us our debts, as we forgive our debtors. And lead us not into temptation, but deliver us from evil: For thine is the kingdom, and the power, and the glory, for ever. Amen" (King James version).

52. Former southeastern French province.

53. Reference to old Germanic winter festivals and supernatural activities centered around Midwinter.

54. Desert: deserving, worth, excellence.

55. Pygmalion's story of the Greek sculptor and his woman carved out of ivory became known as the story of breath of life in a statue.

56. Deportment: conduct, behavior.

57. Temerity: boldness, rashness.

58. The Seven Years' War was a global conflict (1756–63) between Great Britain, France, Spain, Prussia, and Austria at the head of the Holy Roman Empire. In North America, it was known as the French and Indian War.

59. Joseph II (1741–90), Holy Roman Emperor. Given his many social reforms, historians count him among the eighteenth century's enlightened despots.

60. The reference to Leopold II (1747–92) is improbable, as he became Grand Duke of Tuscany in 1765. It is more likely that the author wanted to emphasize the young proponents of enlightened absolutism.

61. Constancy: determination, firmness.

62. Palpitate: to tremble, to quiver, irregular heartbeat.

63. Baron Ernst Gideon von Laudon (1717–90) was an Austrian general who successfully fought against the Prussian king Frederick the Great.

64. Frederick II (1712–86) became King in Prussia in 1740. Henry (1726–1802) was general, statesman, and Prince of Prussia. In 1786, the president of the Continental Congress suggested him to become the president or king of the United States; the offer, however, was revoked.

65. Distraction: disturbance of the mind and feelings, temporary madness.

66. Vestige: mark or trace.

67. Flambeaus: torchlights used in night processions.

68. Solemnize: to celebrate with proper ceremonies and in due form.

Suggestions for Further Reading

Orientalism

"Hamet and Rashid. With an Engraving." 1794. *New-York Magazine; or, Literary Repository* 5 (9): 526–27.

"Hamet: A Tale." 1812. *Port Folio* 8 (2): 184–89.

"The Happy Vale: Extract of a Letter from a Gentleman at Smyrna, to his Friend in Philadelphia, dated 15th February, 1791. With an Engraving." 1792. *New York Magazine; or, Literary Repository* 3 (1): 3–4.

"Omar and Fatima, or The Apothecary of Ispahan." 1807. *Literary Magazine* 8 (46): 5–10; 8 (47): 59–64; 8 (48): 136–42; 8(49): 177–83; 8 (51): 291–301.

Migrant Fictions

"Adventure of a Young English Officer Among the Abenakee Savages." 1775. *The Royal American Magazine, or Universal Repository of Instruction and Amusement* 2 (2): 59–61.

[Friedrich Schiller]. 1797. "The Sport of Fortune: An Anecdote Taken from Real History." *The Literary Museum, or, Monthly Magazine* (Jan.): 5–8; (Feb.): 92–98.
"Some Account of a Remarkable Dream." 1797. *New York Weekly Museum* 9 (447): n.p.
"The Story of Captain Nevill." 1797. *The Philadelphia Minerva* 3 (125): n.p.

Sensationalism

"Account of a Solitary Anthropophagite." 1783. *The Universal Magazine of Knowledge and Pleasure* 72 (502): 214.
Bradford, William. (1642) 1898. "[Thomas Granger's Sodomy]." In *Bradford's History Of Plimoth Plantation*, 475–78. Boston: Wright and Potter Printing Co., State Printers.
Brown, Charles Brockden. 1805. "Somnambulism." *The Literary Magazine, and American Register* 3 (20): 335–47.
"The Horrors of a Monastery: A Tale." 1796. *Philadelphia Minerva* 2 (80–83): n.p.
"The Torture of the Manheim Sisters." 1786. *New Hampshire Spy* 1 (2): 7.

PART V
GHOST STORIES

THIS SECTION FEATURES the presence of the supernatural in narratives from the Americas and its transformation into ghost stories, legends, and myths. The ghost story has been one of the most prolific genres in Western literary history. In contrast, Native American myths have only recently entered into surveys and anthologies, their presence closely allied with the attempt to recognize literary—if often oral—traditions that precede the European presence on the continent. While the nineteenth century saw the rise of Gothic tales by authors such as Charles Brockden Brown and Edgar Allen Poe, this particular form of the supernatural not only refers to the medieval romance but also occurs during a period in which the young American Republic explored and valued Native American civilization. While the United States sought to present itself as the "quintessentially modern nation" (Giles 2011, 71), it remains a construct that obscures the nation's past—a past that includes both European tradition and Native American civilizations. The avenue into this distant past has opened through the exploration of Native American heritage—especially the discovery of burial mounds dating back to 1050—and the engagement with medieval sources by classic nineteenth-century authors such as Washington Irving, James Fenimore Cooper, and Henry Wadsworth Longfellow. In addition, writers like Nathaniel Hawthorne connected the young nation with a "prehistory," a term coined in the 1850s that gave the newly founded nation a sense of pride and purpose, but that also complicated the forging of a national identity. Likewise, the sacred Mayan traditions in the

Popol Vuh have been recorded to perpetuate the memory of a people shortly before its extinction at the hand of Spanish colonists. In the nineteenth century, conversely, Latin American nations invoked indigenous civilizations to justify their existence and create a prehistory of their own that excluded Spanish rule (Echevarría 1997).

Supernatural tales thus emerge as a narrative ground on which various strands of ancient and early modern American culture merge. While the American Republic did not have a medieval past to which it could relate, writers like Irving combined German and English folklore in narratives that echo forms of oral storytelling and combine them with local legends and Native myths that are tied to specific locations in North America (Forbes 2007). Strong links to the supernatural also persisted in Native American cultures and in the numerous religious creeds of the first settlers; tales of hauntings, ghosts, and apparitions filled colonial religious texts as well as the pages of early national magazines and ethnographic accounts of Native myths. In the seventeenth century, prodigious signs and natural phenomena became part of a transatlantic "culture of wonder" in which the European settlers participated by incorporating Native American myths and dramatizing their experience as a battle of good and evil in the "wilderness" of the new continent (Hall 1995, 29–30; Winship 1996, 29; Cohen 2010). In Latin America, folk superstitions, Native legends, and local myths play an important role in the sketches of the *costumbrista* movement in the nineteenth century. Writers like Peruvian José Joaquín de Larriva y Ruiz and Columbians J. de Dios Restrepo and José María Vergara y Vergara used the local characters and landscapes in their tales. In these stories, they developed literary types, such as the South American gaucho, and transmitted oral anecdotes into prose. Earlier periods likewise saw the intrusion of odd incidents, strange events, and local myths into the records of the conquest and subsequent colonization of Middle and South America.

Wonder tales—a commonplace of medieval hagiography—were first rejected as "superstition" by Protestant reformers, but Alexandra Walsham (2003) has demonstrated how their supernatural elements and use as exempla lived on in Protestant writing and dominated early modern print culture.[1] At the same time, accounts of uncanny events from religious or secular sources have become more and more exchangeable as ministers sought to endow their sermons with forceful narratives, and hack writers masked their commercial interests with a few stereotypical religious remarks. Scholars have shown how popular and religious culture also merged on the print market as chapbooks, pamphlets, and broadsides of wonder tales that were hawked by peddlers, hung and read in public places, or perpetuated orally on both sides of the Atlantic (Brown 2007). While most scientists and theologians of the age accepted ghosts and witches as real because they appear in the Bible, radical Enlightenment skeptics, such as Thomas Hobbes and Baruch Spinoza, denied the existence of anything beyond the reach of human sensory perception. As the existence of God was imminently connected to the invisible and spiritual world, however, negating the possibility of the supernatural equaled atheism. Members of the Royal Society, such as Henry More and Joseph Glanvill in England and Increase and Cotton Mather in America, thus sought to verify the existence of the supernatural by means of empirical firsthand observation and detailed reporting (Wise 2010, 231–45).[2] Thus, Cotton Mather operates within and mediates between different transnational cultural influences that can be traced in his report of a ghost in "A Narrative of an Apparition" (1692). On the one hand, Mather participated in a transatlantic Protestant network of correspondents who shared a popular interest in the supernatural with its medieval folkloric background; his record of the Salem witchcraft trials, *The Wonders of the Invisible World* (1692), echoes, for example, cycles of oral storytelling (Dorson 1973, 42). On the other hand, Mather uses a method inspired by the scientific revolution of the seventeenth century, marked by the establishment of the Royal Society in 1660, of which he became a member (Smolinski 2010, 1:14–17).

From the eighteenth century onward, stories with supernatural elements have proven one of the most diverse and vibrant genres in American literature. Many stories centered upon apparitions of ghosts, as evident from the case of Joseph Beacon, which was reprinted three times in different works of Cotton Mather; it was also reissued by Daniel Defoe in a different version in *An Essay on the History and Reality of Apparitions* (1717). With regard to form, Joseph Beacon's narrative of an apparition anticipates the role of detailed description and the investigation of the narrator in Defoe's "A True Relation of the Apparition of Mrs. Veal" (1711), often considered one of the first English short stories. At the same time, the apparition of the ghost and its request to bring the murderer to justice are reminiscent of the ghost of Hamlet's father. That ghosts and other apparitions reveal murderers and ask for justice or revenge is an old folklore motif that enters religious literature, for example, in Glanvill's *Saducismus Triumphatus* (1681), a collection of supernatural and apparition tales. This section juxtaposes European folk traditions that are perpetuated in eighteenth-century Protestant writings and Native American conceptions of the underworld and the interaction between spirits and humans.

While popular belief in the existence of ghosts and witchcraft persists on both sides of the Atlantic, the scientific revolution and the development of empirical methods challenged theologians like Glanvill and Mather to provide evidence of the invisible world and counter what they perceived as a rise of atheism. Cotton Mather thus sought to validate Joseph Beacon's credibility from the outset of the narrative as well as in a closing paragraph that details how he received a signed and sealed report of the apparition from Beacon shortly before his death. The narrator first establishes Beacon's spotless reputation and cites him directly as his source. What follows is a comprehensive account of the apparition that renders in great detail what Beacon sees and hears. As a sign of recognition, the ghost of Beacon's brother wears "the Bengale Gown, which [Beacon's brother] usually wore" and carries a visible wound that is explained by the apparition's account of the murder. These sensory data and the report obtained from the ghost are corroborated by the matching facts of the murder case that Beacon receives about two months later "by common ways of communication." These facts act as proof of the apparition, as Beacon would have had no other way of knowing about his brother's death in London and its circumstances at the very hour it occurred.

Instead of biblical precedents or providential patterns, the narrative's claim to authority rests on a description that corresponds to scientific standards and the witness's reliability. Apparition narratives apply empirical methods that rely on sensory data and a narrative structure that follows the steps of uncovering and interpreting the evidence for apparitions. While narratives like Joseph Beacon's tale play an important role in convincing skeptics of the reality of the invisible world, they also serve as springboards for theorizing the relationship between spirit and matter, the afterlife, and other supernatural phenomena that the Bible mentions only marginally. In *Triparadisus* (written 1712, 1720–27), for instance, Cotton Mather explains apparitions by asserting the existence of a "second paradise" inhabited by the souls of the deceased before they enter eternity, and with the "nishmath chajim," the breath of life that forms human bodies from their inception onwards but can also leave them to appear elsewhere in their shape (Smolinski 1995). While Mather's narrative reflects the hostile climate of the day, in which the pure existence of God has to be verified, it also secures a relevant position for Puritan thought in the emergence of a new scientific discourse. Contrary to notions of Mather as a narrow-minded conservative, he emerges as a scholar-theologian engaging with contemporary scientific discourse by exploring material and spiritual phenomena for the glory of God.

"The Ghost of Falkner Swamp" (1744) and "A Chiricahua Woman Visits the Underworld" (n.d.) demonstrate that American ghost stories draw upon a variety of cultural and regional influences. While the first story was collected and edited by Pennsylvanian-German printer Christopher Sauer, the Elder, "A Chiricahua Woman Visits the Underworld" is a Chiricahua Apache myth recorded by anthropologist Morris Opler during his research in modern-day Arizona (Opler [1941] 1996; Stockel 2008). Sauer's collection of ghost stories, *Of Sundry Old and New Tales of Appearances of Ghosts and Glimpses of the Souls' Condition after Death as it Happened in Oly*, mingles pietist mysticism with American regional folklore; it appeared in Germantown in three editions, but was never translated into English. Sauer's collection combines local ghost tales with material from the German pietist magazine *Geistliche Fama* (*Spiritual News*, 1730–40), and from the German mystic Jacob Böhme (1575–1624), thus demonstrating the extent of the transnational exchange of stories inspired by the pietist interest in the spiritual world and the afterlife. Set in the region of New Hanover, a German settlement in Pennsylvania, "The Ghost of Falkner Swamp" presents the ghost as a man whose rest is disturbed by "unfinished business." As in Mather's relation, it combines realistic details that make it possible to identify the apparitions with enduring folklore motifs that have found their way into the Americas; "A Narrative of an Apparition" and "The Ghost of Falkner Swamp" continue typical plot elements of ghost stories that can also be found in differing ethnic contexts and their forms of storytelling. Both stories provide detailed descriptions and contain a narrator or characters attempting to determine whether an apparition actually occurred or whether the claims of the ghost can be verified.

In Washington Irving's "The Devil and Tom Walker" (1824), the truthfulness of events is of minor importance, as the narrator freely combines elements from folklore and refrains from fitting them into a convincing argument or didactic message. After introducing the two characters of the title, the narrative voice evaluates the unfolding tale by surmising that "it has almost too familiar an air to be credited." Repeatedly, the narrator refers to the circulation and variation of the story that has itself become a local legend and presents the reader with the version he finds most likely or generally believed. The many references to other legendary entities—such as Native American ghosts and the treasure grove of the pirate William Kidd—are tightly woven into the description of the woods as dark and mysterious. Set in Puritan New England, the story refers to the general suspicion of a devilish undermining of its society in the witchcraft trials and parallels the hypocrisy of superficial piety with the cutthroat market economy that evolved in the colonies. Through these references and elements of oral storytelling, "The Devil and Tom Walker" endows New England with a legendary past that it previously had not possessed, developing American folkloric figures such as the devil roaming the woods, heathen Natives, and dangerous pirates in a way that supersedes Irving's most famous stories, "Rip Van Winkle" and "The Legend of Sleepy Hollow."

The taste for Gothic literature also goes back—in an etymological sense—to the Middle Ages, as the term was often used as a pejorative for a "barbaric," "dark," and "rude" state of mankind. Accordingly, eighteenth-century literature witnessed a return of elements from legends, epics, and fairy tales in narratives revolving around valiant knights entering dark castles or enchanted landscapes on quests of love and adventure. In Anna Lætitia Barbauld's "Sir Bertrand: A Fragment," for example, a traveling knight enters a dark castle and releases a lady from her enchanted confinement. Barbauld and her brother, John Aikin, originally published her story in England in *Miscellaneous Pieces, in Prose* (1773); it was then reprinted numerous times in North America, for example by the *Columbia Magazine* in 1787. A prolific English poet, writer, and political activist, Barbauld used the fragment to test her theories about the power of literature to evoke effects like horror. Using medieval settings and infusing them with a Gothic atmosphere, Barbauld's narratives—and others like them—enlarged the American sense of history by incorporating references to the European Middle Ages. Likewise, Washington Irving's "The Devil and Tom Walker" adopts the European folkloric conception of the devil as a black man, but it also alludes to the Native Americans, pirates, and Puritans who helped create a mythological impact on a particular place. With this tale that is so rich in allusions and elements from legends, superstitions, and folklore, Irving invokes a pleasure of storytelling that is far from moral or scientific reasoning, but is not without satirical comments at the Puritan settlers and their morality.

In spite of these attempts to create a legendary and usable past in the Americas, the many regions and cultural contact zones have a rich oral and literary tradition reaching back thousands of years (Brotherston 1979; Nabokov 2002).

Often called the "Mayan Bible," the *Popol Vuh* is a record of Guatemalan K'iche' Maya oral traditions that have been recorded by Mayan scribes to preserve and bundle the knowledge of ancient codices and the "pre-Hispanic centers of learning" (Costa 1997, 534). The Mayas were a literate culture, and the scribes, often descending from nobles and priests, also preserved chronicles, medicine books, and—as its most encompassing and important work—the *Chilam Balam*, a collection of prophecies, mythical and historical passages, songs, poetry, and traditions. Its wisdom section already shows influences of Christianity. The *Popol Vuh* contains creation accounts that are similar to other Native American myths of origin, but it also has sections on myths and religion as part of a general history of the Maya until the time of contact. As Roberto González Echevarría (1995, 28) notes in his introduction of the section reprinted here, the *Popol Vuh*'s status as a sacred text has also become part of a fiction developed in its nineteenth-century reprinting in the wake of the emergence of a new national culture independent from Spain. These contradictory assessments of the text's authenticity are representative of all records of Native American storytelling that have generally undergone various steps of recording, translation, and reprinting.

In North America, the first records of Native myths, religion, and folklore can be found in colonial diaries and in the reports of missionaries, like those of the Jesuits and the Moravians, whose missions could also be found in the Caribbean and South America. Like the Mayan culture, whose agriculture was based on maize, the Penobscot tribes in what is today Maine record the creation of two plants from the dead body of First Mother (Nicolar [1893] 2007, 133–44). In Benjamin Franklin's "Origin of Tobacco" (1787), a similar myth is told by Susquehannock Natives and is satirically compared to the creation and fall of men in the Bible. While it extends the patterns of Native American myth to the biblical use of fruit, it also serves as an indictment of the missionary's narrow-minded rejection of this parallel and concept of truth. Thus the story could serve as a reminder that this Christian perspective and bias was shared by many of the recorders of Native American culture and is present in the various intentions and translation processes involved in preserving this culture in writing. Franklin's short narrative first appeared in a Massachusetts newspaper and was quickly reprinted in a number of magazines and other newspapers from Pennsylvania and throughout New England.

Stripped of their theological implications, eighteenth-century ghost tales use the supernatural as a means to question human perception as well as evoke a certain mood or effect. Still, through various allusions and references, Washington Irving incorporates English legends and writers such as Chaucer and Shakespeare into the American context. The role of the narrator also shifts as epistemological uncertainty increases. For example, while Glanvill's, Mather's, and Defoe's first-person narrators act as rational investigators, Irving and Barbauld contrast Enlightenment thinking with medieval legends and create moods based on fragmentation and unclear perception. While their innovative use of the narrator and description in supernatural tales anticipates formal characteristics of the later short story, the tales in this section also demonstrate the vitality of oral storytelling and legends in a transnational setting.

GHOSTS

COTTON MATHER

*A Narrative of an APPARITION which a Gentleman in Boston, had of his Brother, just then Murdered in London (1692)**

It was, on the Second of *May* in the Year 1687 that a most ingenious, accomplished and well-disposed young Gentleman, Mr. *Joseph Beacon*, by Name, about Five a clock in the Morning, as he lay, whether Sleeping or Waking he could not say, (but judged the latter of them,) had a View of his Brother then at *London*, altho' he was now himself at Our *Boston*, distanced from him a Thousand Leagues. This his Brother appear'd unto him,[3] in the Morning, about five a Clock at *Boston*, having on him a *Bengale* Gown,[4] which he usually wore, with a Napkin Ty'd about his Head; His Countenance was very Pale, Ghastly, Deadly, and he had a Bloody Wound On one Side of his Forehead![5] *Brother*! saies the Affrighted *Joseph*. Brother! Answered the Apparition. Said *Joseph, What's the matter, Brother! How came you here*! The Apparition reply'd, *Brother, I have been most Barbarously and Injuriously Butchered, by a Debauch'd, Drunken Fellow, to whom* I *never did any wrong in my life*. Where-

* SOURCE: Mather, Cotton. 1692. "A Narrative of an APPARITION which a Gentleman in *Boston*, had of his Brother, just then Murdered in *London*." In *The Wonders of the Invisible World*, 79–81. Boston.

PUBLICATION HISTORY: As an embedded story, the apparition of Joseph Beacon's brother appears without direct reference to the title in Cotton Mather's *Magnalia Christi Americana* (1702); Mather included the story again in his handwritten compilation *Triparadisus* (1720–27); Daniel Defoe was probably Beacon's trading partner in London and recorded a version of the story in *An Essay on the History and Reality of Apparitions*, published in London in 1727.

upon he gave a particular Description of the Murderer; adding, *Brother, This Fellow, changing his Name, is attempting to come over unto* New-England, *in* Foy *or* Wild; *I would pray you, on the first Arrival of either of these, to get an Order from the Governour, to Seiz the person, whom I have now described; and then do you Indict him for the Murder of me your Brother: I'le Stand by you, and prove the Indictment.*[6] And so he vanished. Mr. *Beacon* was extreamly astonished at what he had seen and heard; and the People of the Family not only observed an extraordinary Alteration upon him, for the Week following, but have also given me under their Hands a full Testimony, that he then gave them an Account of this Apparition.

All this while, Mr. *Beacon* had no Advice of any thing amiss attending his Brother then in *England*; but about the latter end of *June* following, he understood by the common ways of communication, that the *April* before, his Brother going in hast[e] by night to call a coach for a Lady, mett a fellow then in drink, with his *Doxy*[7] in his hand. Some way or other the fellow thought himself affrontted in the hasty passage of this *Beacon*, & immediately ran in to the Fire-side of a Neighbouring Tavern, from whence he fetch'd out a Fire-fork, wherewith he grievously wounded *Beacon* in the skull; even in that very part, where the Apparition show'd his wound. Of this Wound he Languished until he Dy'd, on the second of *May*, about five of the Clock in the morning at *London*. The murderer it seems, was endeavouring an escape, as the Apparition affirm'd, but the Friends of the Deceased *Beacon* siezed him: and prosecuting him at Law, he found the help of such Friends, as brought him off without the loss of his Life; since which, there has no more been heard of the Business.

This History I received of Mr. *Joseph Beacon* himself; who, a little before his own Pious & Hopeful Death, which follow'd not long after, gave me the Story written and signed with his own Hand; and Attested with the Circumstances I have already mentioned.

ANONYMOUS

*The Ghost of Falkner Swamp (1744)**

A day-laborer, who used to go around thatching roofs, died on a small farm not far from here.[8] And four years later, when Frederick Rimer moved on the same

* SOURCE: Sauer, Christopher. 1951. *The Pennsylvania Dutchman* 2 (16): 2.
PUBLICATION HISTORY: Sauer pirated the story from the German radical pietist periodical *Geistliche Fama* (*Spiritual News*), where the story first appeared in 1739. *Spiritual News* was widely known among German-speaking pietists on both sides of the Atlantic. The story was

place his nine-year-old daughter saw the previous occupant's ghost several times. One time she saw him sitting on a stump; another time he was standing alongside the maid of a neighbor. And on still another occasion she saw him sitting on the straw roof of the stable; he was pulling off the straw, throwing it right and left. The girl went and told her parents, for no matter how much straw he ripped off, there still was no hole in the roof. (She didn't know as yet that she was seeing a ghost). Once, when the father was absent from home this same girl coaxed her 17-year-old sister to come with her to question the man. But the older sister could see nothing, nor could she hear anything. Nonetheless, she told her younger sister what to ask him.

She began, "What are you doing here? What do you want?" In a subdued voice came the answer, "I've been waiting for help for a long time. Save me, for you can."

She asked, "From what shall I save you though?"

He answered, "I came here five years ago from the old country. On the way I borrowed 30 Gulden[9] from a woman in Holland and I never paid it back. And I won't find rest until this debt is paid."

She asked, "Is this woman married?"

"Yes," he said.

"And what is her name?"

He said, "Steinman."

She asked, "Can't your wife save you?"

"No," he said.

"But why not?" asked the girl.

"Because she's my wife, that's why," he answered.

"Why didn't you take care of this when you were living?" she asked him.

"I didn't have time; I died too soon," he answered.

---

rewritten by Sauer and translated into an American context. Sauer's reprint tells the story of a "Neuländer's Geist" (newcomer's ghost) who has come "five years ago from the old country," as the ghost reveals in one of the dialogue scenes. It appeared in Sauer's 1744 collection of ghost tales, titled *Of Sundry Old and New Tales of Appearances of Ghosts and Glimpses of the Souls' Condition after Death as it Happened in Oly* (*Verschiedene alte und neue Geschichten von Erscheinungen der Geister, und etwas von dem Zustand der Seelen nach dem Tode bey Varanlassung der Begegebenheit in Oly*). The book developed into a colonial steady seller. Sauer's collection went through several editions in 1748, 1755, and 1792, growing from a slim octavo volume of 96 pages into a bulk of tales and authorial comments, with 202 pages in its third edition. An English translation of the short narrative was first published under the title "The Ghost of Falkner Swamp" in *The Pennsylvania Dutchman* published by the Pennsylvania Dutch Folklore Center.

The girl asked him, "But are you sure that you will have peace when the debt is paid?"

Upon prompting from her sister, the girl said they wanted to help. This seemed to cheer the ghost and he began to walk across the field.

"Where are you going?" asked the girl.

"To my house," came the reply.

She asked, "But where is your house?"

"Come," he said, "and I'll show you." And he walked so fast the sisters could see the yellow soles of his feet.

She called to him, "Wait, we want to join you."

He waited a moment and then continued on his way. When he came to the creek he lifted the underbrush. He went on and soon came to the burial ground on Sieber's farm; he crawled through the fence. Then the girl saw his grave and in it there was a hole; and the next moment he was gone.

During the time they talked, the girls saw that the ghost had two red fangs protruding from either side of his mouth. She had the feeling they pained him. This condition impaired his speech. When she couldn't understand what he was saying, she put the question a second, sometimes even a third time. When her sister prodded her on she answered, "He'll get angry if I keep on asking him to repeat so often." Because of this she got her sister close to his side so she could understand what he was saying. She got so close, in fact, she felt she was stepping on his shroud.[10] (This time the ghost appeared as he looked in the coffin.)

The neighbors recalled that when his body was placed in the coffin his cap fell from his head. They then pulled the shroud over his head. And this is the way he appeared to the girl this time.

Prior to this, however, she always saw him dressed in his usual garb. The girl had never seen him alive. (The family, remember, moved on the farm four years after his death.) Yet her description of him is coincided with that of the neighbors—both as to height and dress. The girl also said he never seemed able to stand still.

The neighbors reported that on the very same farm a man had taken ill four years before. They said he lost his speech after two day's illness and died two days after that.

They went to the ghost's wife, but she didn't own up to her husband's debt. Others in the neighborhood who crossed the ocean on the same ship as the two, recollected that the couple fell out with the woman who had lent the money and that they denied receiving the loan. They remembered, too, how she cursed him, wishing him no peace in death.

The neighbors tried to find the woman to pay her back, but they met with failure. They began to feel in the end that the girl might have misunderstood the name, particularly since he had such great difficulty in talking.

After this, no one ever saw the ghost of the thatcher[11] again.

CHIRICAHUA

*A Chiricahua Woman Visits the Underworld (n.d.; publ. 1942)**

A Chiricahua woman was very sick. Though they spoke to her she recognized nothing. Later she recovered her senses and got well. She said that her ghost had gone from her body and had come to a high bluff. Below there was darkness. Below she could see cottonwoods and a stream. She jumped off and landed on a great cone of sand. When she landed the sand began to move and she continued to go further down. Finally she reached the bottom and saw many camps. The people were living there just as we live here. It was light in that place.

She started to go toward the camps and recognized some of her relatives there. Two of her youngest relatives met her and were happy to see her. All the people she met looked as they had in life and she could see no difference between life down there and life here. Her relatives led her to the camps and she came to her father and mother. On the way her two relatives warned her not to accept food at her father's camp if she wished to get back to earth again.

She followed this advice. Her relatives were happy to see her again and prepared food, but she refused to eat. This woman had had two husbands and when they saw her they started to come to her and fought over her. Her two younger relatives seemed to be protecting her through all this. They advised her to go back to earth and told her how to do so. Her ghost came back to her body and she opened her eyes.

* SOURCE: Chiricahua. "A Chiricahua Woman Visits the Underworld." 1942. *Myths and Tales of the Chiricahua Apache Indians*, edited by Morris Edward Opler, 83. New York: Kraus Reprint. Reprinted with permission of the American Folklore Society (afsnet.org).
PUBLICATION HISTORY: The Chiricahua originate in a band of Apachean-speaking Native Americans in the Southwest of the United States. The anthropologist Morris E. Opler conducted fieldwork among the Navajo and Apache throughout the 1930s and 1940s. Opler studied the rich culture of storytelling and myth of the southwestern tribes; he published numerous anthologies of Native American underworld and ghost stories.

LEGENDS

ANONYMOUS [ANNE LÆTITIA BARBAULD]

*Sir Bertrand: A Fragment. By Mrs. Barbauld (1787)**

Sir Bertrand turned his steed towards the woods, hoping to cross these dreary moors before the cur-few. But ere he had proceeded half his journey, he was bewildered by the different tracks; and not being able, as far as the eye could reach, to espy any object but the brown heath surrounding him, he was at length quite uncertain which way he could direct his course. Night overtook him in this situation. It was one of those nights when the moon gives a faint glimmering of light through the thick, black clouds of a lowering sky. Now and then she suddenly emerged in full splendor from her veil; and then instantly retired behind it, having just served to give forlorn Sir Bertrand a wide extended prospect over the desolate waste. Hope and native courage a while urged him to push forwards, but at length the increasing darkness and fatigue of body and mind overcame him; he dreaded moving from the ground he stood on, for fear of unknown pits and bogs, and alighting from his horse in despair he threw himself on the ground. He had not long continued in that posture when the sullen tone of a distant bell struck his ear—he started up, and turning towards the sound, discerned a dim, and twinkling light. Instantly he seized his horse's bridle, and with cautious steps advanced towards it. After a painful march he was stopt by a moated ditch, surrounding the place from whence the light proceeded; and by a momentary glimpse of moon-light he had a full view of a large antique mansion, with turrets at the corners, and an ample porch in the centre. The injuries of time were strongly marked on every thing about it. The roof in various places was fallen in, the battlements were half demolished, and

* SOURCE: Barbauld, Anna Lætitia. 1787. "Sir Bertrand: A Fragment. By Mrs. Barbauld." *The Columbian Magazine* 1 (15): 743–45.
PUBLICATION HISTORY: Originally published as part of the essay "On the Pleasure Derived from Objects of Terror; with Sir Bertrand, A Fragment" in John and Anne Lætitia Aikin. 1773. *Miscellaneous Pieces, in Prose*, 127–37. The story was reprinted in a number of British magazines: "Sir Bertrand: A Fragment. By Mrs. Barbauld." 1786. *The European Magazine, and London Review* (December 1): 399–400; 1787. *The Scots Magazine* 49 (January): 17–19. In America, it was first reprinted by *The Columbian Magazine* in 1787 and turned into verse in 1792 in *The Weekly Entertainer: Or, Agreeable and Instructive Repository* 19 (476): 294–96; 19 (477): 318–20; a reprint of the original story appeared in 1795. *The Literary Miscellany* 1 (8): 12–17. Another wave of reprints occurred in the opening decades of the nineteenth century: "Sir Bertrand: A Fragment." 1802. *Walker's Hibernian Magazine, or Compendium of Entertaining Knowledge*, 93–96; 1807. Mrs. Barbauld. "Sir Bertrand: A Fragment, in Imitation of an Ancient Romance." 1807. *The Literary Tablet; or, a General Repository of Useful Entertainment* 4 (17): 66.

the windows broken and dismantled. A draw-bridge, with a ruinous gateway at each end, led to the court before the building—he entered, and instantly the light, which proceeded from a window in one of the turrets, glided along and vanished; at the same moment the moon sunk beneath a black cloud, and the night was darker than ever. All was silent, Sir Bertrand fastened his steed under a shed, and approaching the house traversed its whole front with light and slow footsteps—All was still as death—He looked in at the lower window, but could not distinguish a single object thro' the impenetrable gloom. After a short parley with himself, he entered the porch, and seizing an iron massy knocker at the gate, lifted up, and hesitating, at length struck a loud stroke—The noise resounded through the whole mansion with hollow echoes. All was still again—He repeated the stroke more boldly and louder—another interval of silence ensued——A third time he knocked, and a third time all was still. He then fell back to some distance, that he might discern whether any light could be seen in the whole front.—It again appeared in the same place, and quickly glided away as before—At the same instant a deep, sullen toll sounded from the turret, Sir Bertrand's heart made a fearful stop—He was a while motionless; then terror impelled him to make some hasty steps towards his steed—but shame stopped his flight; and urged by honour, and a resistless desire of finishing the adventure, he returned to the porch; and working up his soul to a full steadiness and resolution, he drew forth his sword with one hand, and with the other lifted up the latch of the grate. The heavy door, creaking upon its hinges, reluctantly yielded to his hand—he applied his shoulder to it and forced it open—he quitted it and stept forward—the door instantly shut with a thundering clap. Sir Bertrand's blood was chilled—he turned back to find the door, and it was long ere his trembling hands could seize it—but his utmost strength could not open it again. After several ineffectual attempts he looked behind him, and beheld, across a hall, upon a large stair case, a pale bluish flame, which cast a dismal gleam of light around. He again summoned forth his courage and advanced towards it——it retired. He went slowly up, the flame retiring before him, till he came to a wide gallery—The flame proceeded along it, and he followed it in silent horror, treading lightly, for the echoes of his footsteps startled him. It led him to the foot of another stair-case, and then vanished!—At the same instant, another toll sounded from the turret—Sir Bertrand felt it strike upon his heart. He was now in total darkness, and with his arms extended, began to ascend the second stair-case. A dead cold hand met his left hand, and firmly grasped it, drawing him forcibly forwards—he endeavoured to disengage himself, but could not—he made a furious blow with his sword, and instantly a loud shriek pierced his ears, and the dead hand was left powerless in his—he dropped it, and rushed forward with a desperate valour.

The stairs were narrow and winding, and interrupted by frequent breaches, and loose fragments of stone. The staircase grew narrower and narrower, and at length terminated in a low iron gate. Sir Bertrand pushed it open—it led to an intricate winding passage, just large enough to admit a person upon his hands and knees. A faint glimmering light served to shew the nature of the place. Sir Bertrand entered—A deep hollow groan resounded from a distance through the vault.—He went forwards, and proceeding beyond the first turning, he discerned the same blue flame which had before conducted him—He followed it. The vault, at length, suddenly opened into a lofty gallery, in the midst of which a figure appeared, completely armed, thrusting forward the bloody stump of an arm, with a terrible frown and menacing gesture, and brandishing a sword in his hand. Sir Bertrand instantly sprang forwards; and aiming a fierce blow at the figure, it instantly vanished, letting fall a massy iron key to a brazen lock——with difficulty he turned the bolt——instantly the doors flew open, and discovered a large apartment, at the end of which was a coffin rested upon a bier, with a taper burning on each side of it. Along the room on both sides were gigantic statues of black marble, attired in the Moorish habit, and holding enormous sabres in their right hands. Each of them reared his arm, and advanced one leg forwards, as the knight entered; at the same moment the lid of the coffin flew open, and the bell tolled. The flame still glided forwards, and Sir Bertrand resolutely followed, till he arrived within six paces of the coffin. Suddenly a lady in a shroud and black veil rose up in it, and stretched out her arms towards him—at the same time the statues clashed their sabres and advanced. Sir Bertrand flew to the lady, and clasped her in his arms—she threw up her veil and kissed his lips; and instantly the whole building shook as with an earthquake, and fell asunder with a horrible crash. Sir Bertrand was thrown into a sudden trance, and on recovering, found himself seated on a velvet sofa, in the most magnificent room he had ever seen, lighted with innumerable tapers, in lustres of pure crystal. A sumptuous banquet was set in the middle. The doors opening to soft music, a lady of incomparable beauty, attired with amazing splendour, entered surrounded by a troop of gay nymphs more fair than the Graces.[12] She advanced to the knight, and falling on her knees thanked him as her deliverer. The nymphs placed a garland of laurel upon his head, and the lady led him by the hand to the banquet, and sat beside him. The nymphs placed themselves at the table, and a numerous train of servants entering, served up the feast, delicious music playing all the time. Sir Bertrand could not speak for astonishment—he could only return their honours by courteous looks and gestures. After the banquet was finished, all retired but the lady, who leading back the knight to the sopha, addressed him in these words: - - - - - - - - -

WASHINGTON IRVING

*THE DEVIL AND TOM WALKER (1824)**

A few miles from Boston, in Massachusetts, there is a deep inlet winding several miles into the interior of the country from Charles Bay, and terminating in a thickly wooded swamp, or morass. On one side of this inlet is a beautiful dark grove; on the opposite side the land rises abruptly from the water's edge, into a high ridge on which grow a few scattered oaks of great age and immense size. It was under one of these gigantic trees, according to old stories, that Kidd the pirate buried his treasure.[13] The inlet allowed a facility to bring the money in a boat secretly and at night to the very foot of the hill. The elevation of the place permitted a good look out to be kept that no one was at hand, while the remarkable trees formed good landmarks by which the place might easily be found again. The old stories add, moreover, that the devil presided at the hiding of the money, and took it under his guardianship; but this, it is well known, he always does with buried treasure, particularly when it has been ill gotten. Be that as it may, Kidd never returned to recover his wealth; being shortly after seized at Boston, sent out to England, and there hanged for a pirate.

About the year 1727, just at the time when earthquakes were prevalent in New-England, and shook many tall sinners down upon their knees, there lived near this place a meagre miserly fellow of the name of Tom Walker. He had a wife as miserly as himself; they were so miserly that they even conspired to cheat each other. Whatever the woman could lay hands on she hid away: a hen

* SOURCE: Irving, Washington. 1824. "The Devil and Tom Walker." In *Tales of a Traveller. By Geoffrey Crayon, Gent.* Vol. 2. 23–49. Philadelphia: Carey and Lee.
PUBLICATION HISTORY: *Tales of a Traveller* is a collection of 32 interwoven stories, conceived for a "story-telling and story-reading age," as Geoffrey Crayon, Irving's fictitious author, puts it in his preface. "The Devil and Tom Walker" is included in "Part IV," entitled "Money Diggers," and told by a "Cape-Cod whaler." It is preceded by a tale about "Kidd the Pirate," followed by another one, "Wolfert Webber, or Golden Dreams," told by John Josse Vandermoere. Irving's collection of tales ran through various editions in England, America, and France. The story was also reprinted in numerous American magazines throughout the nineteenth century, along with anonymous and abridged versions.

could not cackle but she was on the alert to secure the new-laid egg. Her husband was continually prying about to detect her secret hoards, and many and fierce were the conflicts that took place about what ought to have been common property. They lived in a forlorn-looking house, that stood alone and had an air of starvation. A few straggling savin trees, emblems of sterility, grew near it; no smoke ever curled from its chimney; no traveller stopped at its door. A miserable horse, whose ribs were as articulate as the bars of a gridiron, stalked about a field where a thin carpet of moss, scarcely covering the ragged beds of pudding stone, tantalized and balked his hunger; and sometimes he would lean his head over the fence, look piteously at the passer by, and seem to petition deliverance from this land of famine. The house and its inmates had altogether a bad name. Tom's wife was a tall termagant, fierce of temper, loud of tongue, and strong of arm. Her voice was often heard in wordy warfare with her husband; and his face sometimes showed signs that their conflicts were not confined to words. No one ventured, however, to interfere between them; the lonely wayfarer shrunk within himself at the horrid clamour and clapper-clawing; eyed the den of discord askance, and hurried on his way, rejoicing, if a bachelor, in his celibacy.

One day that Tom Walker had been to a distant part of the neighbourhood, he took what he considered a short cut homewards through the swamp. Like most short cuts, it was an ill chosen route. The swamp was thickly grown with great gloomy pines and hemlocks, some of them ninety feet high; which made it dark at noonday, and a retreat for all the owls of the neighbourhood. It was full of pits and quagmires, partly covered with weeds and mosses; where the green surface often betrayed the traveller into a gulf of black smothering mud; there were also dark and stagnant pools, the abodes of the tadpole, the bullfrog, and the water snake, and where trunks of pines and hemlocks lay half drowned, half rotting, looking like alligators, sleeping in the mire.

Tom had long been picking his way cautiously through this treacherous forest; stepping from tuft to tuft of rushes and roots which afforded precarious footholds among deep sloughs; or pacing carefully, like a cat, along the prostrate trunks of trees; startled now and then by the sudden screaming of the bittern, or the quacking of a wild duck, rising on the wing from some solitary pool. At length he arrived at a piece of firm ground, which ran out like a peninsula into the deep bosom of the swamp. It had been one of the strong holds of the Indians during their wars with the first colonists. Here they had thrown up a kind of fort which they had looked upon as almost impregnable, and had used as a place of refuge for their squaws and children. Nothing remained of the Indian fort but a few embankments gradually sinking to the level of the surrounding earth, and already overgrown in part by oaks and other forest trees, the foliage of which formed a contrast to the dark pines and hemlocks of the swamp.

It was late in the dusk of evening that Tom Walker reached the old fort, and he paused there for a while to rest himself. Any one but he would have felt unwilling to linger in this lonely, melancholy place for the common people had a bad opinion of it from the stories handed down from the time of the Indian wars; when it was asserted that the savages held incantations here and made sacrifices to the evil spirit. Tom Walker, however, was not a man to be troubled with any fears of the kind.

He reposed himself for some time on the trunk of a fallen hemlock, listening to the boding cry of the tree toad, and delving with his walking staff into a mound of black mould at his feet. As he turned up the soil unconsciously, his staff struck against something hard. He raked it out of the vegetable mould, and lo! a cloven skull with an Indian tomahawk buried deep in it, lay before him. The rust on the weapon showed the time that had elapsed since this death blow had been given. It was a dreary memento of the fierce struggle that had taken place in this last foothold of the Indian warriors.

"Humph!" said Tom Walker, as he gave the skull a kick to shake the dirt from it.

"Let that skull alone!" said a gruff voice.

Tom lifted up his eyes and beheld a great black man, seated directly opposite him on the stump of a tree. He was exceedingly surprised, having neither seen nor heard any one approach, and he was still more perplexed on observing, as well as the gathering gloom would permit, that the stranger was neither negro nor Indian. It is true, he was dressed in a rude Indian garb, and had a red belt or sash swathed round his body, but his face was neither black nor copper colour, but swarthy and dingy and begrimed with soot, as if he had been accustomed to toil among fires and forges. He had a shock of coarse black hair, that stood out from his head in all directions; and bore an axe on his shoulder.

He scowled for a moment at Tom with a pair of great red eyes.

"What are you doing in my grounds?" said the black man, with a hoarse growling voice.

"Your grounds?" said Tom, with a sneer; "no more your grounds than mine: they belong to Deacon Peabody."

"Deacon Peabody be d——d," said the stranger, "as I flatter myself he will be, if he does not look more to his own sins and less to his neighbour's. Look yonder, and see how Deacon Peabody is faring."

Tom looked in the direction that the stranger pointed, and beheld one of the great trees fair and flourishing without, but rotten at the core and saw that it had been nearly hewn through, so that the first high wind was likely to blow it down. On the bark of the tree was scored the name of Deacon Peabody. He now looked round and found most of the tall trees marked with the name of some great men of the colony, and all more or less scored by the axe. The one on which he had been seated, and which had evidently just been hewn down, bore the name of Crowninshield; and he recollected a mighty rich man of that name, who made a vulgar display of wealth, which it was whispered he had acquired by buccaneering.

"He's just ready for burning!" said the black man, with a growl of triumph. "You see I am likely to have a good stock of firewood for winter."

"But what right have you," said Tom, "to cut down Deacon Peabody's timber?"

"The right of prior claim," said the other. "This woodland belonged to me long before one of your white-faced race put foot upon the soil."

"And pray who are you, if I may be so bold?" said Tom.

"Oh, I go by various names. I am the Wild Huntsman in some countries; the Black Miner in others. In this neighbourhood I am known by the name of the Black Woodsman. I am he to whom the red men devoted this spot, and now and then roasted a white man by way of sweet smelling sacrifice. Since the red men have been exterminated by you white savages, I amuse myself by presiding at the persecutions of quakers and anabaptists; I am the great patron and prompter of slave dealers, and the grand master of the Salem witches."

"The upshot of all which is, that, if I mistake not," said Tom, sturdily, "you are commonly called Old Scratch."

"The same, at your service!" replied the black man, with a half civil nod.

Such was the opening of this interview, according to the old story, though it has almost too familiar an air to be credited. One would think that to meet with such a singular personage in this wild lonely place, would have shaken any man's nerves: but Tom was a hard-minded fellow, not easily daunted, and he had lived so long with a termagant wife, that he did not even fear the devil.

It is said that after this commencement, they had a long and earnest conversation together, as Tom returned homewards. The black man told him of great sums of money which had been buried by Kidd the pirate, under the oak trees on the high ridge not far from the morass. All these were under his command and protected by his power, so that none could find them but such as propitiated his favour. These he offered to place within Tom Walker's reach, having conceived an especial kindness for him: but they were to be had only on certain conditions. What these conditions were, may easily be surmised, though Tom never disclosed them publicly. They must have been very hard, for he required time to think of them, and he was not a man to stick at trifles where money was in view. When they had reached the edge of the swamp the stranger paused.

"What proof have I that all you have been telling me is true?" said Tom.

"There is my signature," said the black man, pressing his finger on Tom's forehead. So saying, he turned off among the thickets of the swamp, and seemed as Tom said, to go down, down, down, into the earth, until nothing but his head and shoulders could be seen, and so until he totally disappeared.

When Tom reached home he found the black print of a finger burnt, as it were, into his forehead, which nothing could obliterate.

The first news his wife had to tell him was the sudden death of Absalom Crowninshield, the rich buccaneer. It was announced in the papers with the usual flourish, that "a great man had fallen in Israel."

Tom recollected the tree which his black friend had just hewn down, and which was ready for burning. "Let the freebooter roast," said Tom, "who cares!" He now felt convinced that all he had heard and seen was no illusion.

He was not prone to let his wife into his confidence; but as this was an uneasy secret, he willingly shared it with her. All her avarice was awakened at the mention of hidden gold, and she urged her husband to comply with the black man's terms and secure what would make them wealthy for life. However Tom might have felt disposed to sell himself to the devil, he was determined not to do so to oblige his wife; so he flatly refused out of the mere spirit of contradiction. Many and bitter were the quarrels they had on the subject, but the more she talked the more resolute was Tom not to be damned to please her. At length she determined to drive the bargain on her own account, and if she succeeded, to keep all the gain to herself.

Being of the same fearless temper as her husband, she set off for the old Indian fort towards the close of a summer's day. She was many hours absent. When she came back she was reserved and sullen in her replies. She spoke something of a black man whom she had met about twilight, hewing at the root of a tall tree. He was sulky, however and would not come to terms; she was to go again with a propitiatory offering, but what it was she forebore to say.

The next evening she set off again for the swamp, with her apron heavily laden. Tom waited and waited for her, but in vain: midnight came, but she did not make her appearance; morning, noon, night returned, but still she did not come. Tom now grew uneasy for her safety; especially as he found she had carried off in her apron the silver teapot and spoons and every portable article of value. Another night elapsed, another morning came; but no wife. In a word, she was never heard of more.

What was her real fate nobody knows, in consequence of so many pretending to know. It is one of those facts that have become confounded by a variety of historians. Some asserted that she lost her way among the tangled mazes of the swamp and sunk into some pit or slough; others, more uncharitable, hinted that she had eloped with the household booty, and made off to some other province; while others assert that the tempter had decoyed her into a dismal quagmire on top of which her hat was found lying. In confirmation of this, it was said a great black man with an axe on his shoulder was seen late that very evening coming out of the swamp, carrying a bundle tied in a check apron, with an air of surly triumph.

The most current and probable story, however, observes that Tom Walker grew so anxious about the fate of his wife and his property that he sat out at length to seek them both at the Indian fort. During a long summer's afternoon he searched about the gloomy place, but no wife was to be seen. He called her name repeatedly, but she was no where to be heard. The bittern alone responded to his voice, as he flew screaming by; or the bull frog croaked dolefully from a neighbouring pool. At length, it is said, just in the brown hour of twilight, when the owls began to hoot and the bats to flit about, his attention was attracted by the clamour of carrion crows that were hovering about a cypress tree. He looked and beheld a bundle tied in a check apron and hanging in the branches of the tree, with a great vulture perched hard by, as if keeping watch upon it. He leaped with joy, for he recognized his wife's apron, and supposed it to contain the household valuables.

"Let us get hold of the property," said he, consolingly to himself, "and we will endeavour to do without the woman."

As he scrambled up the tree the vulture spread its wide wings, and sailed off screaming into the deep shadows of the forest. Tom seized the check apron, but, woful sight! found nothing but a heart and liver tied up in it.

Such, according to the most authentic old story, was all that was to be found of Tom's wife. She had probably attempted to deal with the black man as she had been accustomed to deal with her husband; but though a female scold is generally considered a match for the devil, yet in this instance she appears to have had the worst of it. She must have died game however; from the part that remained unconquered. Indeed, it is said that Tom noticed many prints of cloven feet deeply stamped about the tree, and several handsful of hair, that looked as if they had been plucked from the coarse black shock of the woodsman. Tom knew his wife's prowess by experience. He shrugged his shoulders as he looked at the signs of a fierce clapper-clawing. "Egad," said he to himself, "Old Scratch must have had a tough time of it."

Tom consoled himself for the loss of his property with the loss of his wife; for he was a little of a philosopher. He even felt something like gratitude towards the black woodsman, who he considered, had done him a kindness. He sought, therefore, to cultivate a further acquaintance with him, but for some time without success; the old black legs played shy, for whatever people may think, he is not always to be had for calling for; he knows how to play his cards when pretty sure of his game.

At length, it is said, when delay had whetted Tom's eagerness to the quick, and prepared him to agree to any thing rather than not gain the promised treasure, he met the black man one evening in his usual woodman dress, with his axe on his shoulder, sauntering along the edge of the swamp, and humming a tune. He affected to receive Tom's advance with great indifference, made brief replies, and went on humming his tune.

By degrees, however, Tom brought him to business, and they began to haggle about the terms on which the former was to have the pirate's treasure. There was one condition which need not be mentioned, being generally understood in all cases where the devil grants favours; but there were others about which, though of less importance, he was inflexibly obstinate. He insisted that the money found through his means should be employed in his service. He proposed, therefore, that Tom should employ it in the black traffick; that is to say, that he should fit out a slave ship. This, however, Tom resolutely refused; he was bad enough in all conscience; but the devil himself could not tempt him to turn slave dealer.

Finding Tom so squeamish on this point, he did not insist upon it, but proposed instead that he should turn usurer; the devil being extremely anxious for the increase of usurers, looking upon them as his peculiar people.

To this no objections were made, for it was just to Tom's taste.

"You shall open a broker's shop in Boston next month," said the black man.

"I'll do it to-morrow, if you wish," said Tom Walker.

"You shall lend money at two per cent. a month."

"Egad, I'll charge four!" replied Tom Walker.

"You shall extort bonds, foreclose mortgages, drive the merchant to bankruptcy—"

"I'll drive him to the d—l," cried Tom Walker, eagerly.

"You are the usurer for my money!" said the black legs, with delight. "When will you want the rhino?"

"This very night."

"Done!" said the devil.

"Done!" said Tom Walker.—So they shook hands, and struck a bargain.

A few days' time saw Tom Walker seated behind his desk in a counting house in Boston. His reputation for a ready moneyed man, who would lend money out for a good consideration, soon spread abroad. Every body remembers the days of Governor Belcher,[14] when money was particularly scarce. It was a time of paper credit. The country had been deluged with government bills; the famous Land Bank had been established; there had been a rage for speculating; the people had run mad with schemes for new settlements; for building cities in the wilderness; land jobbers went about with maps of grants, and townships, and Eldorados, lying nobody knew where, but which every body was ready to purchase. In a word, the great speculating fever which breaks out every now and then in the country, had raged to an alarming degree, and every body was dreaming of making sudden fortunes from nothing. As usual the fever had subsided; the dream had gone off, and the imaginary fortunes with it; the patients were left in doleful plight, and the whole country resounded with the consequent cry of "hard times."

At this propitious time of public distress did Tom Walker set up as a usurer in Boston. His door was soon thronged by customers. The needy and the adventurous; the gambling speculator; the dreaming land jobber; the thriftless tradesman; the merchant with cracked credit; in short, every one driven to raise money by desperate means and desperate sacrifices, hurried to Tom Walker.

Thus Tom was the universal friend of the needy, and he acted like a "friend in need;" that is to say, he always exacted good pay and good security. In proportion to the distress of the applicant was the hardness of his terms. He accumulated bonds and mortgages; gradually squeezed his customers closer and closer; and sent them at length, dry as a sponge from his door.

In this way he made money hand over hand; became a rich and mighty man, and exalted his cocked hat upon change. He built himself, as usual, a vast house, out of ostentation; but left the greater part of it unfinished and unfurnished out of parsimony. He even set up a carriage in the fullness of his vain glory, though he nearly starved the horses which drew it; and as the ungreased wheels groaned and screeched on the axle trees, you would have thought you heard the souls of the poor debtors he was squeezing.

As Tom waxed old, however, he grew thoughtful. Having secured the good things of this world, he began to feel anxious about those of the next. He thought with regret on the bargain he had made with his black friend, and set his wits to work to cheat him out of the conditions. He became, therefore, all of a sudden, a violent church goer. He prayed loudly and strenuously as if heaven were to be taken by force of lungs. Indeed, one might always tell when he had sinned most during the week, by the clamor of his Sunday devotion. The quiet christians who had been modestly and steadfastly travelling Zionward, were struck with self-reproach at seeing themselves so suddenly outstripped in their career by this new-made convert. Tom was as rigid in religious, as in money matters; he was a stern supervisor and censurer of his neighbors, and seemed to think every sin entered up to their account became a credit on his own side of the page. He even talked of the expediency of reviving the persecution of quakers and anabaptists. In a word, Tom's zeal became as notorious as his riches.

Still, in spite of all this strenuous attention to forms, Tom had a lurking dread that the devil, after all, would have his due. That he might not be taken unawares, therefore, it is said he always carried a small bible in his coat pocket. He had also a great folio bible on his counting-house desk, and would frequently be found reading it when people called on business; on such occasions he would lay his green spectacles on the book, to mark the place, while he turned round to drive some usurious bargain.

Some say that Tom grew a little crack brained in his old days, and that fancying his end approaching, he had his horse new shod, saddled and bridled, and buried with his feet uppermost; because he supposed that at the last day the world would be turned upside down; in which case he should find his horse standing ready for mounting, and he was determined at the worst to give his old friend a run for it. This, however, is probably a mere old wife's fable. If he really did take such a precaution it was totally superfluous; at least so says the authentic old legend, which closes his story in the following manner.

One hot afternoon in the dog days, just as a terrible black thundergust was coming up, Tom sat in his counting house in his white linen cap and India silk morning gown. He was on the point of foreclosing a mortgage, by which he would complete the ruin of an unlucky land speculator for whom he had professed the greatest friendship. The poor land jobber begged him to grant a few months indulgence. Tom had grown testy and irritated, and refused another day.

"My family will be ruined and brought upon the parish," said the land jobber. "Charity begins at home," replied Tom; "I must take care of myself in these hard times."

"You have made so much money out of me," said the speculator.

Tom lost his patience and his piety—"The devil take me," said he, "if I have made a farthing!"

Just then there were three loud knocks at the street door. He stepped out to see who was there. A black man was holding a black horse which neighed and stamped with impatience.

"Tom, you're come for!" said the black fellow, gruffly. Tom shrunk back, but too late. He had left his little bible at the bottom of his coat pocket, and his big bible on the desk buried under the mortgage he was about to foreclose: never was sinner taken more unawares. The black man whisked him like a child astride the horse and away he galloped in the midst of a thunder storm. The clerks stuck their pens behind their ears and stared after him from the windows. Away went Tom Walker, dashing down the streets; his white cap bobbing up and down; his morning gown fluttering in the wind, and his steed striking fire out of the pavement at every bound. When the clerks turned to look for the black man he had disappeared.

Tom Walker never returned to foreclose the mortgage. A countryman who lived on the borders of the swamp, reported that in the height of the thundergust he had heard a great clattering of hoofs and a howling along the road, and that when he ran to the window he just caught sight of a figure, such as I have described, on a horse that galloped like mad across the fields, over the hills and down into the black hemlock swamp towards the old Indian fort; and that shortly after a thunderbolt fell in that direction which seemed to set the whole forest in a blaze.

The good people of Boston shook their heads and shrugged their shoulders, but had been so much accustomed to witches and goblins and tricks of the devil in all kinds of shapes from the first settlement of the colony, that they were not so much horror struck as might have been expected. Trustees were appointed to take charge of Tom's effects. There was nothing, however, to administer upon. On searching his coffers all his bonds and mortgages were found reduced to cinders. In place of gold and silver his iron chest was filled with chips and shavings; two skeletons lay in his stable instead of his half starved horses, and the very next day his great house took fire and was burnt to the ground.

Such was the end of Tom Walker and his ill gotten wealth. Let all griping money brokers lay this story to heart. The truth of it is not to be doubted. The very hole under the oak trees, from whence he dug Kidd's money is to be seen to this day; and the neighbouring swamp and old Indian fort is often haunted in stormy nights by a figure on horseback, in a morning gown and white cap, which is doubtless the troubled spirit of the usurer. In fact, the story has resolved itself into a proverb, and is the origin of that popular saying, prevalent throughout New-England, of "The Devil and Tom Walker."

MYTH

K'ICHE' MAYA

*A Maiden's Story (c. 1524)**

A girl heard of this tree and came to see for herself. She was the daughter of Gathered Blood, one of the Lords of the Underworld. Her name was Xquic, little blood, woman's blood. She came and stood near the tree and gazed up into its branches. "Such strange fruit," she murmured. "It's impossible that I should die for picking one." Then the skull that nestled in the graveyard of the branches spoke: "What do you want? Skulls are the fruit of this tree. Is that what you want, a skull?"

"Yes, give me one," the girl answered.

"All right," said the skull, "reach up here." The girl reached her hand upward,

* SOURCE: from *Popol Vuh: The Great Mythological Book of the Ancient Maya*. 1977. Newly translated and with an introduction by Ralph Nelson, 54–57. Boston: Houghton Mifflin.

PUBLICATION HISTORY: "A Maiden's Story" is contained in the *Popol Vuh*, a collection of mytho-historical narratives written down by a K'iche' nobleman in mid-sixteenth century Guatemala. It was translated into Spanish in the eighteenth century. The title of the corpus translates as "The Book of the People," and the collection is an important source for Mayan creation myths and epic histories. The stories frequently have their origin in oral performances and have been recycled as Mayan stories.

FIG. 5: "Depósitos del Ynga." Drawing 132. 1619. In Felipe Guamán Poma de Ayala, *El Primer Nueva Corónica y Buen Gobierno*, 337. Manuscript GKS 2232 4° reprinted with permission from the Royal Library, Copenhagen, Denmark. The illustration shows the use of the quipu, a system of strings and knots, to register and manage the contents of the storehouse.

ready to catch the fruit. The skull let a few drops of spittle fall directly into her palm. She looked quickly into the palm of her hand, but the spittle had disappeared into her flesh. "In my saliva and spittle," the voice again came from the tree, "I have given you my descendants. My head has a different look now without flesh, for the beauty of all men lies in their flesh. When death takes a handsome prince, men are frightened by his bones. But descendants are saliva and spit. Saliva and spit are the sons of kings, and when they die they keep their substance. The king or soothsayer or lawyer leaves his image to his son or daughter, and this I have left to you. Now go to the surface of the world and keep your life. Believe in my words, and they will be true."

All that these two did together was under the direction of Huracan, Chipi-Caculha, and Raxa-Caculha. The girl returned home, sons in her belly conceived of spittle. And thus Hunahpu and Xbalanque were conceived. One day, her father noticed her roundness. He went to the Lords. "My daughter is pregnant, Sirs," he told them. "She's a useless little whore."

"At least question her," advised the Lords. "Search her mouth for truth. If she doesn't confess, punish her. Send her far into the hills to be sacrificed." Gathered Blood returned home to question his daughter. "I want a direct answer," he told her. "Who is the father of the children that you carry?"

"I have no child, Father," the girl answered. "I haven't yet known the face of a man."

"A real whore!" the father exploded. "Not another word! Lord Messenger!" he called to the owls. "Take her. Come back with a bowl containing her deceitful heart." The four owls took the bowl and a sacrificial knife of flint. They lifted the girl in their arms, and set out.

Along the way the girl spoke to the owls. "Oh, messengers!" she said. "I can't believe you will kill me! I'm innocent. What I carry in my stomach is no disgrace, it's a miracle! I became pregnant standing by the magic tree. I can't believe that you would sacrifice me!"

"But what can we bring in place of your heart?" asked the owls. "You heard your father's command! Do your duty, he said, bring her heart to me. We can't take back an empty bowl. We don't want to kill you, but what can we do?"

"My heart does not belong to them!" the girl answered. "Don't let them force you to take it. You don't belong here yourselves. Why should you be forced to kill men? The time will come when I will defeat the Lords of Death. The time will come when the real criminals will be at your mercy. Come with me. On earth you will have all that belongs to you. You will be loved there." Just then they were passing a tree from which a red sap flowed. Seeing this the girl stopped. "Here," she said, "fill the bowl with the red sap from this tree. That will satisfy the Lords."

"We shall do it," the owls said, "and we shall go with you to the Upperworld." The red sap gushed out of the tree. The owls filled the bowl. The sap looked exactly like blood. It glistened red as it flowed into the bowl, clotting in the shape of a heart. The tree itself glowed radiantly as the owls and the girl stood there gathering the sap. From that day on the tree was called the Blood Tree. While the girl traveled on toward the upper regions, the owls returned with the sap for the Lords of Death.

The Lords were assembled, waiting, when the owls returned. "Have you finished?" they asked.

"It is finished," the owls replied. "Here is the girl's heart."

"Let's have a look," said Hun-Came, and the bowl broke as he grabbed it in his eager fingers, and the red blood leaked in a stream. "Stir up a fire," he said, "put it on the coals." As soon as it was on the fire, and the wet smoke began to rise, all the Lords of the Underworld drew close and began to sniff. To them the fragrance of the heart was very, very sweet. As the Lords of Death sat deep in thought, the owls rose as one body and flew from the abyss, earthbound to serve their new mistress in the upper regions.

PENOBSCOT

*Corn Mother (n.d.)**

When Kloskurbeh, the All-maker, lived on earth, there were no people yet. But one day when the sun was high, a youth appeared and called him "Uncle, brother of my mother." This young man was born from the foam of the waves, foam quickened by the wind and warmed by the sun. It was the motion of the wind, the moistness of water, and the sun's warmth which gave him life—warmth above all, because warmth is life. And the young man lived with Kloskurbeh and became his chief helper.

Now, after these two powerful beings had created all manner of things, there

* SOURCE: Penobscot. (n.d.) 1984. "Corn Mother." In Erdoes, Richard and Alfonso Ortiz, eds. *American Indian Myths and Legends*, 12–13. New York: Pantheon.
PUBLICATION HISTORY: Stories of the corn maiden and her transformation and later sacrifice as corn mother abound among the Eastern Algonquin nations. This tale from the Penobscot, an indigenous people of the northeastern woodlands, was recorded in the nineteenth century. It can be found in Joseph Nicolar's *The Life and Traditions of the Red Man* (1893). Nicolar was an elder and political leader of the Penobscot Nation of Maine.

came to them, as the sun was shining at high noon, a beautiful girl. She was born of the wonderful earth plant, and of the dew, and of warmth. Because a drop of dew fell on a leaf and was warmed by the sun, and the warming sun is life, this girl came into being—from the green living plant, from moisture, and from warmth.

"I am love," said the maiden. "I am a strength giver, I am the nourisher, I am the provider of men and animals. They all love me."

Then Kloskurbeh thanked the Great Mystery Above for having sent them the maiden. The youth, the Great Nephew, married her, and the girl conceived and thus became First Mother. And Kloskurbeh, the Great Uncle, who teaches humans all they need to know, taught their children how to live. Then he went away to dwell in the north, from which he will return sometime when he is needed.

Now the people increased and became numerous. They lived by hunting, and the more people there were, the less game they found. They were hunting it out, and as the animals decreased, starvation came upon the people. And First Mother pitied them.

The little children came to First Mother and said: "We are hungry. Feed us." But she had nothing to give them, and she wept. She told them: "Be patient. I will make some food. Then your little bellies will be full." But she kept weeping.

Her husband asked: "How can I make you smile? How can I make you happy?"

"There is only one thing that will stop my tears."

"What is it?" asked her husband.

"It is this: you must kill me."

"I could never do that."

"You must, or I will go on weeping and grieving forever."

Then the husband traveled far, to the end of the earth, to the north he went, to ask the Great Instructor, his uncle Kloskurbeh, what he should do.

"You must do what she wants. You must kill her," said Kloskurbeh. Then the young man went back to his home, and it was his turn to weep. But First Mother said: "Tomorrow at high noon you must do it. After you have killed me, let two of our sons take hold of my hair and drag my body over that empty patch of earth. Let them drag me back and forth, back, and forth, over every part of the patch, until all my flesh has been torn from my body. Afterwards, take my bones, gather them up, and bury them in the middle of this clearing. Then leave that place."

She smiled and said, "Wait seven moons and then come back, and you will find my flesh there, flesh given out of love, and it will nourish and strengthen you forever and ever."

So it was done. The husband slew his wife and her sons, praying, dragged her body to and fro as she had commanded, until her flesh covered all the earth. Then they took up her bones and buried them in the middle of it. Weeping loudly, they went away.

When the husband and his children and his children's children came back to that place after seven moons had passed, they found the earth covered with tall, green, tasseled plants. The plants' fruit—corn[15]—was First Mother's flesh, given so that the people might live and flourish. And they partook of First Mother's flesh and found it sweet beyond words. Following her instructions, they did not eat all, but put many kernels back into the earth. In this way her flesh and spirit renewed themselves every seven months, generation after generation.

And at the spot where they had burned First Mother's bones there grew another plant, broad-leafed and fragrant. It was First Mother's breath, and they heard her spirit talking: "Burn this up and smoke it. It is sacred. It will clear your minds, help your prayers, and gladden your hearts."

And First Mother's husband called the first plant *Skarmunal*, corn, and the second plant *utarmur-wayeh*, tobacco.

"Remember," he told the people, "and take good care of First Mother's flesh, because it is her goodness become substance. Take good care of her breath, because it is her love turned into smoke. Remember her and think of her whenever you eat, whenever you smoke this sacred plant, because she has given her life so you might live. Yet she is not dead, she lives: in undying love she renews herself again and again."

BENJAMIN FRANKLIN

*The Origin of TOBACCO, from a Curious Account Given by Dr. Franklin of the Hospitality of Those We Call the Savage Indians (1784)**

A Swedish Minister took occasion to inform the chiefs of the Susquehannah Indians, in a kind of sermon, of the principal historical facts on which the Chris-

* SOURCE: Franklin, Benjamin. 1784. "The Origin of Tobacco, from a Curious Account Given by Dr. Franklin of the Hospitality of Those We Call the Savage Indians." *The Essex Journal and the Massachusetts and New-Hampshire General Advertiser* 25: 2.

PUBLICATION HISTORY: The narrative was reprinted in numerous newspapers and magazines: 1787. *The American Museum, or Repository of Ancient and Modern Fugitive Pieces* 2 (1): 86; 1791. *The Massachusetts Magazine, or Monthly Museum* 3 (3): 167–68; 1794. *The Monthly Magazine; or, Vermont Magazine* 1 (1): 14–15; 1796. *The Philadelphia Minerva* 2 (73): 3, 1798. *The Key* 1 (12): 92–93.

tian religion is founded; and particularly the fall of our first parents, by eating an apple. When the sermon was over, an old Indian orator replied, "What you have told us (said he) is very good; we thank you for coming so far to tell us those things you have heard from your mothers; in return, we will tell you what we heard from our's.

"In the beginning we had only flesh of animals to eat, and if they failed we starved; two of our hunters having killed a deer, and broiled a part of it, saw a young woman descend from the clouds, and seat herself on a hill hard by. Said one to the other, "It is a spirit, perhaps, that has smelt our venison; let us offer some of it to her." They accordingly gave her the tongue; she was pleased with its flavour, and said, 'Your kindness shall be rewarded; come here thirteen moons hence, and you will find it.' They did so, and found, where her right hand had touched the ground, maize growing; where her left hand had been, kidney-beans; and where her back-side had been, they found tobacco." The Swedish Minister was disgusted. 'What I told you (said he) is sacred truth; yours is fable, fiction, and falsehood.' The Indian, offended in his turn replied, 'My friend, your education has not been a good one; your mothers have not done you justice; they have not well instructed you in the rules of common civility. You saw that we, who understand and practice these rules, believed all your stories; why then do you refuse to believe our's? We believe, indeed, as you have told us, that it is bad to eat apples; it had been better (said he) that they had all been made into cider; but we would not have told you so, had you not disbelieved the method by which we first obtained maize, kidney-beans, and tobacco."

Notes

1. Exempla are short narrative illustrations of a sermon's argument. While they existed in nearly all cultures, they became popular in England through the Mendicant friars, who preached in English to the crowds on marketplaces throughout the country, and were quickly adapted by Protestants as well. Various collections of exempla were published in the sixteenth and seventeenth centuries. Among the most famous is Thomas Beard's *Theater of God's Judgments* (1597)—a translation from French and German sources—that was cited by Increase and Cotton Mather in New England.

2. The Royal Society was founded in 1660 in London to promote "knowledge of the natural world through observation and experiment" and became a leading scientific institution. New findings were published in the yearly *Philosophical Transactions*, and while its founding members were natural philosophers from various disciplines, the society admitted a great many members who were not professional scientists, including, for example, Joseph Glanvill and Cotton Mather, who were both ministers.

3. Apparitions of ghosts have been recorded throughout history in many cultures; see, for example, their representation in the Egyptian *Book of the Dead* (c. 1550 BC). They are also rooted in folk beliefs that in turn have informed oral and written storytelling. To account for apparitions of people in places where they are not bodily present, Cotton Mather developed a theory based on the concept of "nishmath chajim" (breath of life) that inhabits human beings from the moment of conception, forms their body, and guides their functioning. According to Mather, this spirit not only helps to explain the so far unknown origin of muscular motion or the many reflexes and instincts by which humans survive but also how the shape of a person can be seen when this person is not bodily present. Occupying a middle ground between spirit and matter, the "nishmath chajim" encapsulates the form of the body that unfolds during its time in the womb and thus could also re-create it as the basis of an apparition of the deceased as well as their resurrection for the afterlife.

4. Bengale goods, especially cloth and silk, were exported from Bengal to England in the seventeenth century.

5. The visible cause of death is a staple of killed people's ghosts asking for revenge on their murderers. The ghost appearing to a miller can be found in John Webster's *The Displaying of Supposed Witchcraft* (1677) and Joseph Glanvill's *Saducismus Triumphatus* (1681).

6. The lore surrounding ghosts frequently uses an unsolved murder case as the motif for their appearing; see, for example, the ghost of Hamlet's father in Shakespeare's play.

7. Doxy: mistress, prostitute (slang).

8. Falkner Swamp is another name for New Hanover, an area in Pennsylvania that was settled in the 1740s by German immigrants.

9. *Gulden* is the old Dutch word for "golden." Gulden is the common name for a base metal coin. Here it is probably a reference to the Rheingulden, minted in the trade centers along the Rhine River valley; see Sauer's travel account in Part I for currency rates.

10. Shroud: garment, clothing.

11. Thatcher: from to thatch, "cover," someone who builds roofs for houses with straw or reed.

12. In Greek mythology the goddesses of beauty, charm, and creativity.

13. Captain William Kidd (1645–1701) was a well-known pirate and privateer who was hanged in chains in London. Legend has it that he buried his treasure somewhere in New England. Rumors about his wealth influenced Edgar Allan Poe in writing "The Gold-Bug" (1843).

14. Jonathan Belcher (1682–1757) was a Massachusetts-born colonial politician and merchant who became governor of the British provinces of Massachusetts Bay, New Hampshire, and New Jersey. During his governorship Massachusetts faced a currency crisis in the late 1730s.

15. Corn is a sacred food to many Native people of the East and Southwest. It is the central theme of many myths, legends, and rituals.

Suggestions for Further Reading

Ghosts

F.R. [pseud.]. 1799. "On Apparitions: In a Letter from a Country Gentleman to His Friend in Town." *The Monthly Magazine, and American Review* 1 (1): 3–8.

Mather, Cotton. 1692. "Trial of Martha Carrier." In *Wonders of the Invisible World*, 132–38. Boston, 1692.

Mather, Increase. 1684. "[William Morse]." In *An Essay for the Recording of Illustrious Providences*, 142–55. Boston, 1684.

Z.P. [pseud.]. 1789. "Something Unaccountable." *The Massachusetts Magazine, or Monthly Museum of Knowledge and Rational Entertainment* 1 (9): 553–55.

Legends

Brackenridge, Hugh Henry. 1779. "The Cave of Vanhest." *United States Magazine* 1 (1): 14–15; 1 (2): 61–63; 1 (3): 106–10; 1 (4): 149–50; 1 (5): 213–16; 1 (6): 253–55; 1 (7): 311–13.

Dunwell, Jonathan [pseud. of William Austin]. 1824–27. "Peter Rugg: The Missing Man." *The New England Galaxy* 7 (361): 2–3; 9 (464): 2–3; 10 (484): 3.

Irving, Washington, [and James Kirke Paulding?]. 1807. "The Little Man in Black." *Salmagundi; or, The Whim-Whams and Opinions of Launcelot Langstaff, Esq., and Others* 2 (18): 317–26.

Myth

Celadon [pseud.]. 1785. *The Golden age; or, Future Glory of North-America Discovered by an Angel to Celadon, in Several Entertaining Visions*. n.p.

"Extract of a Letter from an Officer Stationed at Miami." 1786. *The Daily Adviser: Political, Historical, and Commercial* 2 (483): 2.

Freneau, Philip. (1797). "Tomo Cheeki." *The Time Piece; and Literary Companion* 1 (3): 10.

Josselyn, John. 1674. *An Account of Two Voyages to New-England*, 28–29. London.

WORKS CITED

Allison, Robert J. (1995) 2000. *The Crescent Obscured: The United States and the Muslim World, 1776–1815*. Reprint, Chicago: Univ. of Chicago Press.

Altman, Rick. 2008. *A Theory of Narrative*. New York: Columbia Univ. Press.

Amory, Hugh, and David D. Hall, eds. 2007. *The Colonial Book in the Atlantic World*. Vol. 1 of *A History of the Book in America*, edited by David D. Hall. Chapel Hill: Univ. of North Carolina Press.

Axelrad, Jacob. 1967. *Philip Freneau: Champion of Democracy*. Austin: Univ. of Texas Press.

Babb, Valerie. 1998. *Whiteness Visible: The Meaning of Whiteness in American Literature and Culture*. New York: New York Univ. Press.

Baepler, Paul. 1999. *White Slaves, African Masters: An Anthology of American Barbary Captivity Narratives*. Chicago: Univ. of Chicago Press.

Baine, Rodney M. 1962. "Daniel Defoe and 'The History and Reality of Apparitions.'" *Proceedings of the American Philosophical Society* 106 (4): 335–47.

Baker, Dorothy Z. 2007. *America's Gothic Fiction: The Legacy of Magnalia Christi Americana*. Columbus: Ohio State Univ. Press.

Bannet, Eve T. 2011. *Transatlantic Stories and the History of Reading, 1720–1810: Migrant Fictions*. Cambridge: Cambridge Univ. Press.

Basseler, Michael. 2011. "Theories and Typologies of the Short Story." In *A History of the American Short Story: Genres, Developments, Model Interpretations*, edited by Michael Basseler and Ansgar Nünning, 41–64. WVT Handbücher zum literaturwissenschaftlichen Studium 14. Trier, Ger.: Wissenschaftlicher Verlag Trier.

Bauer, Ralph, ed. 2009. *Themes in American Literature, 1492–1820*. Vol. 1. Boston, MA: Wadsworth.

Bauer, Ralph, and José Antonio Mazzotti, eds. 2009. *Creole Subjects in the Colonial Americas: Empires, Texts, Identities*. Chapel Hill: Univ. of North Carolina Press.

Bendixen, Alfred, and James Nagel, eds. 2010. *A Companion to the American Short Story*. Chichester, UK: Wiley-Blackwell.

Bertsch, Janet. 2004. *Storytelling in the Works of Bunyan, Grimmelshausen, Defoe, and Schnabel*. Rochester, NY: Camden House.

Boddy, Kasia. 2011. *The New Penguin Book of American Short Stories: From Washington Irving to Lydia Davis*. Penguin Classics. London: Penguin.

Bonheim, Helmut. 1982. *The Narrative Modes: Techniques of the Short Story*. Cambridge: Brewer.

Bourdieu, Pierre. 1993. *The Field of Cultural Production: Essays on Art and Literature*. New York: Columbia Univ. Press.

Boyer, Patricio. 2010. "Criminality and Subjectivity in Infortunios de Alonso Ramírez." *Hispanic Review* 78 (1): 25–48. doi: 10.1353/hir.0.0090.

Brander Rasmussen, Birgit. 2012. *Queequeg's Coffin: Indigenous Literacies and Early American Literature*. Durham, NC: Duke Univ. Press.

Brewer, David A. 2005. *The Afterlife of Character, 1726–1825*. Philadelphia: Univ. of Pennsylvania Press.

Bross, Kristina, and Hilary E. Wyss, eds. 2008. *Early Native Literacies in New England: A Documentary and Critical Anthology*. Amherst: Univ. of Massachusetts Press.

Brotherston, Gordon. 1979. *Image of the New World: The American Continent Portrayed in Native Texts*. London: Thames and Hudson.

Brown, Matthew P. 2006. "The Thick Style: Steady Sellers, Textual Aesthetics, and Early Modern Devotional Reading." *PMLA* 121 (1): 67–86.

———. 2007. *The Pilgrim and the Bee: Reading Rituals and Book Culture in Early New England*. Philadelphia: Univ. of Pennsylvania Press.

Bryant, John. 2002. *The Fluid Text: A Theory of Revision and Editing for Book and Screen*. Ann Arbor: Univ. of Michigan Press.

Buscaglia-Salgado, José F. 2005. "The Misfortunes of Alonso Ramírez (1690) and the Duplicitous Complicity between the Narrator, the Writer, and the Censor." *Dissidences: Hispanic Journal of Theory and Criticism* 1 (1): 1–41. http://digitalcommons.bowdoin.edu/dissidences/vol1/iss1/3.

Carocci, Max, ed. 2012. *Native American Adoption, Captivity, and Slavery in Changing Contexts*. New York: Palgrave Macmillan.

Carretta, Vincent. 1996. *Unchained Voices: An Anthology of Black Authors in the English-Speaking World of the Eighteenth Century*. 2nd ed. Lexington: Univ. Press of Kentucky.

Carter, Donald Martin. 2010. *Navigating the African Diaspora: The Anthropology of Invisibility*. Minneapolis: Univ. of Minnesota Press.

Castiglia, Christopher. 1996. *Bound and Determined: Captivity, Culture-Crossing, and White Womanhood from Mary Rowlandson to Patty Hearst*. Chicago: Univ. of Chicago Press.

Certeau, Michel de. 2008. *The Practice of Everyday Life*. Translated by Steven Rendall. Berkeley: Univ. of California Press.

Coclanis, Peter A. 2005. Introduction to *The Atlantic Economy during the Seventeenth and Eighteenth Centuries: Organization, Operation, Practice, and Personnel*, edited by Peter A. Coclanis, xi–xix. Columbia: Univ. of South Carolina Press.

Cohen, Lara L. 2012. *The Fabrication of American Literature: Fraudulence and Antebellum Print Culture*. Philadelphia: Univ. of Pennsylvania Press.

Cohen, Matt. 2010. *The Networked Wilderness: Communicating in Early New England*. Minneapolis: Univ. of Minnesota Press.

Costa, Elena de. 1997. "Mayan Literature" In *Encyclopedia of Latin American Literature*, edited by Verity Smith, 533–35. London: Fitzroy Dearborn.

Curnutt, Kirk. 1997. *Wise Economies: Brevity and Storytelling in American Short Stories*. Moscow: Univ. of Idaho Press.

Current-García, Eugene. 1985. *The American Short Story before 1850: A Critical History*. Boston: Twayne.

Derounian-Stodola, Kathryn Zabelle, and James A. Levernier. 1993. *The Indian Captive Narrative, 1550–1900*. Twayne's United States Authors Series 622. New York: Twayne.

Dimock, Wai C. 2001. "Deep Time: American Literature and World History." *American Literary History* 13 (4): 755–75.

Dorson, Richard M. 1973. *America in Legend: Folklore from the Colonial Period to the Present*. New York: Pantheon.

Dowling, David. 2011. *The Business of Literary Circles in Nineteenth-Century America*. New York: Palgrave Macmillan.

Ebersole, Gary. 1995. *Captured by Texts: Puritan to Postmodern Images of Indian Captivity*. Charlottesville: Univ. Press of Virginia.

Echevarría, Roberto González. 1997. Introduction to *The Oxford Book of Latin American Short Stories*, 2–22. New York: Oxford Univ. Press.

Edwards, Brian T. 2011. "Logics and Contexts of Circulation." In *A Companion to Comparative Literature*, edited by Ali Behdad and Dominic Thomas, 454–72. Chichester, UK: Wiley-Blackwell.

Engel, Katherine Carte. 2008. *Religion and Profit: Moravians in Early America*. Philadelphia: Univ. of Pennsylvania Press.

Erben, Patrick. 2012. *A Harmony of Spirits: Translation and the Language of Community in Early Pennsylvania*. Chapel Hill: Univ. of North Carolina Press.

Fergus, Jan. 2006. *Provincial Readers in Eighteenth-Century England*. Oxford: Oxford Univ. Press.

Flint, Christopher. 2011. *The Appearance of Print in Eighteenth-Century Fiction*. Cambridge: Cambridge Univ. Press.

Forbes, Jack D. 2007. *The American Discovery of Europe*. Urbana and Chicago: Univ. of Illinois Press.

Frow, John. 2006. *Genre*. New York: Routledge.

Gardner, Jared. 2012. *The Rise and Fall of Early American Magazine Culture: The History of Communication*. Urbana: Univ. of Illinois Press.

"The General Observer No. 1." 1789. *The Massachusetts Magazine, or, Monthly Museum of Knowledge and Rational Entertainment* (Jan.): 9–10.

"General Preface." 1790. *The Massachusetts Magazine, or, Monthly Museum of Knowledge and Rational Entertainment* (Jan.): i–iii.

Giffen, Allison. 1999. "Ann Eliza Bleecker." In *American Women Prose Writers to 1820*, edited by Carla Mulford, Angela Vietto, and Amy E. Winans, 55–61. Detroit, MI: Thomson Gale.

Giles, Paul. 2011. *The Global Remapping of American Literature*. Princeton, NJ: Princeton Univ. Press.

Gillman, Susan, and Kirsten S. Gruesz. 2011. "Worlding America: The Hemispheric Text-Network." In *A Companion to American Literary Studies*, edited by Caroline F. Levander and Robert S. Levine, 228–47. Blackwell Companions to Literature and Culture 78. Chichester, UK: Wiley-Blackwell.

Gilroy, Paul. 1993. *The Black Atlantic: Modernity and Double Consciousness*. Cambridge, MA: Harvard Univ. Press.

Goudie, Sean X. 2006. *Creole America: The West Indies and the Formation of Literature and Culture in the New Republic*. Philadelphia: Univ. of Pennsylvania Press.

Gross, Robert A., and Mary Kelley, eds. 2010. *An Extensive Republic: Print, Culture, and Society in the New Nation, 1790–1840*. Vol. 2 of *A History of the Book in America*. Chapel Hill: Univ. of North Carolina Press.

Gura, Philip F. 2013. *Truth's Ragged Edge: The Rise of the American Novel*. New York: Farrar, Straus, and Giroux.

Haberman, Robb K. 2008. "Magazines, Presentation Networks, and the Cultivation of Authorship in Post-Revolutionary America." *American Periodicals* 18 (2): 141–62.

Hall, David D. 1990. *Worlds of Wonder, Days of Judgment: Popular Religious Belief in Early New England*. Cambridge, MA: Harvard Univ. Press.

———. 1995. "Worlds of Wonders: The Mentality of the Supernatural in Seventeenth-Century New England." In *Religion and American Culture: A Reader*, edited by David G. Hackett, 27–52. New York: Routledge.

———. 2008. *Ways of Writing: The Practice and Politics of Text-Making in Seventeenth-Century New England*. Philadelphia: Univ. of Pennsylvania Press.

Harris, Sharon M. 2005. *Executing Race: Early American Women Narratives of Race, Society, and the Law*. Columbus: Ohio State Univ. Press.

———, ed. 1996. *American Women Writers to 1800*. New York: Oxford Univ. Press.

———, ed. 2003. *Women's Early American Historical Narratives*. Penguin Classics. London: Penguin.

Hartman, James D. 1999. *Providence Tales and the Birth of American Literature*. Baltimore, MD: Johns Hopkins Univ. Press.

Hayot, Eric. 2012. *On Literary Worlds*. New York: Oxford Univ. Press.

Heidegger, Martin. (1927) 2010. *Being and Time*. Translated by Joan Stambaugh. Revised and with a foreword by Dennis J. Schmidt. Albany: State Univ. of New York Press.

Hewitt, Elizabeth. 2004. *Correspondence and American Literature, 1770–1865*. Cambridge: Cambridge Univ. Press.

Hochbruck, Wolfgang, Aynur Erdogan, and Philipp Fidler, eds. 2008. *Origins of the American Short Story*. Los Gatos, CA: Slack Water Press.

Hunter, Paul J. 1990. *Before Novels: The Cultural Context of Eighteenth Century English Fiction*. New York: Norton.

Imbarrato, Susan C. 2012. "Life Writing." In *Transatlantic Literary Studies, 1660–1830*, edited by Eve T. Bannet and Susan Manning, 60–74. Cambridge: Cambridge Univ. Press.

Jackson, Leon. 2008. *The Business of Letters: Authorial Economies in Antebellum America*. Stanford, CA: Stanford Univ. Press.

Jackson, Maurice. 2009. *Let This Voice Be Heard: Anthony Benezet, Father of American Abolitionism*. Philadelphia: Univ. of Pennsylvania Press.

Johnson, Joe E. 2009. "The Baron de Saint Castin, Bricaire de la Dixmerie, and *Azakia* (1765)." In *An American Voltaire: Essays in Memory of J. Patrick Lee*, edited by E. Joe Johnson and Byron R. Wells, 201–20. Newcastle: Cambridge Scholars Publishing.

Kamrath, Mark, and Sharon M. Harris, eds. 2005. *Periodical Literature in Eighteenth-Century America*. Knoxville: Univ. of Tennessee Press.

Kittler, Friedrich A. 1990. *Discourse Networks 1800, 1900*. Foreword by David E. Wellbery. Stanford, CA: Stanford Univ. Press.

Krise, Thomas W., ed. 1999. *Caribbeana: An Anthology of English Literature of the West Indies, 1657–1777*. Chicago: Univ. of Chicago Press.

Lanzendörfer, Tim. 2013. *The Professionalization of the American Magazine: Periodicals, Biography, and Nationalism in the Early Republic*. Paderborn, Ger.: Schöningh.

———, and Oliver Scheiding, eds. Forthcoming. *American Lives: An Anthology of Early American Biographies*. Trier, Ger.: Wissenschaftlicher Verlag Trier.

Lázaro, Fabio López. 2011. *The Misfortunes of Alonso Ramírez: The True Adventures of a Spanish American with 17th-Century Pirates*. Austin: Univ. of Texas Press.

Lee, Benjamin, and Edward LiPuma. 2002. "Cultures of Circulation: The Imaginations of Modernity." *Public Culture* 14 (1): 191–213.

Levander, Caroline F. 2013. *Where Is American Literature?* Chichester, UK: Wiley-Blackwell.

———, and Robert S. Levine. 2011. Introduction to *A Companion to American Literary Studies*, 1–12. Chichester, UK: Wiley-Blackwell.

Levernier, James Arthur. 1999. "Hannah Duston." In *American Women Prose Writers to 1820*, edited by Carla Mulford, Angela Vietto, and Amy E. Winans, 107–12. Detroit, MI: Thomson Gale.

Levy, Andrew. 1993. *The Culture and Commerce of the American Short Story*. Cambridge: Cambridge Univ. Press.

Lindstrom, Naomi. 2004. *Early Spanish American Narrative*. Austin: Univ. of Texas Press.

Lockley, Timothy James. 2009. Introduction to *Maroon Communities in South Carolina. A Documentary Record*, ix–xxiii. Columbia: Univ. of South Carolina Press.

Lohafer, Susan, and Jo Ellyn Clarey, eds. 1989. *Short Story Theory at a Crossroads*. Baton Rouge: Louisiana State Univ. Press.

Loughran, Trish. 2007. *The Republic in Print: Print Culture in the Age of U.S. Nation Building, 1770–1870*. New York: Columbia Univ. Press.

Love, Herald. 1993. *Scribal Publication in Seventeenth-Century England*. Oxford: Clarendon Press.

March-Russell, Paul. 2009. *The Short Story: An Introduction*. Edinburgh: Edinburgh Univ. Press.

Marcus, Greil, and Werner Sollors, eds. 2009. *A New Literary History of America*. Cambridge, MA: Belknap Press of Harvard Univ. Press.

Mather, Cotton. 1726. *Manuductio ad Ministerium. Directions for a Candidate of the Ministry*. Boston.

Matthews, Brander. (1885) 1994. "The Philosophy of the Short-Story." In *The New Short Story Theories*, edited by Charles E. May, 73–80. Athens: Ohio Univ. Press.

May, Charles E. 2002. *The Short Story: The Reality of Artifice*. New York: Routledge.

Mayo, Robert Donald. 1962. *The English Novel in the Magazines, 1740–1815: With a Catalogue of 1375 Magazine Novels and Novelettes*. Evanston, IL: Northwestern Univ. Press.

McGill, Meredith L. 2003. *American Literature and the Culture of Reprinting, 1834–1853*. Philadelphia: Univ. of Pennsylvania Press.

McKeon, Michael. 1987. *The Origins of the English Novel, 1600–1740*. Baltimore, MD: Johns Hopkins Univ. Press.

Medovoi, Leerom. 2011. "'Terminal Crisis?' From Worlding of American Literature to World-System Literature." *American Literary History* 23 (3): 643–59.

Moore, Lisa L., Joanna Brooks, and Caroline Wigginton, eds. 2012. *Transatlantic Feminisms in the Age of Revolutions*. Oxford: Oxford Univ. Press.

Moretti, Franco. 2005. *Graphs, Maps, and Trees: Abstract Models for a Literary History*. London: Verso.

Mulford, Carla. 2002. *Early American Writings*. New York: Oxford Univ. Press.

———, Angela Vietto, and Amy E. Winans. 1999. Introduction to *American Women Prose Writers to 1820*, edited by Carla Mulford, Angela Vietto, and Amy E. Winans, xvii–xxix. Detroit, MI: Thomson Gale.

Nabokov, Peter. 2002. *A Forest of Time: American Indian Ways of History*. Cambridge: Cambridge Univ. Press.

Nagel, James, ed. 2008. *Anthology of the American Short Story*. Boston, MA: Houghton Mifflin.

Nicolar, Joseph. (1893) 2007. *The Life and Traditions of the Red Man*. Edited by Annette Kolodny. Durham, NC: Duke Univ. Press.

O'Brien, Edward J. (1931) 1969. *The Advance of the American Short Story*. Reprint, Folcroft, PA: Folcroft Press.

Opler, Morris Edward. (1941) 1996. *An Apache Life-Way: The Economic, Social, and Religious Institutions of the Chiricahua Indians*. Lincoln: Univ. of Nebraska Press.

Pattee, Fred L. (1924) 1966. *The Development of the American Short Story: An Historical Survey*. New York: Biblio and Tannen.

Pease, Donald. 2007. "From American Literary Studies to Planetary Literature: The Emergence of Literary Extraterritoriality." In *Transnational American* Studies, edited by Winfried Fluck, Sebastian Brandt, and Ingrid Thaler, 9–35. Yearbook of Research in English and American Literature 23. Tübingen, Ger.: Narr.

Peskin, Lawrence A. 2009. *Captives and Countrymen: Barbary Slavery and the American Public, 1785–1816*. Baltimore, MD: Johns Hopkins Univ. Press.

Pitcher, Edward W. R. 2000. Introduction to *An Anthology of the Short Story in 18th and 19th Century America*. 2 vols. Studies in British and American Magazines 5. 1–47. Lewiston, NY: Mellen.

———, and D. Sean Hartigan, eds. 2000. *Sensationalist Literature and Popular Culture in the Early American Republic: An Anthology of Exotic Nonfiction, Wonder Tales, and Whoppers*. Lewiston, NY: Mellen.

Poe, Edgar Allan. 1846. "The Philosophy of Composition." *Graham's Magazine* 28 (4): 163–67.

Powell, Manushag N. 2011. "New Directions in Eighteenth-Century Periodical Studies." *Literature Compass* 8 (5): 240–57.

Prendergast, Christopher. 2001. "Negotiating World Literature." *New Left Review* 8: 100–21.

Rediker, Marcus. 2007. *The Slave Ship: A Human History*. London: Viking.

Rhodes, Evans. 2012. "Beyond the Exceptionalist Thesis, a Global American Studies 2.0." *American Quarterly* 64 (4): 899–912.

Roach, Joseph. 1996. *Cities of the Dead: Circum-Atlantic Performance*. New York: Columbia Univ. Press.

Round, Phillip H. 1999. *By Nature and by Custom Cursed: Transatlantic Civil Discourse and New England Cultural Production, 1620–1660*. Hanover: Univ. Press of New England.

Scheiding, Oliver. 2012. "Migrant Fictions: The Early Story in North American Magazines." In *Mobility in Literature and Culture, 1500–1900*, edited by Ingo Berensmeyer, Christoph Ehland, and Herbert Grabes, 197–218. Yearbook of Research in English and American Literature 28. Tübingen, Ger.: Narr.

———. Forthcoming. "'Small Tales': Brevity and Liminality in Early American Magazines." In *Liminality and the Short Story: Boundary Crossings in American, Canadian, and British Writing*, edited by Jochen Achilles and Ina Bergmann. Routledge Interdisciplinary Perspectives on Literature. London: Routledge.

———, and Martin Seidl. 2011. "Early American Short Narratives: The Art of Story-Telling Prior to Washington Irving." In *A History of the American Short Story: Genres, Classics, Model Interpretations*, edited by Michael Basseler and Ansgar Nünning, 67–81. Trier, Ger.: Wissenschaftlicher Verlag Trier.

Schmidt, Benjamin. 2001. *Innocence Abroad: The Dutch Imagination and the New World, 1570–1670*. Cambridge: Cambridge Univ. Press.

Scofield, Martin. 2006. *The Cambridge Introduction to the American Short Story*. Cambridge: Cambridge Univ. Press.

Shapiro, Stephen. 2008. *The Culture and Commerce of the Early American Novel: Reading the Atlantic World-System*. University Park: Pennsylvania State Univ. Press.

Silver, Peter. 2008. *Our Savage Neighbors: How Indian War Transformed Early America*. New York: Norton.

Smith, Sidonie, and Julia Watson. (2001) 2010. *Reading Autobiography: A Guide for Interpreting Life Narratives*. Minneapolis: Univ. of Minnesota Press.

Smolinski, Reiner. 2010. "'Biblia Americana': America's First Bible Commentary." In Cotton Mather, *Biblia Americana: America's First Bible Commentary; a Synoptic Commentary on the Old and New Testaments*. Vol. 1, *Genesis*, edited by Reiner Smolinski, 3–76. Tübingen, Ger.: Mohr Siebeck.

———, ed. 1995. *The Threefold Paradise of Cotton Mather: An Edition of "Triparadisus."* Athens: Univ. of Georgia Press.

Snyder, Christina, ed. 2010. *Slavery in Indian Country: The Changing Face of Captivity in Early America*. Cambridge: Harvard Univ. Press, 2010.

Sobel, Mechal. 2000. *Teach Me Dreams: The Search for Self in the Revolutionary Era*. Princeton, NJ: Princeton Univ. Press.

Stockel, Henrietta H. 2008. *Salvation through Slavery: Chiricahua Apaches and Priests on the Spanish Colonial Frontier*. Albuquerque: Univ. of New Mexico Press.

"Theories and Methodologies: Early American Literature." 2013. *PMLA* 128 (4): 938–1003.

Toulouse, Teresa. 2007. *The Captive's Position: Female Narrative, Male Identity, and Royal Authority in Colonial New England*. Philadelphia: Univ. of Pennsylvania Press.

Ulrich, Laurel Thatcher. 1982. *Good Wives: Image and Reality in the Lives of Women in Northern New England, 1650–1750*. New York: Knopf.

Voigt, Lisa Beth. 2009. *Writing Captivity in the Early Modern Atlantic: Circulations of Knowledge and Authority in Iberian and English Imperial Worlds*. Omohundro Institute of Early American History and Culture. Chapel Hill: Univ. of North Carolina Press.

Voss, Arthur. 1973. *The American Short Story: A Critical Survey*. Norman: Univ. of Oklahoma Press.

Walsham, Alexandra. (1999) 2003. *Providence in Early Modern England*. Oxford: Oxford Univ. Press.

Walters, Kerry. 2011. *Revolutionary Deists: Early America's Rational Infidels*. Amherst, MA: Prometheus.

Weber, Alfred. 1987. Introduction to *Charles Brockden Brown: Somnambulism and Other Stories*, edited by Alfred Weber, vii–xxi. Studien und Texte zur Amerikanistik 4. Frankfurt am Main, Ger.: Lang.

Weis, Ann-Marie. 1998. "The Murderous Mother and the Solicitous Father: Violence, Jacksonian Family Values, and Hannah Duston's Captivity." *American Studies International* 36 (1): 46–65.

Werlock, Abby H. P., ed. 2010. *The Facts on File Companion to the American Short Story*. 2nd ed. New York: Facts on File.

Weyler, Karen A. 2013. *Empowering Words: Outsiders and Authorship in Early America*. Athens: Univ. of Georgia Press.

White, Hayden. 2008. "Commentary: 'With No Particular Place to Go': Literary History in the Age of the Global Picture." *American Literary History* 39: 727–45.

Williams, Daniel E. 1993. "The Gratification of That Corrupt and Lawless Passion: Character Types and Themes in Early New England Rape Narratives." In *A Mixed Race: Ethnicity in Early America*, edited by Frank Shuffelton, 194–224. New York: Oxford Univ. Press.

Wilsdorf, Heinz G. F. 1999. *Early German-American Imprints*. New York: Lang.

Winship, Michael P. 1996. *Seers of God: Puritan Providentialism in the Restoration and Early Enlightenment*. Baltimore, MD: Johns Hopkins Univ. Press.

Winthrop, John. 1996. *The Journal of John Winthrop, 1630–1649*, edited by Richard S. Dunn, James Savage, and Laetitia Yeandle. Cambridge, MA: Belknap Press of Harvard Univ. Press.

Wise, Paul. 2010. "Cotton Mather and the Invisible World." In *Cotton Mather and 'Biblia Americana' America's First Bible Commentary; Essays in Reappraisal*, edited by Reiner Smolinski and Jan Stievermann, 227–61. Tübingen, Ger.: Mohr Siebeck.

Zahedieh, Nuala. 2010. *The Capital and the Colonies: London and the Atlantic Economy, 1660–1700*. Cambridge: Cambridge Univ. Press.

Zantop, Susanne M. 1997. *Colonial Fantasies: Conquest, Family, and Nation in Precolonial Germany, 1770–1870*. Durham, NC: Duke Univ. Press.

The authorized representative in the EU for product safety and compliance is:
Mare Nostrum Group
B.V Doelen 72
4831 GR Breda
The Netherlands

www.ingramcontent.com/pod-product-compliance
Lightning Source LLC
Chambersburg PA
CBHW060806310726
48980CB00002B/254

* 9 7 8 0 8 0 4 7 9 0 8 0 2 *